Miles Davis and Jazz as Religion

Miles Davis and Jazz as Religion

The Politics of Social Music Culture

Earnest N. Bracey

LEXINGTON BOOKS
Lanham • Boulder • New York • London

Published by Lexington Books
An imprint of The Rowman & Littlefield Publishing Group, Inc.
4501 Forbes Boulevard, Suite 200, Lanham, Maryland 20706
www.rowman.com

6 Tinworth Street, London SE11 5AL, United Kingdom

Copyright © 2021 The Rowman & Littlefield Publishing Group, Inc.

All rights reserved. No part of this book may be reproduced in any form or by any electronic or mechanical means, including information storage and retrieval systems, without written permission from the publisher, except by a reviewer who may quote passages in a review.

British Library Cataloguing in Publication Information Available

Library of Congress Cataloging-in-Publication Data Available

ISBN 978-1-7936-5359-8 (cloth : alk. paper)
ISBN 978-1-7936-5361-1 (pbk : alk. paper)
ISBN 978-1-7936-5360-4 (electronic)

∞™ The paper used in this publication meets the minimum requirements of American National Standard for Information Sciences—Permanence of Paper for Printed Library Materials, ANSI/NISO Z39.48-1992.

*This book is dedicated to my brother,
Professor Jerry A. Bracey.*

Contents

Preface		ix
Acknowledgments		xiii
Introduction		xv
1	The Evolution of Miles Davis's Social Music	1
2	The Start: Of Youth and Old Music Men	9
3	Band Members: Turning Ideas into Music	15
4	The Art of Stage Presence	21
5	Of Missed Notes and Technique	27
6	The Man and His Horn	35
7	Of Spanish Music, Cool Jazz, and Style	41
8	Of Politics and Civil Rights	51
9	The Meaning of His Blues	57
10	Europe or Bust: Concerts and Touring	65
11	In Love with Paris	75
12	The Twilight of Avant-Garde	85
13	Fusion: The Heart of the Matter	93
14	Drugs and Retirement	97
15	The Catalytic Return	105

16	Transformations	113
17	The New Music	121
18	Of Critics and Jazz Purists	127
19	Montreux and Death	137
20	After an Ending	143
21	In a Quiet Way	153

Conclusion	163
Bibliography	171
Index	183
About the Author	189

Preface

I have always wanted to write a book about the late and brazen jazz trumpeter Miles Dewey Davis and add to the discussion of this infamous jazz man. Or at least pick up on (or present) some issues his (Davis's) 1990 autobiography left out. Davis became my hero when I was a youngster, as I am also a musician, and I have been playing the trumpet since I was fourteen years old. I just wanted to be like Miles Davis, to even play my trumpet like him. Indeed, his music encapsulates everything that I personally wanted to hear when I became a musician. Davis was the jazz trumpeter *everyone* in my orbit wanted to listen to when I was a teenager growing up in segregated Mississippi. For a time, I even tried to talk with a raspy voice like Davis, and I carried my trumpet everywhere, in a *gig* bag, as I was dazzled by his powerful image and innovative music. My earliest memory of Miles Davis was at the tender age of ten, as I attentively listened to my sister's vinyl records of him (Davis) on our broken-down stereo in the front room of the house, where I grew up, which was a predominantly black neighborhood in Jackson, the state capital. We called my sister Virginia, and she played a beautiful jazzy piano.

I tried to play the piano, but I opted to play the trumpet. My father, who played the guitar, didn't hesitate to buy me a new trumpet at a pawn shop on Ferris Street in the segregated black, business area downtown, for which I was eternally grateful, because I thought I was Miles Davis. I later became first trumpet chair in my segregated High School Band. I was basically self-taught, but our band leader, whose name I now forget, taught me the basics, but his main instrument was the saxophone. When I started college, I played in the famous Jackson State University Jazz Big Band as a trumpet soloist. I also played in a jazz combo for a while in Japan. Although I am now a political science professor, I still occasionally play my horn, as I am passionate about jazz. As great jazz musicians go, we are sometimes graced by individuals, who through the sheer brilliance of their performances can lead jazz fans and others to unfamiliar places, by listening to unique music that they wouldn't even previously consider. Miles Davis, in this regard, became the driving force behind jazz music for quite some time. While he lived, I remember anxiously anticipating Davis's next extraordinary album that would come out, because I would buy the LPs without giving it a second thought. So it was all about hero worship for me.

Whether people love jazz or not, Miles Davis's music makes listeners think, particularly when it comes to the dynamics in his very unusual sound, which is most curious, special, and exhilarating. Therefore, Davis has been foremost on my mind in writing this book, as I have tried to learn everything about his life. To be sure, it has been irresistible, and an enlightening experience for me. What no one should dispute is that Miles Davis was a musical genius. And paradoxically, his uncompromising artistry and jazz work is more accessible today than it was during his exceptional life. His prolific and creative output was nothing short of brilliant. I have always had a strong sense of enjoyment listening to records by Miles Davis. And when I played my horn in the past, and even today, sometimes, I consciously try to emulate his sound in my trumpet solos. There has always been something achingly relevant about Davis's music for me, especially as it relates to religion, because his sound gives me a sort of spiritual calm. It must be noted that Davis made his music a very compelling thing, in a notable or significant way. Davis also served as a highly visible jazz hero for many, because he made his own place in the jazz world. Most importantly, Davis's music today provides me with eternal joy. And his brand of jazz has sustained me spiritually over the years.

Furthermore, I always liked that Davis seriously challenged conventional wisdom, when it came to jazz, as he developed a distinguishable and specific way of performing his music. I personally feel that Davis was very much ahead of his time, and was still going strong artistically and musically before he died. As an influential musician, Davis was from another time and place—that is, when jazz musicians were idealized and worshiped more than they are today. In this respect, I firmly believe that Davis's life is still worthy of further examination and consideration. To say the least, Davis's musical accomplishments deserve to be put in the complete context of his existence. And if readers want to know what drove Davis to excel as a band leader and jazz trumpeter, or what shaped his musical views and values or virtues, they must all start with his background. In writing this book about Miles Davis, I have tried to stay true to what this great jazz man was all about. However, it is not a day-by-day account of his life. Such biographical treatment has already been done in other published works. But this narrative is my personal contribution, as I wanted to elaborate on his "social music," and the artistic creed of Miles Davis. This biographical work also assesses some of the musical achievements of the jazz man, while discussing how he reached his potential and esteemed position in the jazz world, which was really by virtue of his talent.

This book also attempts to debunk some of the myths surrounding Davis's life, as it addresses a particular side of the man that no one, perhaps, knew existed. Moreover, this book tries to present a clear perspective on Davis's true legacy, while providing additional, pertinent information. For readers that are unfamiliar with Miles Davis, they should know that the hand of God was entwined in the very act of him playing jazz improvisation. Or so I believe. And the fact that Davis's music is sometimes bluesy, in a silent way, it is as though the listener can hear *nothing* or *everything* in the background on his recordings, even a pin drop. Therefore, it is not a stretch to believe that Miles Davis was able to play his trumpet like a musical angel. Indeed, Davis was not just another jazz *pretender*, because it takes talent and *authenticity*, to create music on the spot, or to play something that isn't there. I firmly believe that Miles Davis played music that many (like jazz *purists*) would come to envy, as they (his harshest critics) touted the traditional jazz orthodoxy. I also believe that all of Davis's music is more than a variegated, patchwork of sounds. For me, listening to jazz has always been based upon or measured by the music of Miles Davis.

Hence, the heart or thrust of this book is an analysis of Davis's spiritual and artistic vision in terms of jazz. It also takes a political and critical look at Davis in all his glory and *ugliness* as a human being, while attempting to flesh out the complexity of the man and his music. Additionally, I have tried to provide more insight into Davis's politics and musical creativity, as it explores the workings of his remarkable mind. In other words, I explain what Miles Davis was really all about. Although biographers, critics, historians, and others have dealt exhaustively with his life, in a general way, they failed to address Davis's humanity. Therefore, people think that they know *everything* they need to know about Miles Davis as a person and jazz musician. But their understanding is only superficial; or many jazz enthusiasts have only some very basic information about the iconic Davis. In so many words, people shouldn't believe whatever they want about the jazzman. In this regard, I have presented a glimpse into his sometimes-perplexing existence. Furthermore, this work explores the eccentricities of his life, to allay the preconceived, negative notions about Miles Davis.

That said, Davis was no musical lightweight, as he was able to become someone big in the jazz world movement. Widely credited with modernizing the sound of modern jazz, Davis's music was antithetical to the smiley face of the great entertainer and trumpeter Louis Armstrong, which was nothing short of revolutionary. But there was always something unspoken, at the end of the day, about Miles Davis's artistry and public persona, which was never understated by those who loved him. It should be noted that Davis wasn't answerable to anyone but himself. For me personally, Davis still has an overwhelming influence on almost every aspect of my life, as I listen to his music every day. And whatever my personal likes and dislikes about Davis's music, his jazz has always been a part of my existence.

Gradually, Miles Davis would become an energy and something else musically when it came to jazz, particularly with his lyrical (music) transformation. I finally believe that Davis's significance to jazz is incalculable, because of his creative spirit. With nothing but his smooth sound to go on, Davis's music can lead the listener to extraordinary places, as it has done with me. In the final analysis, this book is a psycho-political study of Miles Davis, as it reflects on his courage against many odds; and his self-sacrifice, and being a jazzman extraordinaire. But it would be an exaggeration to say that this book is the final word on Miles Davis.

Acknowledgments

I would like to acknowledge my brother, Jerry A. Bracey, for suggesting that I complete this book about Miles Davis, in 2003, when I was teaching at Hampton University, as the chairman of the Political Science and History Department during some late night brainstorming sessions. Jerry is my older brother, and he is currently a professor of Music at Hampton University, and the director of the Jazz Band and String Orchestra. My brother, Jerry, is a musical genius; and he plays the violin, piano, viola, and saxophone.

Growing up in segregated Jackson, Mississippi, it seemed like music was really the only thing that piqued my brother's interest. Unfortunately, he has never been given his due, as Jerry is a brilliant musician. Jerry is also an outstanding violinist, who plays the string instrument beautifully; and he is a better musician than I will ever be. During our college years, we both played in the famous Jackson State University's Jazz Big Band. As I recall, we recorded a competition jazz album, in the late 1970s, where listeners can hear me playing my trumpet on a couple of tunes, as a soloist.

I hope that my brother, Jerry, who I affectionately call "the Maestro," is pleased with my efforts in this book, as this is a scholarly endeavor. To be sure, Jerry clarified my thinking about the direction I should take in writing this biography.

I actually started the research for this book, in earnest, several years ago at Hampton University—that is, before I left to later become the chairman of the Political Science Department at Jackson State University. Some of the sources identified and used herewith are the result of a diligent effort on my part, as I searched the libraries at Hampton University, Jackson State University, the University of Nevada, Las Vegas, and at Sophia University, in Japan. But I am also particularly grateful to the librarians at the College of Southern Nevada.

As I finished this difficult book, I found myself often thinking about my brother, Jerry, who has been an inspiration to me when it comes to music. We both also love Miles Davis, and grew up listening to a lot of music, in a family of twelve. To say the least, all my siblings were musically inclined. Of course, we knew that Davis's music is never stagnant; and listening to his recordings is like taking a master class in jazz. Finally, I would like to thank the Hollis brothers, who inspired me to play my trumpet. I particularly want to thank Kermit Hollis who gave me the opportunity to play with the Jackson State University Jazz Big Band, as he was the director at the time I attended the university.

To my brother, Jerry, I don't know if there are any words that can express my deep appreciation to you for giving me the push that I needed to complete this book about Miles Davis. Thanks, Jerry, for everything. Finally, I am indebted to my wife, Atsuko. As far as my writing is concerned, Atsuko has always been supportive; and she has never let me down.

Introduction

This work is both a biography-like and interpretive history of jazz as it relates to religion, music, spirituality, politics, and the life of Miles Dewey Davis. Jazz, of course, can be an *all-consuming* musical quest, particularly in the realm of social science and music. Jazz is also a global and political force. Although the book is not an exhaustive treatment, the scope of this work focuses specifically on Miles Davis and on African American contributions to *all* music. Moreover, this work is not intended to serve as a comprehensive, chronological reference about jazz and Miles Davis. But this book does tell us that jazz and religion are intimately associated with American culture, black life, and black music, in general, as it relates to politics and the place or *agency* of African Americans. Davis, an absolutely brilliant trumpeter, and "one of the most original and influential musicians in jazz,"[1] during his era was hardly a man of religion or faith; nor was he devoted to some supernatural entity or *Supreme Being*. But through his exceptional music, Miles Davis was indeed a political and spiritual black man. Or he had a deep spiritual side to himself. To be sure, when Davis wasn't ill or struggling with his demons and personal challenges, his otherworldly recordings and national and international concerts were like a (televangelist's) religious event, or some kind of ritualistic ceremony in a *megachurch*, as he pushed the boundaries of the jazz *genre*. The late Tony Williams, who played drums in one of Davis's greatest bands once wrote that "Audiences had a desire to be touched" by Miles Davis's music, and "his vision and [musical] courage."[2] Perhaps they (his audiences) wanted to be a part of his very spiritual existence, as Davis was the genuine musical article, so to speak, with a reservoir of musical talent. According to famed black poet and prolific writer, the late Amiri Baraka (formerly LeRoi Jones), "Miles Davis was one constant source of emotional and intellectual revelation through his music." In regard to his veracity of faith in jazz, Baraka goes on to write:

Figure 0.1 Photograph of a young Miles Davis. *Source*: Photograph in public domain.

Miles was among the most mercurial of recent jazz masters. His music was a constantly shifting expression of his whole self, though the "persona," [or] what was projected to his . . . audiences, might seem less so in that he was not so easily understood, i.e. what he felt and how he presented it, as a person. [His] music is somewhat skewed in this sense. . . . [But] he could play, would play, whatever he wanted to, always with that provocative "Me-ness" that allows us to identify his playing instantly.[3]

Although Miles Davis didn't have *any* religious beliefs per se, or "never espoused a systematic [or religious] philosophy, he was always conscious of the broader context of his own situation"[4] (see Figure 0.1 and 0.2). Also, it would be inaccurate to say that Davis was a sort of living god, because of his unearthly and superlative trumpet playing. Yet, it is perhaps fair to point out that his music is memorable, and immortalized in many ways. Unfortunately, his son, Gregory Davis, noted that his father only believed in himself.[5] To say the least, Miles Davis would have nothing to do with any organized religion, because he perhaps felt that jazz allowed for musical innovation (and a certain visionary, spiritual, musical belief system), without any type of regimentation, or religious compliance. Indeed, jazz (a black American musical form) permits musical extemporaneousness, on the *spur-of-the-moment* worship, or improvisational *mysticism*. Unfortunately, Davis's hierarchy in jazz is often glossed over in similar works, especially as it concerns faith and religion; but this book attempts to rectify these slights. About his father's religious beliefs, Gregory Davis put it this way:

> My father [Miles Davis] knew there was a God out there and that if he'd do some of the work then God would do the rest. [But] with my father, it got to the point where he felt he was doing most of the work.[6]

Equally important, Miles Davis was considered the *Dark Magus*, or the "Prince of Darkness," a living, musical deity, or a devil, because of his sometimes uncouth, calculating evil, or his "kiss-my-black-ass" behavior and attitude. According to Davis's former band member, David Liebman, you couldn't help being pulled in or affected by the spirituality in the music of Miles Davis.[7] Moreover, "he [Davis] surrounded himself with young visionaries, [which] summoned an entire ecosystem of sound into being and then sat in its center, an inscrutable Buddha."[8] Was this because of his unique take on the "social music" genre? Davis clearly believed that to have good music, and "a great band," you must also have "sacrifice and compromise from everyone; [because] without it, *nothing* [my emphasis] happens."[9] This book also identifies the impact Davis has had on young (jazz) musicians today, because of his brilliant, musical innovations. In purely musical terms, Davis's trumpet playing could sometimes be shrouded in silence, like in his mystical album, *In a Silent Way*. As such, his music had a distinctive personal feel, which "seemed to bend the air around him to fit his ever-growing [spiritual] vision."[10] Davis, from the standpoint of his self-image, and as far as embracing any kind of religion, as already mentioned, wasn't something he was really interested in, as he believed, for over fifty years, in creating a divine sound, or a spiritual music for essentially himself, his friends, and avid listeners, and fans. After all, jazz, or "social music" was (in a sense) Davis's specific faith, as well as his loving mistress, his sine qua non, or essential purpose. Another former band member of Miles Davis, the great black jazz pianist, Herbie Hancock thought that Davis was something akin to a mystic; or he had some higher connection or communion with the ultimate reality. Hancock, for example, once stated that Miles Davis

> is a sorcerer. His whole attitude, the way he is, is kind of mysterious. I know him well but there's still a kind of musical mystique about him. His music sounds like witchcraft. There are times I don't know where his music comes from. It doesn't sound like he's doing it. It sounds like it's coming from [God, or] somewhere else.[11]

Furthermore, Miles Davis was more at home playing his different, nimble trumpet at some well-known jazz clubs and jazz festivals, where he was able to cut his musical teeth, like when he first started out playing, as a young man, in (jazz) big bands in the 1940s and 1950s. Davis especially liked playing in Europe, where he was always warmly received. No doubt, he was certainly comfortable playing in many musical venues or Jazz Clubs in New York, Paris, or Japan, where Davis "learned the secret of meaningful communication: [To] speak only when you have something to say."[12] Professor of music at the College of Fine Arts, Jeremy Yudkin wrote that Miles Davis's "thoughtful, laconic phrasing, his careful choice of notes, the personal quality of his sound, the sense that he is constantly striving for expression—these [made] his conversations with us like that of no other musician in jazz."[13] Indeed, there was/is a sort of quiet, serene, loneliness in his brilliant trumpet playing, which is both spare and thoughtful. Equally, there is a vulnerability about his playing, an innocence that was unmatched by others, with the possible exception of the late Donald Byrd, an excellent black, jazz trumpeter, who also played with a deft, Miles-Davis-esque and *evocative* touch, just like Miles Davis, particularly his outstanding rendition of "I Will Wait for You," on his 1981 *The Creeper* album. Listening to this ballad, we might easily mistake Byrd's exquisite trumpet playing for that of Miles Davis: such was his musical influence.

In a renowned jazz concert, "at the *Teatro dell' Arte* in Milan, on October 11, 1964, with his second [great] quintet," jazz writer John Lingan describes Miles Davis's trumpet playing and stage presence this way: "Head down, he [Davis was] almost in prayer. His subtly ballooning cheeks reveal the huge respiratory power behind that simmering, sneaky tone,"[14] as well as his elegant jazz renditions and musical mindset. Of course, Miles Davis, while he lived, was one of the most consequential jazz musicians in American history and on the planet—that is, besides the legendary black trumpet player, Louis "Satchmo" Armstrong. And with Davis's famous name, even today, he is spoken of in revered terms, especially among jazz musicians, as if he (Miles Dewey Davis) was some (par excellent) religious figure.

Figure 0.2 Miles Davis statue at Ed Dwight's Studio in Colorado. *Source*: Author's personal photograph.

Finally, this book addresses Davis's influence in the history of jazz and twentieth-century music, especially as it concerned his radical experiment with rock music, bebop, African Rhythms, cool jazz, gospel, blues, funk, and the music of electronic fusion.

NOTES

1. "Miles (Dewey) Davis," in *Merriam-Webster's Collegiate Encyclopedia*, edited by Mark A. Stevens (Springfield, MA: Merriam-Webster, Inc., 2000), 44. It should be noted here that Miles Davis had very little time for organized religion. But

he had a deep interest in the spiritual realm, or the existence of a God. To say the least, Davis was a musical warrior and spiritual genius, who used a holistic, musical approach to playing jazz. And for the most part, he played his soulful trumpet with a supernatural diligence and determination.

2. Tony Williams, liner notes to "A Tribute to Miles" (Burbank, CA: Qwest Records, 1992), recording. Audiences would often sit and carefully listen in silence to Miles Davis during his many concerts, except to applaud. And for some fans, Davis was even considered a sex-symbol.

3. Amiri Baraka, liner notes to "Miles after Miles – Panthalassa: The Music of Miles Davis, 1969–1974" (New York: Sony Music Entertainment, Inc., 1998), recording. Davis, of course, developed his own playing ideology, like a modern-day philosopher. He was tenacious when it came to recording his remarkable music and making beautiful, memorable albums, which were unorthodox and wonderfully nuanced and voluminous in scope.

4. Brian Morton, *Miles Davis* (London, England: Haus Publishing Limited, 2005), 26. Miles Davis incorporated several different musical mediums, to play what he wanted, which can be considered symbolically spiritual. And his minimalist, on-the-spot improvisations is or was the stuff of legend. That is, Miles Davis defied conventional musical theory and history.

5. Gregory Davis and Les Sussman, *Dark Magus: The Jekyll and Hyde Life of Miles Davis* (San Francisco, CA: Backbeat Books, 2006), 147. Jazz instrumentalists can especially make *impromptu* musical decisions, individually, when improvising or playing "off the cuff," so to speak (or without practice or musical preparation) separate from the other musicians in a jazz band, with different choices in playing chords or presenting other musical clichés, of which Miles Davis was a master.

6. Davis and Sussman, *Dark Magus*, 147. Note that Miles Davis would later reject the word "jazz" or such derogatory terminology, because he liked the term "social music." See Brian Morton, *Miles Davis*, 1. Furthermore, Davis could not stand the thought that his unique repertoire of "social music" was not accepted or ignored by the mainstream music scene.

7. David Liebman, liner notes to "Dark Magus: The Legacy of Columbia Jazz" (New York: Sony Music Entertainment, 1977), recording. So did Miles Davis personify some supreme spirit of evil? There is no doubt that Davis's efforts made a big difference in jazz. And, if anything, Miles Davis thought that the most important thing to have was great and talented band members like John Coltrane or Sonny Rollins; and later, the white saxophonist Bill Evans. And Davis played at a very high level with his young band members.

8. John Lingan, "Jazz on European TV," *The New York Times Magazine*, December 2, 2018, 23.

9. Miles Davis and Quincy Troupe, *Miles: The Autobiography* (New York: Simon & Schuster Paperbacks, 1989), 273.

10. Lingan, "Jazz on European TV," 23.

11. Nat Hentoff, liner notes to "Herbie Hancock's Speak like a Child" (Manhattan Records, a division of Capitol Records, Inc., 1987) recording. Time and again, Miles

Davis gave life to the jazz movement in the United States. Was it magic or divine intervention? Or was it just the normal progression of his "social music"?

12. Jeremy Yudkin, *Miles Davis, Miles Smiles, and the Invention of Post Bop* (Indianapolis: Indiana University Press, 2008) xi. This work also explores several issues in regard to how Miles Davis contributed to jazz, and the modern-day Civil Rights Movement, as he played several important concerts (like at Carnegie Hall in the 1960s) that enhanced his overall status in both the African American and white American communities—that is, particularly in terms of politics; and his undeniably influential music.

13. Yudkin, *Miles Davis*, xi.

14. Lingan, "Jazz on European TV," 23. Miles Davis was more than just an average or competent enough trumpet player, even though he often played his amazing trumpet sparingly, but with an intensity all his own.

Chapter 1

The Evolution of Miles Davis's Social Music

Miles Dewey Davis profoundly influenced the so-called Jazz Church, as well as the jazz musical agenda or broader jazz culture, for six decades. Many fans and others became passionate advocates, worshiping jazz and the music of Miles Davis openly, particularly at "the dawn of the jazz-meets-world-music revolution."[1] But understanding jazz is not a foregone conclusion, as it requires a deep commitment, with a sense of urgency, like some religions. Broadly speaking, jazz is "primarily a vehicle for profoundly personal expression through improvisation and composition";[2] and Davis would become the master of this music work. More importantly, Miles Davis's name would become synonymous with jazz, especially in the public imagination. Furthermore, jazz, or what Davis called "social music" is actually "tailored for celebration or ceremony,"[3] as in religious rituals, or faith worshiping. Of course, to "worship is probably the most basic element of religion," besides "moral conduct, right belief, and participation in religious institutions."[4] No doubt, this assessment is what jazz is all about, because it addresses "the human condition with a unique intensity and [musical] depth," while "building on its own discoveries and producing works that [can] withstand and reward [spiritual] contemplation."[5] Miles Davis understood this "inherent need to transform"[6] jazz long before he became famous. He also thought deep thoughts about the spellbinding music. As a youngster, Miles Davis didn't blink when it came to what he wanted to do, or who he wanted to be. Davis was born May 25, 1926, in Alton, Ill., the son of an affluent dental surgeon, and grew up in East St. Louis, Ill." Significantly, "on his 13th birthday," thanks to his beloved father, Davis was given "a trumpet and lessons with a local jazz musician, Elwood Buchanan,"[7] who later thought the world of the young Miles Davis. The incomparable Buchanan took the younger Davis under his wing, and taught the budding musician everything that he knew about playing the trumpet. Accordingly, as a young, ambitious black man, Davis, with self-awareness about his place in the music world (at that time) would eventually gain a great passion for playing his horn, even getting "his musicians' union card at 15 so he could perform around St. Louis with Eddie Randall's Blue Devils."[8] To say the least, jazz was a powerful attraction for the young Miles Davis.

Equally important, "Davis may also have been the first important Black trumpeter from a comfortable middle-class background,"[9] which set him apart from others. Musically, Davis heard what he wanted to hear. And, as if summoning some higher power, he played what he wanted to play. In this way, Davis found many ways to play the music he loved so much. And he was perfectly suited for taking the reign of jazz. Perhaps it was Davis's early training and dedication that helped shape him as the remarkable jazz musician he would become. When he first heard *suave* black men, as a youngster, playing jazz, the new music of the time, Davis really knew that he had found his vocation. But as a young man, Davis probably didn't know that he would become a titular giant, and the most influential jazz trumpeter of his day; but he had a good head on his shoulders and knew what the music was all about and what it could ultimately become. Or Davis focused on things that he wanted to focus on when it came to jazz, or "social music." And no matter how he changed musically over time, one thing was certain: Davis decided that he would be *somebody* in jazz, no matter what. Indeed, Miles Davis would do different things to make people pay attention to him; and through force of personality he was able to create excitement with his music, where listeners noticed. Perhaps just as important, Davis was able to take center stage and carve out his own jazz career—that is, apart from other great luminaries, like Clark Terry, Fats Navarro, Clifford Brown, or Dizzy Gillespie. Of course, Davis believed that there were so many music avenues and things that a jazzman could use to be musically different that it didn't necessarily take a genius to figure it out. The young Miles Davis had no illusions that the road would be easy as a black musician. Indeed, he would weather many challenges, like getting recognized or trying to be a good husband to his three wives, the dancer Frances Taylor, singer Betty Mabry, and the actress Cicely Tyson, whom he would later respectively divorce. Davis also often made the headlines for allegedly slapping around prostitutes and beating up women, his wives, or various lovers; but there is no evidence that he hated women. So was Davis really a *vulgar* womanizer? Additionally, Davis wasn't the perfect father to his children: his daughter, Cheryl, and sons, Gregory Miles IV and Erin. Therefore, his fame had drawbacks. Or was Davis simply a complicated man? Or was he just a bad man?

As an unknown musician, upon his arrival in New York, in 1944, Miles Davis knew that if he was able to succeed as a jazz man, as described in this book, he would be able to make it *anywhere*. Later in life, Davis never felt any ambivalence about living a charmed life as a (jazz) musician. Or was he like some "court jester," or musical god, who only wanted to entertain or upset the masses? To be sure, Davis brought a potent blend of different music mediums to the forefront of jazz. Jazz singer and Mississippi native, Cassandra Wilson never met Miles Davis, but she firmly believed that he "went fearlessly into so many directions with his music and he was always so confident about it . . . [that he] never compromised and . . . always followed his intuition."[10] Fortunately, many in the jazz world would ultimately realize that Davis was *somebody* who was important. The most significant thing is that in the world of jazz, listeners can't avoid his music, as Davis is still loved by a *coterie* of jazz fans. Back in 1939, however, jazz critic George M. Avakian, to be specifically political, wrote that "Jazz is jazz; [and] it can't be modernized or streamlined."[11] But what Avakian wrote isn't exactly true, because Miles Davis was able to make the necessary changes in jazz, while "reinventing its traditional interaction with the wider culture."[12] Miles Davis set a sort of musical precedent that would affect jazz for all time, particularly in terms of jazz or "social music" being some kind of religious faith. In 2011, the late sideman of Miles Davis and great saxophonist, Sonny Rollins stated that "Jazz is a spirit. It is freedom. It is reality put into musical form. It will never leave until this planet leaves."[13] Generally speaking, in terms of jazz, people listen to the music of Miles Davis, perhaps, to be transported, to absorb the essence and beauty of the jazz form. And for others, Davis's jazz can allow us to also escape sometimes from reality. All in all, his instantly recognizable music (or sound) provides a spiritual connection to the listener; or the *ooh-aah* factor, which is no small feat, as Davis added an extra dimension or spiritual perspective to the music of jazz.

When it was all said and done, some fans interpreted Davis's "plaintive, aching, sometimes fragile and delicate, but beautiful rendering of [jazz or] the blues,"[14] as a deeply emotional listening experience. As will be discussed in this book, Miles Davis wasn't religious, but he had a kind of personal spiritualism and faith in himself and his music that strengthened most of his new, musical inclinations—and artistic vision. Davis dared to be a different kind of jazz man. But during his life, some jazz purists thought that Davis was simply being disagreeable or "inconvenient" to the notion of traditional jazz itself; or that he (Davis) was only following the current musical trends. However, according to jazz critic John Rockwell, Davis "was more of a musical thinker than a virtuoso. He constantly thought about how music could work, tending toward a minimalist removal of notes compared with the onslaughts of the bop *pyro technicians*."[15] After all, the young Miles Davis was thrust onto the world stage at an early age, playing with the legendary Charlie "Bird" Parker, who saw something in him. In this respect, Davis "developed a quieter bop style on the trumpet that was more accessible and less virtuosic, fitting in quite well with Charlie Parker's [hard-bop] quintet."[16] Of course, some of Davis's music is mysterious, dramatic, poignant, and purposeful, and he was able to garner eccentric jazz fans from almost everywhere in the world. These jazz enthusiasts were always looking for different music that they had never heard before. And many who found his (Davis's) music were "totally fascinated by [the] melancholy, beautiful sound of Miles Davis,"[17] as it is very much like a faithful music, or meditative chants, evoking a spiritual mood. For some, Davis's jazz or "social music" is close to something *godly*. Journalist Nekesa Mumbi Moody tells us that Davis's music like today's Hip-Hop and Rap music incites "a fervor in fans" that is "reminiscent of a religious experience."[18] Davis was extraordinarily perceptive and had the courage, talent, and *stamina* to pursue his musical goals. Put another way, Miles Davis was blessed with a certain spiritual countenance and innate ability as a musician. His strength was his talent to maximize his horn playing by incorporating bluesy ballads into his musical repertoire. No doubt, Davis could connect with jazz fans on many levels; and playing ballads was one of the musical things that he could do extremely well. It is equally important to acknowledge that "jazz" is a learning experience, especially for the uninitiated, because it imparts spiritual lessons that we should all take to heart.

Miles Davis's philosophy was always to make a pleasing sound, although "he wasn't afraid to dwell in the darkness."[19] In his idiosyncratic way, Davis made the "social music" his own. Indeed, the black jazz man created some of the most interesting and innovative new jazz music during his lifetime. More importantly, Davis, like an evangelical minister, always made waves in the jazz world, as some of his music is very risqué, like *Bitches Brew*. Years from now, we will still be talking about Miles Davis and his incredible recordings, as he is linked with jazz. Jazz critic Mark Zanger explained that "It's black magic that keeps a man dangerous past his years, and Miles's pact with the devil is of long standing and well respected by both parties."[20] So was Davis possessed by demonic forces or the angels? For certain, many thought that Davis was the great black Satan. Nevertheless, jazz fans were awestruck by the likes of Miles Davis, because he was able to make or exert an impressive musical sound that was altogether different from other jazz musicians during his era. Moreover, Davis's dynamic personality and legendary status was a cut above the average jazz man, as he used the act of playing his horn as a metaphor for what he was feeling about life and being a black man in a systemically racist society. Davis also was able to communicate his abstract musical ideas or notions with his trumpet, which was about the beauty of "Blackness." He also had tremendous listening skills. It is quixotic to talk about Miles Davis in terms of him seizing the musical imagination of jazz acolytes or those devoted fans who loved his music. Davis created a gigantic niche for himself in the jazz world. Die-hard jazz fans took him on his own terms, as they had a reverence for his music; and he gave people a bit of himself. Therefore, "the key to understanding Miles [Davis] is to realize that he was a reserved individual and a minimalist. He would just as soon not say anything unless he had something he really wanted to say, and when he did speak, he tended to tell the truth regardless of how anyone might react to it. And his music reflected this aspect of his personality totally."[21] Perhaps no one since Louis Armstrong, who created his own unique jazz sound, has had such a profound impact on the jazz world as Miles Davis. Nevertheless, he spent almost his entire musical career fighting the technical and creative limitations in the music called jazz. And Davis was resolute and breathed life into the most engaging music of the day. Yet, jazz critics came to loathe him for embracing deconstructed rhythms, rock, and popular music, and his *duplicity* when it came to jazz music commercialism. Still, Davis's musicianship and genius shows through miraculously in his many recordings and albums, because he had the willingness to be an extraordinary jazz musician. Davis was certainly beyond the ordinary as a jazz trumpeter.

The movie actor Elijah Wood, who wasn't even born when Davis first started out as a jazz musician, was quoted as saying, Miles Davis "had a kind of influence over music at large because he dipped into areas of music that a lot of others didn't explore. He messed around with rock, soul, funk," and later even Hip-Hop or Rap, you name it.[22] In other words, Davis (with mental fortitude) concocted a new way of thinking and presenting jazz, or "social music," while maintaining his musical bearings. So was this attitude what made Miles Davis so appealing? Without doubt, Davis understood that "jazz is the greatest contribution [made by black musicians in] the U.S. to the culture of mankind, though it is [still] greatly underrated by the American people.[23] Furthermore, *jazz* did not begin abruptly or precisely," or deliberately, but its "beginnings are rather to be thought of as a gradual culmination of all the [musical] influences which precede."[24] The point as Dr. William "Billy" Taylor writes:

> Americans of African descent, in producing music which expressed themselves [like jazz], not only developed a new musical vocabulary, they created a *classical* music—an authentic [African] *American* music which articulated uniquely American feelings and thoughts, which eventually came to transcend ethnic boundaries.[25]

So can *jazz* be resurrected from the dismal state that it is in today—that is, without the musical voice of Miles Dewey Davis? Let us hope so. Otherwise, jazz will suffer the fate of European classical music, which is hardly listened to today by the larger public. In other words, many young people are not all

Figure 1.1 Miles Davis statue in downtown Alton, IL. *Source*: Author's personal photograph.

that interested in such music today, as it is not "the dominant style of popular music." On the other hand, jazz is "instantly addictive," and all about "excitement, romance, tunefulness and virtuosity,"[26] and the spirit. In this regard, Miles Davis was an example of a man with many musical ideas, who had a single-minded purpose when it came to jazz and the *efficacy* of his artistic methods [see Figure 1.1]. We should remember that Davis always believed in different musical notions. So was Davis the *Genghis Khan* of jazz, because he conquered all the various forms of the musical (jazz) idiom? Finally, what manner of jazzman was Miles Davis? Finally, why did he become the stuff of legend? In the end, Davis deserves credit for changing the music of jazz, while making it palatable for almost everyone.

NOTES

1. "3 Jazz Profiles-Miles Davis," *BBC Radio*, February 16, 2006, http://www.bbc.co.uk/radio3/jazz/profiles/.

2. "Jazz," in *Merriam-Webster's Collegiate Encyclopedia*, ed. Mark A. Stevens (Springfield, MA: Merriam-Webster, Inc., 2000), 841.

3. "Jazz," 841.

4. "Religion," in *Merriam-Webster's Collegiate Encyclopedia*, ed. Mark A. Stevens (Springfield, MA: Merriam-Webster, Inc., 2000), 1360.

5. Larry Kart, "Provocative Opinion: The Death of Jazz," *Black Music Research Journal*, vol. 10, no. 1 (1990): 78.

6. Kart, "Provocative Opinion," 78.

7. "Miles Davis Obituary," *Race Matters.org The New York Times Company*, April 27, 2001, http://www.racematters.org/milesdavisobituary.htm. It should be noted that Miles Davis's musical spirit probably came from his mother, Cleota Mae Henry; who played the piano and was a musician in her own right. But she wanted Davis, her son, to start his musical journey with a violin.

8. "Miles Davis Obituary." Davis believed that he had a knack for playing jazz, or "social music." As a young man, he also had a lot of moxie, as we discuss in this work. And to be unfairly blunt, Davis gave some people headaches with his racial and controversial political views. Nevertheless, jazz fans who revered Davis thought that everything he said or did was relevant or significant (to them).

9. Krin Gabbard, "Signifyin(g) the Phallus: Mo' Better Blues and Representation of the Jazz Trumpet," *Cinema Journal* 33, no. 1 (Fall 1992): 47.

10. Steve Jones, "Instrumental to Her Voice: For Cassandra Wilson, Shades of Miles Davis," *USA Today*, sec. 6E, March 26, 1999. And Davis's music cannot be taken for granted. Additionally, Miles Davis showed that he was willing to go against doctrinaire jazz; and there should an asterisk next to his name in this regard.

11. George M. Avakian, "Where is Jazz Going," *Down Beat*, September 1939, 9. It is noteworthy that jazz should always be approached from alternative points of view, especially when discussing the phenomenon around Miles Davis and his inventive music. Furthermore, jazz purists still see Davis as a false prophet when it came to the music.

12. Seth Mnookin, "The Keys to the Future," *Newsweek*, March 10, 2003, 62. With his music, Miles Davis was probably meant to represent the artistic, musical, and cultural ideas of the time and during his life. Moreover, in order for him to create the kind of music he wanted, Davis had to stay focused always on what he was doing, while putting his mind and soul into his great music.

13. Jerry Shriver, "For Rollins, The Spirit of Jazz Is Freedom," *USA Today*, sec. 2D, May 6, 2011.

14. Jones, "Instrumental to Her," 6E.

15. John Rockwell, "Miles Davis: Theme with restless variations built In," *The New York Times*, December 27, 2002, 46. Davis also embodied the quality of defiance and fearlessness when it came to his music. And for these reasons, Davis attracted so much interest, especially from other jazz musicians. He also struck an emotional pose through his critical words, as he openly spoke out against the hatred and viciousness of racist whites.

16. Scott Yanow, "Miles Davis," *Jazz Heritage* Society, 1990, 15. Davis's more explicit attraction to jazz developed not from his time at Juilliard, but it was when he started working with other jazz musicians. Indeed, what the young Miles Davis saw in Charlie Parker captured his musical imagination.

17. Jerry Fink, "No Desire to Settle Down," *Las Vegas Sun*, November 12, 2007, 7. It should be noted also that "any record [or recordings] that Miles Davis played on deserves to be called legendary as there was no talent quite like him." See "Serenade

Music Catalogue," *The Miles Davis Quintet: The Prestige Quintet Sessions*, August 2007, 22.

18. Nekesa Mumbi Moody, "Lil Jon Works to Expand His Kingdom of Crunk," *Las Vegas Review-Journal*, sec. 7E, November 23, 2004. Davis was clearly not a devout religious person, nor a devotee of some organized faith. But he did speak of his personal failures, admitting his problems with drugs, such as cocaine and heroin. Finally, Miles Davis didn't hesitate to tell those who he thought had wronged him, to go to hell, even in public.

19. Flying Lotus, "Psychedelic Funk and Fusion Barreling Into the Future," *The New York Times*, October 12, 2014, 17.

20. Mark Zanger, "Miles Davis Blowing Hot and Cool at 56," *The Real Paper*, August 11, 1976, 7.

21. Scott McFarland, "Miles Davis: The "Electric" Years," *Perfect Sound Forever*, August 1997, http://www.furious.com/pervect/miles.html (2/16/2006). It seemed like Davis was always able to stick to his plans and finish what he started out musically to do. In addition, Davis was noted for unapologetically being himself.

22. Elijah Wood, "Quote on Miles Davis," *USA Weekend*, November 10–12, 2006, 23. When listening to Davis's holistic, electric jazz music, fans are faced with two choices: To love it or hate it. In this regard, Miles Davis was able to move forward regardless of what others thought about what he was doing.

23. Eric Vogel, "Jazz in Nazi Concentration Camp," *Down Beat*, December 7, 1961, 20. In addition, according to Eric Vogel, "the strong mission of jazz [is] the mission of brotherhood and understanding," where "jazz musicians are the 'better people,' free of hate and bias." See the same reference and page number.

24. Paul Eduard Miller, "Roots of Hot White Jazz Are Negroid," *Down Beat*, April 1937, 5.

25. William "Billy" Taylor, "Jazz: America's Classical Music," *The Black Perspective in Music*, vol. 14, issue 3 (1986): 21. Even today, jazz strenuously calls for our attention to this black music. And Davis's music is meant to be heard. Unfortunately, "Jazz hasn't had a consistent mainstream profile in decades." Is this because of the absence of Miles Davis? See Alex Suskind, "Music Review: Adrian Younge, Ali Shaheed Muhammad & Roy Ayers," *Entertainment Weekly*, July 2020, 75.

26. Charles Spencer, "Let Yourself Be Seduced by jazz," *The Daily Telegraph*, July 26, 2010, 22.

Chapter 2

The Start

Of Youth and Old Music Men

It is well known that Miles Davis was an early sideman of the great jazz tenor saxophonist, Charlie "Bird" Parker, who had been extremely important in his (Miles's) early career development. Davis learned by watching and listening to Parker and many others. Davis, at this time, never knew that he would become famous one day, he just wanted to play his trumpet. According to jazz writer Ransom Riggs, "Miles's musical education took place occasionally at the Julliard School of Music but mostly in the smoky clubs of 52nd Street, where he was trained in the esoteric art of 'hot jazz,' a hyper-complex, acrobatic style of playing torrential melodies at breakneck tempos."[1] And Davis was honing his craft under the tutelage of Charlie "Bird" Parker. But it also took discipline and hours of practice on the part of Miles Davis. He was also writing music all the time, thinking and breathing music, so to speak, as if it was part of his DNA. Prior to this time, before he was able to develop his potential talent even more:

> Miles Dewey Davis grew up in East St. Louis, Illinois, the son of a prominent dentist and landowner. He was given his first trumpet [as mentioned] by his father for his 13th birthday. Among his early idols were Bobby Hackett (particularly because of the lyrical solo that Hackett took on a 1939 recording of "Embraceable You"), Harry James, and Clark Terry (a local star at that time). Davis played with his high school band, worked with Eddie Randall's Blue Devils during 1941–43, and had what he described as the greatest musical experience of his life when he had the opportunity to sit in with the Billy Eckstine Orchestra in 1944; among its stars were Dizzy Gillespie and Charlie Parker.[2]

Charlie "Bird" Parker allowed Davis to not only hone his skills as a musician, or jazz trumpeter, but this strange relationship might have been regarded

Figure 2.1 Miles Davis statue in downtown Alton, IL. *Source*: Author's personal photograph.

as Davis's apprenticeship, or his musical or seminary training, where the two famous jazz men essentially melded their creative juices, having faith in jazz—that is, having a shared belief in new musical directions. No doubt, Miles Davis had an outsized personality, but at the start of his musical career, he was incredibly shy. In a soft tone, almost as if he was embarrassed to even play his trumpet sometimes, reminded the young Davis that he had work to do. Perhaps at the time, Davis didn't know that he was going to build a new musical *paradigm* and jazz movement, personally around him [see Figure 2.1]. Indeed, as jazz writers Joachim-Ernst Berendt and Günther Huesmann write:

> Miles Davis began as a Dizzy [Gillespie] imitator, just as Dizzy had begun by imitating [Roy] Eldridge. But he [Davis] soon found his own, completely new [music] style. Miles is the founder and chief representative of the second phase of modern jazz trumpeting: *lyrical* arcs of melody in which the sophistication of simplicity is admirably cultivated, even less vibrato than Dizzy—and all this with a tone less glowing than loaded with coolly smoldering protest.[3]

Even playing with Charlie "Bird" Parker, the young Miles Davis tried to improve on his trumpet playing each and every day with Bird's fast-pace saxophone playing and improvisations. But Davis would play on, because he thought he played well enough; and Davis personally thought that he was making progress, especially with his own improvisations. According to jazz enthusiast and photographer Kathy Sloane, "to make this [jazz] music of improvisation demands a highly imaginative and creative mind, not only to blow, but also to live a life that enables one to make the music."[4] And the young Miles Davis had the imagination and creativeness and power to blow his horn in spades. Which is to say, Miles Davis made an ingenious effort to interpret Be-bop jazz with gumption, bravado, and enthusiasm. Therefore, with Charlie "Bird" Parker, Davis was on the cusp of musical greatness, even though his trumpet playing was a bit shaky at that time in the 1940s. And in the backrooms of jazz clubs "was where the elders [like Charlie "Bird" Parker] taught the youngsters [like Miles Davis] the things they'd need to know in addition to mouthpieces and harmony."[5] Jazz critic for the BBC, Alyn Shipton explains:

> Unlike Gillespie, Davis was not a technical innovator on the trumpet. His playing lacked the rapidity, verve, range, and brilliance of the most consummate bebop trumpeters, who also included Fats Navarro, Howard McGhee, and Clifford Brown. Yet Davis created an immediately identifiable personal voice: a clear vibrato-free tone with a logic about the placement of each note that stamped his authority on all his groups and dictated how those around him would [eventually] approach his music.[6]

As a young jazz musician, Davis dedicated his time to practicing fast, particularly the high notes on his trumpet; but it was more challenging than he had expected, especially keeping up with Charlie "Bird" Parker. If Davis looked at you while on stage at some nightclub, then, his face revealed nothing, as he was fearless. Or he would sometimes clench his jaws in frustration. Ultimately and abruptly, Davis would sometimes look upward, toward the ceiling, as if he was beseeching the gods. Then, he would *titch* his tongue before bringing his trumpet to his sensitive lips and begin to seriously blow his horn. Also, on stage during the late 1940s, Davis was known for creating a surprising mellow mood or an emotive sound, which was sometimes wanting, and often delivered in an imprecise or unsophisticated manner. But as he matured as a musician, his solos evolved into something beautiful. Moreover, the force of his presence was great, especially standing head-to-head with Charlie "Bird" Parker. And when Davis played, he put *everything* he had into his solos; but he was often overshadowed by the great Charlie "Bird" Parker, as there was a stark difference in the way they both played their respective instruments. Also, performing on-stage during that time, the young, skinny-looking Miles Davis had other insecurities, like his reserved trumpet playing. Nevertheless, Davis was able to conquer his fear of playing before a live audience, as he wanted to bring to the forefront the best of himself (as a trumpeter) to *any* performance, where he was a sideman. On the other hand, Davis never really liked being scrutinized in public—that is, all of the time, because he also relished his privacy. Consequently, with Charlie "Bird" Parker in the background, Davis played with his head and heart, taking a holistic approach to the music. This is to say, Davis played with an earnest spirit, even when there was nothing particularly extraordinary about his trumpet playing at that time.

But Davis had it in him to use his apprenticeship with Parker, to learn marvelous new things. Davis also knew that he was not going to be a typical jazz trumpeter. Although he would later be described as "the conqueror, the innovator, the great introducer and discoverer of talent as well as the creative lover and hateful destroyer,"[7] Davis, however, never liked such accolades. The turning point came for Davis when he decided to strike out on his own, because he felt he was ready. In the end, Miles had "added a quality of elegance to "Bird's" image of raw authenticity, and it was embodied in the [Davis] sound that fit him perfectly."[8] No doubt, Charlie "Bird" Parker was appreciative of Miles; but sometimes good things must come to an inevitable end. Jazz writer Ransom Riggs put it this way:

> Miles was a quick study, but after a year touring as a rising star in Charlie Parker's band, he dropped out [completely] in 1958. Miles found that the "hot" stuff didn't speak to his soul; instead, he was captivated by the pensive, intimate sounds of pianist Thelonious Monk, singer Billie Holiday and composer Gil Evans. Their songs cut deeper and played more slowly than popular "hot jazz" tunes, and with those musician's help and influence, he pioneered a style known as "cool jazz," which focused the genre's intensity into a laser beam of sound.[9]

Obviously, Miles Davis learned and grew as a musician from his relationship with Charlie "Bird" Parker, when he was desiring to be *somebody* in the jazz world—that is, after a sort of dissolute youth. And his experiences were worth every bit of his time and efforts. Davis even learned how to be a bandleader from Charlie "Bird" Parker. Of course, Parker understood the essence of what he wanted to do musically, because of his passionate devotion to jazz. The young, endlessly curious Miles Davis, in his exuberance to play his trumpet, had sought out and eventually found the elder jazz man; and took what he could (musically) from him, then he let go, or left Parker's band. And perhaps like a musical god, when it was all said and done, Miles Davis learned that he could reach people deeply through his engaging music. Finally, Davis's musical *pragmatism*, which was most revealing, gave him a new, dominant paradigm of jazz, based on musical interrelatedness and independence—and a taste of the ultimate *divine*. There was no doubt that the young Miles Davis was a musical genius, as his compelling, trumpet-playing demonstrated. And for many during the 1950s and early 1960s, Davis's "individuality and constant desire to stretch himself symbolized jazz."[10] Thus, his early music should, at least, be considered unconventional and an exercise in the spiritual.

NOTES

1. Ransom Riggs, "The Genius of Miles Davis: Explained!" *Mental Floss*, August 15, 2008, https://www.mentalfloss.com/blogs/archives/16692. The young Miles Davis was learning and being taught things that you couldn't get in a music school. Or so Davis thought.

2. Scott Yanow, *Trumpet Kings: The Players Who Shaped the Sound of Jazz Trumpet* (San Francisco, CA: Backbeat books, 2001), 117. Charlie "Bird" Parker helped the young Davis navigate the daunting challenge of playing in nightclubs and getting paid.

3. Joachim-Ernst Berendt and Günther Huesmann, *The Jazz Book: From Ragtime to the 21st Century* (Chicago, IL: Lawrence Hill Books, 2009), 251.

4. Sascha Feinstein and Kathy Sloane, *Keystone Corner: Portrait of a Jazz Club* (Bloomington and Indianapolis, IN: Indiana University Press, 2012), 203.

5. Feinstein and Sloane, *Keystone Corner*, 203.

6. Shipton, *Jazz Markers*, 143–144. Davis was extraordinarily committed to the idea of a musical career, because he thought he had the chops and talent.

7. George R. Crips, *Miles Davis: An Impact Biography* (New York: Franklin Watts, 1997), 12.

8. Goodman, "Miles Davis," 12.

9. Riggs, "The Genius of Miles." According to journalist Leonard Feather, "Miles Davis, who served his apprenticeship with Parker in the mid-40s, formed his historic nine-piece band in 1949. With Konitz and baritonist Gerry Mulligan, arrangements by Gil Evans, John Lewis, Johnny Carisi, and Mulligan, it, too, pointed toward the 'cool' jazz movement of the next decade." See Leonard Feather, "Miles and the Fifties," *Down Beat*, July 2, 1964, 44–48, 98.

10. Yanow, "Miles Essentials," 15. It should be pointed out that Davis's "mother wanted him to attend Fisk University, but Miles opposed the plan." Indeed, his determination to stay with music was strengthened by an experience with Billy Eckstine band." Moreover, when Davis "arrived in New York in 1945, [he] immediately sought out Parker and became his good friend and protégé, as well as a disciple of Gillespie." See Leonard Feather, "Miles and the Fifties," 46.

Chapter 3

Band Members

Turning Ideas into Music

As far as Miles Davis being dubbed "the Prince of Darkness" was concerned, which was a sobriquet he liked,[1] we should note that he was once a womanizer, drug addict, a pimp, and a con man, as well as a great jazz musician. And before it became fashionable in some circles and acceptable for some of today's rap artists and other *misogynistic* musicians, Davis was also a foulmouthed child of sometimes unimaginable evil, and a peculiar force to reckon with. In this respect, Davis didn't have any fondness for God; but there was more than a little bit of magic to his personality, especially when dealing with some of his band members. This is to say that Davis could also be a really thoughtful person, compassionate, with good intentions. In many ways, that was the point. Writer and poet Quincy Troupe writes that "Davis was not the kind of person who [concerned] himself with sanitizing his image. He [preferred] to say what he [had] to say, to tell his true feelings, even when what he [had] to say hurts him and others."[2] So was Davis a *demigod* or evil incarnate because of his personal and musical transgressions? Furthermore, Davis *never* liked the language of biblical references, to say the least, to describe his music; nor did he think *any* God would be his personal salvation. However, Davis did use Gospel funk harmony in some of his great classical or acoustic and jazz fusion music. Was this because Davis thought of himself as one of the great ones? *Jazz Review* editor Richard Cook thought that Miles Davis was a mystic, or "the [musical] shaman who conjured unprecedented results out of almost nothing."[3] While Miles Davis lived, he not only achieved the necessary higher consciousness, to reach some special kind of musical *Nirvana*, or perhaps the divine; but he had been in a unique position to witness the spiritual growth and development of jazz with other musicians, which enabled them to free their minds and perhaps their souls. As journalist C. Michael

Bailey writes: "Miles was the conscience of jazz while at the same time reading its horoscope."[4] Bailey goes on to write: "My argument is simple: Miles Davis was present at or instrumental in every major jazz movement after swing."[5] Moreover, and in the view of the great African American jazz pianist Herbie Hancock,

> The genius of [Miles] Davis is rooted in the kind of ethical stance he also finds in his own Buddhist practice: lacing a high value on collaboration, an openness to new ways of seeing and a generosity of spirit. The trumpeter [Davis] often demonstrated this in ways only a master musician could.[6]

Herbie Hancock, "who helped shape the sounds of Davis's path-breaking quintet of the 1960s," firmly believed that Miles Davis could musically turn "poison into medicine"[7]—that is in terms of making a wrong chord played during a performance sound right. In this way, Davis was elevated to one of the jazz gods in that he will remain immortal through his music. Indeed, Miles Davis will forever maintain his status as "the single most important figure in jazz music history."[8] Of course, Davis's ticket to the realm of music god-ship, so to speak, was partly because of the raw talent of some of his young band members, or jazz disciples, who lived vicariously in the shadow of Davis; but they also existed in their own spiritual plane, or political and musical limelight, like the late and great John Coltrane, or Sonny Rollins. As a sideman and "influential saxophonist with Miles Davis, Coltrane 'made vital contributions to numerous Davis albums, including *Relaxin', Steamm', Workin', and Cookin'*." In the end, "Coltrane initiated several new directions in his [own] music, most of which added a dimension of free improvisation to his modal and technical explorations."[9] According to the journalist Bob Blumenthal, "A more pensive and technically limited soloist than most of his generation, Davis recognized the value of musical contrast early on, and found that the aggressive [Sonny] Rollins style offered a perfect complement to his own solos."[10] This is important to note, because "Rollins recorded a number of his own compositions with Davis, including 'Airegin' and 'Oleo,'" before leaving the band in 1954.[11] There were numerous other band members, like Bill Evans, Cannonball Adderly, Paul Chambers, Herbie Hancock, Wayne Shorter, Ron Carter, and the fascinating drummer Tony Williams, to name a few, who made significant contributions to Davis's bands. To play with Davis was an education in itself, and many of his younger sidemen learned from the great jazz man. Tony Williams was once quoted as stating that he had to jump through hoops playing as a drummer with Miles Davis, but it was all worth it.[12] Even Herbie Hancock made the comment that he found the "classroom of Miles Davis to be potent, intoxicating, [and] stimulating."[13] To be sure, playing as a sideman with Davis was educational, or life-fulfilling.

Rarely do jazz musicians today have the same "on-the-job" apprenticeship from some of the elder jazz statesmen like Davis had with Charlie "Bird" Parker and Clark Terry. Indeed, what happened to passing knowledge from one generation to the next? Journalist Nate Chinen writes, "Beginning in the 1990s, a decade that saw the deaths of Blakey, Davis and Carter, jazz's apprenticeship system has routinely been described as woefully diminished."[14] This, of course, is a sad commentary on what jazz apprenticeship means today, or the state of jazz with young musicians of all stripes. According to jazz writer Giovani Russonello:

> "Jazz" today encompasses an entire ocean of past-collegiate musical work: highbrow traditionalism, renegade funk, droning free improvisations. Jazz musicians now have to be improvisers deeply trained in the American tradition, with roots in the blues. Beyond that, almost anything goes.[15]

During the highlight or heyday of jazz, Davis was able to work with several talented musicians, like one of "the great jazz saxophonists of all time," Wayne Shorter. What is poignant here is, Shorter learned from Miles Davis, and "made his name performing" with the jazz trumpeter "from 1964 to 1970." He was also "a prolific composer with Davis, and had a starring role in 'Bitches Brew,' one of the world's bestselling jazz records, [which was] released in 1970,"[16] as discussed earlier. So there is no doubt that, "Playing with Miles Davis was more often than not a tremendous boost to a young musician's career. It was certification that a musician had arrived among the select circle in jazz."[17] Indeed, Davis's jazz apprentices or band members were not only "excellent [musicians] individually, but they "functioned with considerable independence and freedom," complementing each other magnificently in Miles Davis's second greatest quintet.[18] Toward this end, David liked the idea of fine-turning what he played with his young band members, working out the musical glitches. Nevertheless, "Miles was known for allowing the musicians in his band great expressive freedom, and he was not one to limit or dictate to them in any way."[19] Indeed, Davis fiercely guarded his young musicians; and protecting his music was unparalleled. And because of this, his younger, admirable jazz musicians and (mostly Black) band members embraced Davis's way of playing and his style, because he became the standard-bearer of jazz. Davis did his own thing. And later, he would incorporate jazz (or "social music") with soul, rock, and funk traditions. According to the late Dr. Billy Taylor, Miles Davis "was a completely free spirit and had an entirely personalized approach to playing [his music] that was a big contrast to the complex styles of bebop,"[20] or other jazz musical genres. Furthermore, it should be noted that

Davis's insistent matching of musical to ethnic differences over the years bespeaks the collaborative musical variety that he felt compelled to seek by merging various [musical] approaches. There [was] indeed, something in the mix he wanted us—all of us, whites as well as blacks—to hear. Perhaps more than any other contemporary [jazz] musician, Davis made this stylistic, cultural, and ethnic mix the stuff of his music.[21]

No matter that these issues dealt with the racial politics in jazz, his young band members ate it up, because Davis had a genius in navigating his way through the social fires from those days in the late 1950s, 1960s, and 1970s. In an interview by a former band member, Sonny Rollins in 2020, had this to say about culture and Davis's behavior and spirituality: "A lot of people wouldn't think [that] Miles was a very spiritual [individual or] person—though to me he was—and Coltrane was a very spiritual individual. . . . [So] there's [a] connection between the way you behave and your music."[22] Davis's band members over the years, however, didn't care if it was ethical or spiritual with Miles, because many of them stepped away from jazz standards, which jazz purists, ultimately thought was *sacrilegious*.

NOTES

1. Geoffrey C. Ward and Ken Burns, "Miles Davis," *Jazz: A History of America's Music* (New York: Alfred A. Knopf, 2006), 408.
2. Davis and Troupe, *Miles: The Autobiography*, 414.
3. Richard Cook, *It's About That Time: Miles Davis On and Off Record* (New York: Oxford University Press, 2005), 219.
4. C. Michael Bailey, "Miles Davis: Miles Davis at Carnegie Hall," *All About Jazz*, June 1, 1998, https://www.allaboutjazz.com/miles.
5. Bailey, "Miles Davis at Carnegie Hall."
6. Stuart Isacoff, "The Genius of Miles," *The Wall Street Journal*, sec. D5, February 6, 2014.
7. Isacoff, "The Genius of Miles," D5.
8. Bailey, "Miles Davis at Carnegie Hall."
9. Alyn Shipton, *Jazz Makers: Vanguards of Sound* (New York: Oxford University Press, 2002), 173–176.
10. Bob Blumenthal, *Saxophone Colossus: A Portrait of Sonny Rollins* (New York: Abrams, 2009), 16. It should be noted that Sonny Rollins "established himself as one of the leading saxophonists at the cutting edge of jazz development, if not the foremost. See Shipton, *Jazz Makers*, 179–180.
11. Shipton, *Jazz Makers*, 179–180.
12. Nisenson, *Round About Midnight*, 184–185.
13. Isacoff, "The Genius of Miles."

14. Nate Chinen, "Jazz Apprentices," 17.

15. Giovanni Russonello, "A Symbol of Jazz's Past, Aiming to Shape its Future," *The New York Times*, July 28, 2019, 8.

16. "The Jazz of Wayne Shorter: Serious Longevity," *The Economist*, November 16, 2013, 87.

17. Nisenson, *Round About Midnight*, 185.

18. "Miles Davis: 1964–69 Recordings," 8.

19. Billy Taylor and Teresa L. Reed, *The Jazz Life of Dr. Billy Taylor* (Bloomington, IN: Indiana University Press, 2013), 115. According to Dr. Billy Taylor, "Someone once asked him [Davis] how much playing he did on a daily basis. He answered that he never touched his horn unless he had a gig. He claimed that this was the way he kept his musical ideas fresh." See Taylor and Reed, *The Jazz Life*, 115.

20. Taylor and Reed, *The Jazz Life*, 115.

21. "Miles Davis, Musical Dialogician," *Black Music Research Journal*, vol. III, no. 2 (Fall 1991): 255.

22. David Marchese, "Interview with Sonny Rollins on Whether Great Musicians Make Good People," *The New York Times Magazine*, March 1, 2020, 13.

Chapter 4

The Art of Stage Presence

Onstage, when he was performing, Davis was a calming influence for his young band members, as they expected him to give them direction. It was during this time, "between 1955 and 1957, Davis assembled his first quintet with John Coltrane, Red Garland, Paul Chambers, and Philly Joe Jones."[1] Of course, Davis could inspire young musicians to his musical vision, often working so creatively and energetically, that the members of his first quintet felt they had to produce. At this period, Davis's performances were an extravagant event, as he was a formidable jazz presence. Davis loved high-energy performances; and he was very much aware of what was going on onstage, especially with his first quintet band members. In his own way, Davis had a flair for the dramatic. And after his first real band appeared "at the 1955 Newport Jazz Festival and the release of the LP *Round About Midnight*, this quintet hit the big time."[2] Davis was electric to be around, especially on stage, where he ignored his audiences, or left the stage while his band members played their solos. Or sometimes Davis would actually stop playing and glare at his band, particularly when he thought they were being overpowering or too (musically) aggressive. To say the least, Davis always knew how his first quintet was coming off or playing.

Additionally, Davis never interacted or talked to his audiences or announced any of his tunes, as many jazz musicians ordinarily did. Indeed, he would sometimes turn his nose up at *everything*, his audiences included. We must wonder if his audiences ever thought that something was amiss when he walked off the stage during a performance. Was he an angry music god? Davis explained it this way:

> Why I sometimes walk off the stand [or stage] is because when it's somebody else's turn to solo, I ain't going to just stand up there and be detracting [to]

him. What am I going to stand up there for? I ain't no model, and I don't sing or dance, and I damn sure ain't no Uncle Tom just to be up there grinning. Sometimes I go over by the piano or the drums and listen to what they're doing. But if I don't' want to do that, I go in the wings and listen to the whole band until it's the next turn for my horn.[3]

But Davis *did* get into certain situations on stage where he tried to make stuff up, innovatively, just to give his audiences something wonderful or different; because at the end of the day, he believed that you had to give your fans *something* more, *something* special. Therefore, "1958 saw the band leader [Davis] add Julian 'Cannonball' Adderley to the fold, producing what biographer Jack Chambers claims was 'perhaps the finest small band in the history of jazz. [The album] *Milestones* resulted, planting the seeds for future innovations.'"[4] Davis thought of it as creating musical magic on stage—that is, adding "Cannonball" Adderley to his band. And their musical experiences were unforgettable. Davis wasn't bringing his band members together for the sake of just bringing them together; but it was to make good music—on and off the stage. By example, Davis was an exemplary leader, especially when playing his trumpet, in earnest, on stage. Still, Davis could make people angry by his *antics*—his arrogant and sassy attitude. Or wordlessly, Davis could insult his audiences with his "kiss-of-death stare," as if he didn't like you, with sometimes bloodshot eyes that would almost sparkle. But he was fitfully entertaining.

And watching the unexpected chemistry between him and his band members was the price of admissions to his concerts. His audiences also had a keen interest in what he was during on stage during a live performance. There was something vaguely menacing about Davis, as he would lean in with his trumpet. Although Davis wasn't tall, he was an imposing figure just the same. Furthermore, Davis didn't necessarily like people (fans) to become too up close and personal (or familiar) with him; nor did he like members of his audiences coming up to the stage where he was performing, to shake his hands. Yet, Davis's "elegance and extravagance, dramatic outbursts and lyrical moodiness were mirrored in his lifestyle, which fascinated fans who might otherwise know little of jazz."[5] And he (Davis) liked his hold on people.

Davis also attracted attention, because he was a true showman, despite his denial. And his *cocksure* swagger told almost everyone, basically, to kiss his *black ass*. To be sure, his audiences closely watched Davis's every move on stage, as he was an overwhelming presence and more than interesting. Perhaps with appraising eyes, Davis might have viewed the beautiful women in his audiences. Some women fans thought of him as naughty. Many would study his face closely, attentively, as Davis's face would sometimes be grimly stoic, with sometimes eyes blazing, like some latter-day *Svengali*. To say the least, many women found Davis sexy, "fascinating, charismatic, witty and intelligent."[6] Jazz writer Eric Nisenson tells us: "In 1958 Miles was reaching the height of his fame, and he was richly enjoying its rewards. Among those rewards were women. [And] after his divorce from Irene, beautiful, glamorous women were a constant in his life."[7] And suffice to say, these women often took notice of Davis. And during some of his live and taped performances, Davis's jaws even tightened, as he would finally shake his head and turn away from his audiences; then closing his eyes, Davis would place his golden trumpet to his callous lips and blow, displaying a godly virtuosity, while "shooting spikes [of notes] into the upper register and running the changes [in a tune] at breakneck speed."[8] Often, Davis would be worn out by his efforts. Miles also knew that he was being watched by his white audiences, even when he stood in place before a microphone with his horn or walked all over the stage, especially when he was an older jazz man, in his early sixties. Nisenson explained it this way:

> For Miles the existentialist, the physical aspect of playing on stage were as important as such abstract considerations as harmony, melody, and rhythm. Thanks to new technology, he [Davis] no longer had to play into a microphone—his trumpet was wired with its own built-in mike. He could play from any place on stage rather than having to stand in the same place. Once he got used to this new way of playing, he would tell writers that even thinking about the way he formerly had to play "gave [him] a headache."[9]

And because of Davis's incomparable stage presence and flippant attitude, his fans loved him, as if he was a *cult* leader. But his uncouth behavior on stage, for some (to this day) can never be justified. Miles Davis, however, was *never* musically ostentatious, even with his addictive stage presence. To be sure, "Davis could be as arrogant and insulting as he was vulnerable and defensive." Additionally, "he had the kind of personality that drove loved ones close to madness and that only the most eminent [music] artists [could] get away with."[10] Also, Davis had an unearthly (or uncanny) ability to connect with his band members and audiences alike, while performing on stage. Some even found him beguiling. This is to say that, "Davis was clever at being a saint one minute and a cruel despot the next."[11] All in all, and later in life, Davis didn't really get rattled on stage, as he always tried to be in the moment. Furthermore, Davis had a self-assuredness that told you that he was definitely a "bad-ass," punctuated by his spectacular music. But some of his audiences didn't like Davis's snobbish posturing and his sometimes *anemic* trumpet playing. Even Ralph Ellison, the late black writer of *Invisible Man*, "who was a trumpeter and composer before he was an author,"[12] criticized Davis as being "evil" and an inept trumpet player.[13] Nevertheless, Davis's slick movements on stage (for some fans) were of dignity and grace; and he had an almost boyish smile—that is, when he did smile. Of course, some of his audiences also wanted Davis to be a little more mannered, instead of more in their faces. However, Miles Davis was never cooperative or accommodating, as he had a great presence that was a sight to behold, while playing his trumpet and walking around a particular stage. Davis explained:

> I walk around all the time because there's different sounds on stage.... Nobody wants to stand still and play [anymore], you know what I mean? It's old-time, man; it's Jim Crow. [Or] Uncle Tommish when you go to the microphone and you play and you step back and bow to the audience, like the audience is doing something for them [or the jazz musician] when they're really teaching the audience.[14]

Also, as if he was in deep thought, Davis would sometimes quickly look over his right or left shoulder (on stage) at his extraordinary talented, young band members, as if it was his own personal *fiefdom*. He would also, individually, look at them if they pissed him off (in some way) by what they played. But Davis didn't believe that his young sidemen had to be perfect, because they, too, were learning, particularly when they played badly. And, "although Miles was [often] driving the group, making it play at its fullest potential, it appeared to the public, and especially to the so-called jazz critics, that he was being arrogant and almost indifferent."[15] This is to say that sometimes Davis looked uninterested, as if he didn't respect his band members or his respective audiences. But sometimes there probably *was* a wall between Davis and them. Or perhaps this was just his way of involving the audience, in his live performances.

Moreover, Davis was exciting and magnetic during his stage performances, even with his off-putting and unflappable *demeanor*. Davis, of course, had his own sort of gravity on stage, as if he owned the place. Still, audiences wanted to hear something brilliant, or something that would astound them; and they were rarely disappointed. Many of his fans liked that Davis, "effectively [transformed] the trumpet from a showy catcall instrument to something more searching and debonair"—that is, "he [Davis] hit on a sound that married his quest brooding [and stage presence] with a classic fashion sense that included tailoring suits short in the back [as a young man] to account for his slumped-over stage stance."[16] Davis never really played straight. Or he would sometimes hold his trumpet toward the floor, not straight-up the way many trumpeters play their horns. This would become his signature style. In addition, Davis's hunched-over posture was not so much straight, as it was bent backward as he played his trumpet, forming his famous question mark position, with sometimes drooping shoulders. Davis would even tilt his head sideways and pull his ears, even placing his index finger in one of his ears; or cup his ears—to hear the music being played by his band members. Davis actually loved cocking his head, as he would listen some more, harder, deciding on how, perhaps, he would approach his next solo. Moreover, Davis once said that "he'd rather hear a guy miss a couple of notes than hear the same old clichés all the time." He goes on, "often when a man misses [a note], it at least shows he's trying to think of something new to play."[17] Nonetheless, Davis's demeanor always seemed to be somewhat antagonistic, as his face was often in intense concentration, with a fierceness (again) in his eyes—that is, when he wasn't wearing dark sunglasses—as if he was obsessively searching for the right note. According to Nisenson, "All Miles's remaining energy went into just playing his horn," as he simply "wanted to relax on stage, [and] exult in the joy of simply playing his horn rather than [standing] on the razor's edge,"[18] to use the metaphor.

More importantly, Davis was able to grasp onto something tangible, playing his terrific trumpet that was solid, real, profound, and perhaps *godly*. That said, Davis's audiences seemed always to have a ball when he was playing his best, with a supernatural sound like nothing else anyone had ever heard before. Jazz enthusiast Martin Williams writes: "Happily," Miles Davis "found ways to offer" his music onstage, "against both personal odds and a long-enduring public apathy (not to say hostility) toward his [jazz or social music] idiom."[19] Finally, Miles gave his listeners and audiences a rare way to see him onstage—to see his reflective, orgy of beautiful music, as he was most often able to shine brightly. And people and fans were utterly entranced by this black jazz man.

NOTES

1. Bailey, "Miles Davis at Carnegie Hall."
2. Bailey, "Miles Davis at Carnegie Hall."
3. Alex Haley, interview, "Miles Davis: A Candid Conversation with the jazz World's Premier Iconoclast," *Playboy*, September 1962, http://www.honors.umd.edu/HONR2693.
4. Bailey, "Miles Davis at Carnegie Hall."
5. Howard Mandel, "Sketches of Miles," *Down Beat*, December 1991, 18.
6. Eric Nisenson, *Round About Midnight: A Portrait of Miles Davis* (New York: Da Capo Press, 1996), 146.
7. Nisenson, "Round About Midnight," 146.
8. Krin Gabbard, *Hotter Than That: The Trumpet, Jazz, and American Culture* (New York: Faber and Faber, Inc., 2008), 195. It is important to note that Davis's audiences were made up of mostly white fans, who loved his soulful, lyrical music. Unfortunately, as jazz biographer Bill Cole writes, jazz "has never been embraced

[totally] by African-American people, because we have believed that whatever music we create can only benefit from the advice and influence of the dominant [white] culture." See Bill Cole, *Miles Davis: A Musical Biography* (New York: William Morrow & Company, Inc., 1974), 105.

9. Nisenson, "Round About Midnight," 240.

10. Gabbard, *Hotter Than That*, 207.

11. Richard Cook and Frances Stonor Saunders, "Miles Too Popular," *New Statesman*, vol. 130, issue 4533, April 16, 2001, 45, http://web17.epnet.com.

12. Griffin and Washington, *Clawing at the Limits*, 43.

13. Gabbard, *Hotter Than That*, 206.

14. Frank Alkyer, "The Miles Files," *Down Beat*, December 1991, 22.

15. Bill Cole, *Miles Davis: A Musical Biography* (New York: William Morrow, 1974), 79.

16. Andy Battaglia, review of "John Szwed: So What: The Life of Miles Davis," *ADCLUB*, February 28, 2003, 2, https://aux.avclub.com/john-szwed.

17. Nat Hentoff, "Miles: A Trumpeter in the Midst of a Big Comeback Makes a Very Frank Appraisal of Today's Jazz Scene," *Down Beat*, November 2, 1955, 13.

18. Nisenson, "Round About Midnight," 241.

19. Martin Williams, "Miles Davis: A Man Walking," in *The Jazz Tradition* (New York: Oxford University Press, 1970), 189.

Chapter 5

Of Missed Notes and Technique

Some jazz critics believed that Miles Davis's mediocrity and ineptitude as a jazz trumpeter should have limited his stardom. However, in unique ways, Davis was able to showcase and demonstrate his trumpet skills, or "instrumental mastery" on many of his *Tour de Force* recordings. Furthermore, he "remained in the vanguard of jazz exploration from 1949" until his death in 1991, while "developing and advancing several contrasting styles informed by his distinctive, brooding trumpet voice."[1] This is to say that Davis embraced change in the way that he played his music, which was especially important to him. Moreover, Davis had a level of comfort and strength in his trumpet playing, despite what the critics and naysayers had to say to the contrary. Indeed, Davis's nimble adaptability in terms of improvisation was masterful; and his technical expertise was always evolving. Specifically, Davis's trumpet playing improved considerably (in this aspect) over the years while he lived. Also, in this regard, Davis was confident in the fact that he could make or put together aesthetically pleasing music that people liked to listen to. Nevertheless, "critics have always been made uncomfortable by his 'mistakes,' the cracked and missed notes common in his performances."[2] Jazz critic Robert Walser, for example, tells us that Davis had "long been infamous for missing more notes than any other major trumpet player."[3] But Davis never accepted what critics had to say about his trumpet playing, because many inevitably thought that they knew best. Or some white critics had a vague idea about what they thought Miles Davis should be, or how *they* thought he should sound. But it should be understood that Davis "refused to be constrained by *genre* boundaries; his music embraced and explored contradictions; he dismissed questions of authenticity or purity; [and] he was unwilling to separate art, life and politics."[4] Amid the criticism of his trumpet playing and technique, Davis still made beautiful music. Professor Quincy Troupe described Davies's trumpet playing this way:

> Miles Davis was a great poet on his instrument. His horn could blow warm, round notes that spoke to the deepest human emotions, and it could spit out cracked trills that evoked the angry sounds of bullets firing. Sometimes his trumpet seemed to float over and through remarkably complex rhythms and time signatures with heart-stopping speed and efficiency. His sound could penetrate like a sharp knife. It could also be muted, tender and low, like a lullaby, but it was always charged with deeply felt emotion.[5]

Troupe's analysis of Davis's steady trumpet playing is most accurate. And perhaps this was "why so many critics have responded to Davis's music with puzzlement, hostility, or an uneasy silence."[6] And contrary to the reports of the day, Davis could play his trumpet with precise consistency and proficiency. But jazz writer Michael James asks: How could Miles Davis "play so badly a year and more after proving he could play so well" at other times, like "with his splendid solo on *Walkin*,"[7] released in the late 1950s. But we should know that a lot of hard work went into Davis's horn playing, as he opened up new musical vistas and possibilities. For Michael James, there was something intriguingly and aesthetically right about his trumpet playing, even his wrong notes, because Davis liked coming up with a new fluency in the music. James writes:

> Davis preferred to create his own language and his progress was in consequence a good deal slower. [And] if plagiarism was repugnant to him, he had to pay the price for his aversion to it; hence the split notes, faulty intonation and scrambled phrases that mar much of his work in the first five years of his recorded career.[8]

Davis's style of playing his trumpet, however, became his musical *pedigree*. And his stamina and trumpet-playing prowess were always palpable; one just has to listen to his *Kind of Blue* album to test this validity. Davis worked his magic with his horn, as he was prodigiously talented. Indeed, he developed "his own voice—on the horn, based on the St. Louis style of playing—spare and blues-based, but fast, clean, open, lyrical, bold."[9] The one consistent element in Davis's technique, once he decided to play a certain type of music, was the way he improvised and played his solos, especially as he continued to tweak his trumpet sound. Davis's beautiful trumpet voice, in a way, sounds like the breaking of diamonds, perhaps, with a smooth-grooved hammer; or like some precious gem skipping on crystal pools of water. And no one else in the world sounded quite like him, as he had an unmistakable tone. Walser explains: "Davis constantly and consistently put himself at risk in his trumpet playing, by using a loose, flexible *embouchure* that helped him to produce a great variety of tone colors and articulations by striving for dramatic gestures rather than consistent demonstration of mastery, and by experimenting with unconventional techniques,"[10] like bending notes, by depressing "a [trumpet] valve only part of the way down, which [created] a split, unfocused airstream," while allowing for "a variety of timbres and effects,"[11] or an unearthly, godly sound. This was especially true with his improvisations and solos. The great tenor saxophonist and composer Wayne Shorter, a former band member of Miles Davis, was infatuated with his [Davis's] improvisations, as he believed that his trumpet playing "touched the heart of everything, even the act of creating being from nothingness and the art of extracting coolness from boredom."[12] Along the way, Davis exhibited some of the best hand-eye coordination in rendering his improvisations and fingering his trumpet, particularly when it came to the musical ideas in his head that were never seen; and where he reached beyond what he was playing. Also, Davis often "began his improvisations lagging slightly behind the beat, then on it, then to double-time, finishing right on the beat."[13]

After all, what Davis was able to do in jazz music, was uncanny, as he had the capacity to manifest greatness every time he picked up his horn. In other words, Davis would come up with a certain musical concept and find the right musicians to play the music alongside him, to fit his (or that) musical concept. According to jazz pianist Chick Corea, "Miles Davis's improvisational solos are really interesting to look at on music paper, because there's nothing to them." He goes on: With a John Coltrane "solo or Charlie Parker solo, you can string the notes out and see all these phrases and harmonic ideas, patterns, all kinds of things." But Miles Davis "doesn't use patterns. He doesn't string notes out. It's weird. Without the expression, and without the feeling he put in it, there's nothing there."[14] It was as if Davis created, as mentioned earlier in this work, a new *paradigm* for jazz music. James simply states:

> Davis's use of the pause—the audacity with which he ignored the convention that required the soloist to pattern his phrasing on the basic eight-bar divisions—indicates that his conception was inherently more complex.[15]

Moreover, Davis's spare, but almost perfect trumpet sound is musically conveyed in a perfunctory fashion; but when Davis played his horn, he was very intense, *cerebral*, while always working on *not* playing so many notes in his *modal*, improvisational solos. Or he used a minimalist, simple and silent approach. Indeed, Davis's deceptively distant trumpet sound proved that he had a delicate way of playing convincingly. And it was something Davis vigorously pursued, as he learned to concentrate on simply the melodies of a tune, like a language, rather than focusing on all the notes. And, "while his solos may have been expressed simply, they were at the same time highly sophisticated," and even elaborate.[16] Miles Davis was also more concerned with establishing the rhythm with his bands, rather than his trumpet playing. Davis once told Wayne Shorter that he was "not a trumpet player," and that he didn't (really) play the trumpet, because "the trumpet was just a tool," and like "all instruments—it's like a magic wand!"[17] What exactly was Davis talking about, or trying to say? Perhaps when Davis "spoke," like the late alto saxophonist Ornette Coleman commented, "His ideas were often ethereal, more often inscrutable—though you could feel as if you almost understood them."[18] We may never know what Davis meant exactly—that is, by not being a trumpet player, but he was also an "imaginative [horn] player with a knack for making harmonically 'wrong' notes sound right."[19] Maybe Davis was hearing the music differently or in a new way? Also, it would not be an exaggeration to say that Davis was all about finding new connections in the music. Additionally, Davis played to his strengths, with a gentle touch, with an unconventional trumpet voice, particularly when it came to interpreting words to the music, or the spirit of a song. This meant that Davis had a great capacity for understanding the complexity of his "social music," as he often had the ability to play his way out of the *modal* clichés of his own improvisations. Of course, Davis always wanted to play music that was significant to him. In this way, he learned the alchemy of *not* playing anything at all. Or Davis embraced the technique of "less is more."[20] Bob Doerschuck succinctly explains:

> Unlike most of his early colleagues in bebop, Miles [Davis] seldom overplayed. His solos were short and clipped, usually restricted to the trumpet's midrange, and often riddled with broken notes. Whether this style grew out of a chops deficiency is beside the point. What matters is . . . Miles knew his limits.[21]

It is important to be realistic about the limitations of Davis's trumpet playing. Of course, Davis fully acknowledged his shortcomings and musical limitations as a trumpet player; but he was able to change the direction of jazz in almost a nanosecond, so to speak. Ultimately, by applying some of the things that he knew about "social music," Davis concluded that he could, indeed, play the music differently, or in his own way. This was mainly because he had learned the art of listening. To say the least, Davis believed that a musician could learn more by listening to what his band members were playing, rather than playing himself. And "the more latitude Miles [Davis] allowed his band, the more he allowed himself to recede," in the background.[22] But when he did play his horn, Davis, with "an almost perfect melodic order," according to Ornette Coleman, "discovered that he was playing four notes on his trumpet when he played one."[23] Davis also believed that he had perfected his technique or his changing style of playing in the lower trumpet register; and he would immerse himself in the sound, especially when he played ballads. But Davis could play in the higher register too, showing (sometimes) an unmatched facility and expressiveness. For example, his trumpet playing on *Someday My Prince Will Come* is Davis at his very best. Nonetheless, he often struggled with playing his trumpet in the higher register, where he didn't have a lot of control. Yet with ingenuity; he made such efforts work, finding his own voice. Krin Gabbard writes: "He [Davis] could play loud too. But the typical Miles Davis solo primarily communicated vulnerability, emotion, and thoughtfulness."[24] Finally, Davis wanted his trumpet to sound like a guitar, too, if possible, as he was able to take his music to a different place, an unknown realm of sorts, or beyond just an ordinary sound. And with that, he was able to redefine how a trumpet should be played. Jazz critic John Rockwell writes that "Constant throughout his [Davis's] shifting styles were his own rounded tone, wonderfully evocative of the human voice, and spare explorations of the trumpet's middle range."[25] Obviously, when it came to creating new music, Davis probably thought that his trumpet playing was the best ever, or certainly adequate, as he incorporated motifs of blues and gospel traditions, which are beloved by many black Americans [see Figure 5.1]. As journalist Jon Pareles writes:

Figure 5.1 Miles Davis with Charlie "Bird" Parker. *Source*: Photograph in public domain.

The sound of Davis's trumpet was lucid, unforced, never simply quiet or sweet; it had shades of melancholy, of tenderness, of pain, as well as an adamant directness and a determination to probe. He would swing with and against his rhythm sections, but there was often a sense of solitude in his solos. One of Davis's trademarks was to play the note above the expected one, as if reaching for an idea glimpsed just over the horizon.[26]

In the final analysis, Davis's sense of purpose in playing his music continued to flow freely while he was still alive. Indeed, Davis's ultimate goal was to make his trumpet sing, and sound as genuine as possible. Which is to say that his style of trumpet playing was not some gimmick. To be sure, Davis was inventive and played with a lot of depth and enthusiasm. Yet, he was criticized harshly by some for his cracked notes and lackadaisical techniques. But Davis's talents were undeniable; and we have to marvel at the simplicity, completeness, and beauty of his trumpet playing.

NOTES

1. "Davis Miles (1926–1991)," 43.
2. Robert Walser, "Out of Notes: Signification, Interpretation and the Problem of Miles Davis," *Jazz Among the Discourse*, ed. Krin Gabbard (Durham and London: Duke University Press, 1995), 165.
3. Walser, "Out of Notes," 165.
4. Walser, "Out of Notes," 172.
5. Troupe, *Miles and Me*, 1.
6. Walser, "Out of Notes," 172.
7. Michele James, *Kings of Jazz: Miles Davis* (New York: A.S. Barnes and Company, Inc., 1961), 33–34. Finding his way in jazz music, for Miles Davis, was like a divine intervention, or a major (musical) miracle.
8. James, *Kings of Jazz*, 19–20.
9. Quincy Troupe, "Miles Davis: Our 1985 Interview," *Spin*, September 28, 2019, 8, https://www.spin.com/featured/miles-davis.
10. Walser, "Out of Notes," 176.
11. Walser, "Out of Notes," 175. Wayne Shorter was first told that Miles Davis "was making a whole lot of mistakes," as a jazz trumpet player, "screeching all over the place, and had a raucous tone, and some things were smeared" or "some thoughts [with his trumpet playing were] not very clear." But that impression of Davis would all change when he started playing in his band. See Eric Nemeyer, "The Magical Journey—An Interview with Wayne Shorter," *Jazz Improv*, vol. 2, issue 3, January 6, 2000, 74.
12. Michelle Mercer, *Footprints: The Life and Work of Wayne Shorter* (New York: Jeremy P. Tarchee/Penguin, 2007), 120. Musically, Davis could make something out

of nothing almost. And his ability to play how he wanted gave him an edge over other jazz trumpet players. And the way Davis saw things, any personal, creative endeavor that he was involved in was better than doing nothing. It was really about his love for the music.

13. Cole, *A Musical Biography*, 59. Davis was always excited about change and newness in the music; and he had everything going for him, as he explored, perhaps, the depths of his soul. Sometimes it was like you could hear the suffering behind Davis's hard and fierce exterior. And he played his trumpet with refreshing authenticity.

14. Mandel, "Sketches of Miles," 18 and 20. In no uncertain terms, you can hear the depth of Davis's feelings on almost all his recordings, as his music can send shivers up your spine.

15. James, *Kings of Jazz*, 35.

16. *The Definitive Illustrated Encyclopedia*, 1st ed. s.v. "Miles Davis, the Fifties" in Jazz & Blues.

17. Eric Nemeyer, "The Magical Journey—An Interview with Wayne Shorter," *Jazz Improvisation*, vol. 2, issue 3 (2000): 74.

18. Michael J. West, "Ornette Coleman Transformed, Transcended Jazz," *Las Vegas Review-Journal*, sec. 5D, June 15, 2015.

19. Terry Teachout, *Pops: A Life of Louis Armstrong* (New York: Houghton Mifflin Harcourt, 2009), 228.

20. Bob Doerschuck, "Miles Davis: The Picasso of Invisible Art," *Keyboard*, October 1987, 66.

21. Doerschuck, "The Picasso of Invisible Art," 66.

22. Doerschuck, "The Picasso of Invisible Art," 66.

23. Troupe, "Our 1985 Interview," 19.

24. Gabbard, *Hotter Than That*, 155.

25. Rockwell, "Theme with Restless Variations," B46.

26. Jon Pareles, "Miles Davis: The Alchemist and the Terrorist," *The New York Times*, October 4, 1991, 34.

Chapter 6

The Man and His Horn

To say the least, Miles Davis was a towering figure in American music, as well as an influential jazz trumpeter, because of his boundless musical curiosity. Nevertheless, jazz critic and journalist Howard Reich writes: "Davis [proved] capable of both haunting, lyric statements and startling wrong notes, of flashes of improvisational virtuosity followed by passages of less than clean and controlled playing."[1] However, Davis made his wrong notes work with the music somehow. Moreover, many ardent, jazz fans and enthusiasts are infatuated by his *discography* of jazz albums, and great music or trumpet sound, as with Davis's performance on "the best-selling jazz album of all time, *Kind of Blue*," which is a masterpiece of refined, cool, *ethereal*, spiritual music. Developing an entirety idea of "modal chords" in *Kind of Blue*,[2] and other classic recordings, the music on this album is as significant as in some sacred, religious chants. Or, the sound is like the "call-and-response rhythms, and the spirituals of the earliest [black American] slaves."[3] The gifted black saxophonist and jazz composer, Wayne Shorter, another former band member in Davis's second great quintet, rated the trumpeter as one of the best showmen and jazz entertainers in the business while Davis lived, as he created an original musical language.[4] Shorter also stated that "When Miles played the trumpet, he had an *aura*. [And] with his regal bearing, he [Davis] cultivated that aura into a mystique,"[5] in a vulnerable, naked sort of way.

Fortunately, Davis developed this mystique even as he (often) played his horn while he was extremely ill from various ailments. Perhaps Davis played through his pain, as jazz historian Chip Deffaa suggested. Indeed, Davis "channeled his pain into that famed, far-off cry of his trumpet."[6] Jazz critic Nate Chinen writes that some of Davis's former band members, perhaps, could relate to his pain, because they had worked "with Miles Davis, back when they [too] were young men of unnerving composure themselves."[7] No doubt, Davis had his *ups* and *downs*, but he would quickly recover. Deffaa tells us that "The general public hadn't been aware of all of the health problems" Davis had "over the years—sickle-cell anemia, heart palpitations, a liver ailment, ulcers, a stroke, gallstones, drug problems, arthritis, diabetes and more,"[8] as he tried to show *everyone* that he was the epitome of health when he boxed, worked out, and played his trumpet beautifully. Yet, Davis was not a healthy man. Nonetheless, Miles Davis continued to work, play hard, and perform, or tour, because he was a "restless improviser," who "continually evolved," while he lived; and "every five years," or so, he practically created new types of jazz or *social music*.[9] This is to say that Davis was able to survive and thrive musically because of his strong will and desire to leave his mark or musical ideas and concepts behind for all the world to know or hear, or perhaps remember for some spiritual posterity.

Davis also believed that his musical approaches were sometimes necessarily contrived, but would be, ultimately, hard to miss when he left this world. Moreover, Davis was aware of the religious undertones or such unique frames of references in his complex improvisations, which are intricate and otherworldly, *godly*. According to music critic George Goodman, Jr., "by the late 1950s and early 1960s, when Mr. Davis's sound had reached maturity, the musician could bring his listeners to the verge of tears, wrenching the most melancholy qualities from a song without falling into sentimentality."[10] Davis liked the fact that he could make someone cry, or weep, simply by playing beautiful and mournful notes on his trumpet. Or was this all about his ego? To study and listen to Miles Davis's amazing music is to enter a world of profound wonderment and calmness of mind. Or his trumpet playing might put the listener in a deep, contemplative state. Of course, the syncopated rhythms and contrapuntal flow of sounds from his remarkable trumpet playing and music allowed his legions of jazz fans to reach some higher purpose, or an altered state of mind, without drugs or by some artificial means. Or was his music on a higher, spiritual plane? Indeed, if we are to believe in *angels*, the late Miles Davis is probably jamming, or playing with the archangel Gabriel, who is also known (biblically) for blowing a *godly* trumpet, or a mean, bad-ass horn. When it is all said and done, perhaps Davis's music appeals to our better instincts or *angels*. Goodman writes that "to worshipful fans, from Hollywood to Antibes, the sound of Mr. Davis became the perfect signature for his personality, the style and substance of the new archetypical man of jazz."[11] Some might also argue that listening to his music is a "mystical," or religious experience, perhaps a perception of a sacred sound or an exploration of *holy music*.

However, during the 1950s, some critics and harsh reviewers of his music considered Davis to be an arrogant and rude black man, because he would sometimes lay-out, or stop playing (after his trumpet solo), and leave the respective stage while one of his band members played their own solo. Or Davis would turn "his back on audiences and [refuse] to announce his [jazz] tunes. No [smiling face] Louis Armstrong stage tricks for him."[12] According to drama critic Terry Teachout, "Instead of playing to his crowds, Davis turned his back on them [his audiences]—and they ate it up."[13] But Davis firmly believed that he was being totally misunderstood, or sometimes misjudged regarding what he was trying to accomplish (particularly on stage), which was to change "the manners in jazz performance."[14] Or Davis just wanted the opportunity to be heard, without any confrontation. Furthermore, Davis's "attitude of casually shrugging off his [harshest] critics [was] just as much the substance of 'cool' as the sound of his horn."[15] Davis, of course, was a private person with little time and use for critics and naysayers, as "he defined the era's stance and tone, its irreverence, its style, its daring introversion, [and] its brusque belligerence."[16] To be honest, Davis was able to maintain his role as a jazz man because of his personality and supreme, prodigious talent as a path-breaking trumpeter. Indeed, it should be pointed out that

> African-American performers and composers [like Miles Davis], often from a relatively small patch of the south-eastern United States, have shaped many of the greatest musical traditions of the past century: jazz, blues, gospel, soul, R&B, hip-hop, *house*, *rap* and rock'n'roll.[17]

Meanwhile, Miles scrupulously worked his magic, or his influential musical power for his fellow band members and other musicians, as well as his followers and adoring fans—his *congregation*, so to speak. For example, we only have to listen to his unusual trumpet accompaniment to the late jazz singer Shirley Horn's great rendition or tune, "You Won't Forget Me," to know that God spoke through Miles Dewey Davis. Shirley Horn absolutely felt as much when she once stated that listening to early Miles was like being in heaven.[18] As far as playing on Shirley Horn's magnificent and classic album, "You Won't Forget Me," Davis's brilliant accompaniment can be summed up in this way:

> Notes were placed rather than punched out, the timing so exquisite as to force his [accompanying] to generate intense rhythmic energy. When playing . . . with the mute pressed close to the microphone, he [Davis] evoked a sense of skittish abandon one minute and utter desolation the next.[19]

Perhaps it was inevitable that Miles Davis was considered the number one jazz musician in the world for so long, or mostly while he lived, although "he was never the fastest nor the flashiest"[20] trumpet player, like Fats Navarro or Dizzy Gillespie. Davis, however, was tenacious and persistent, with a remarkable, determined presence of mind. He was the black man with the "golden horn," who threw caution to the wind and played whatever he wanted. To that end, Davis had learned to play his trumpet (on stage) when he thought that it was needed or necessary. We only have to listen to his *Round About Midnight, Miles Ahead, Sketches of Spain,* or *Miles Davis at Carnegie Hall* albums, to know that Davis could have been someone's musical or *spiritual* father. At the *Carnegie Hall* concert, for example, Davis played with a sense of excitement, like he was from a different universe, which was flawless from a jazz musician's perspective. Of course, Davis wasn't afraid of stepping up to the plate or spotlight, even with a bit of trepidation, sometimes. He also appeared angelic under the bright lights of the *Carnegie Hall* stage. Or so it seems from the photographs taken at that time of the event.

We can certainly get a sense of the so-called jazz faith and *ardor* from his great music, and uncompromising trumpet playing. No doubt, listeners are seduced by his "golden horn." Indeed, Davis's "best and truest playing" is "compressed into isolated and cryptic phrases that [hang] and [glow] in the air."[21] To be sure, his trumpet playing or musical efforts proved more than worthwhile, because at that time Davis had the *stamina* to play half the night in his late thirties and early forties. Additionally, Davis gave *eclectic*, musical concerts, mainly because he wanted to play a variety of things. Furthermore, his improvisations allowed for open-ended musical conversations that permitted him to expand on his "social music" ideas. At the same time, Davis wanted people to hear what he had to play or say with his trumpet, which he was able to do on multiple (musical) levels and occasions. But sometimes his various illnesses negatively affected the way that he played, gifted or not. Finally, as far as Davis's son, Gregory, was concerned, his "father's talent was a God-given gift, but it tortured him. It was a burden as well as a gift. Miles was like Beethoven and a lot of these great artists over the centuries who were tortured by their genius. They were all given special gifts, but they sure paid a high price for it."[22] In the end, Davis's trumpet playing was his *karmic* debt to the jazz music world. Or so he [Miles Davis] thought. And his "social music" was stripped down to the essence of jazz.

NOTES

1. Howard Reich, "Completely Hot: Live at the Plugged Nickel' Shares Miles Davis's Incendiary Gig with the World," *Chicago Tribune*, June 18, 1995, 17.

2. Jerry Shriver, "1959 Saw Jazz Take Giant Steps in Pop Culture," *USA Today*, sec. 3D, June 30, 2009.

3. "African-American Music: The Blues Had a Baby," *The Economist*, March 30, 2019, 86.

4. Mitchell Mercer, *Footprints: The Life and Work of Wayne Shorter* (New York: The Penguin Group, 2004, 2007), 99.

5. Mercer, *Footprints*, 99.

6. Chip Deffaa, liner notes to "Miles Davis: The Complete Concert, 1964 and My Funny Valentine, Plus Four & More—Columbia Jazz Masterpieces," (New York: Sony Music Entertainment, Inc., 1992), recording.

7. Nate Chinen, "Jazz Apprentices Still Find Their Masters," *The New York Times*, July 22, 2012, 17.

8. Deffaa, "Miles Davis," 4.

9. Scott Yanow, "Miles Essentials," *Jazz Heritage Society*, 1990, 15.

10. George Goodman, Jr., "Miles Davis: I Just Pick Up My Horn and Play," *The New York Times*, June 28, 1981, 12.

11. Goodman, "Miles Davis," 12.

12. Michael Ullman, "Miles Davis in Retrospect," *New Boston Review* (May/June 1981): 18.

13. Terry Teachout, *POPS: A Life of Louis Armstrong* (New York: Houghton Mifflin Harcourt, 2009), 306.

14. Teachout, *POPS*, 306. Davis once said that "he left the stage when not playing his trumpet, so that the audience would focus on the other musicians." See Geoffrey C. Ward and Ken Burns, "Miles Davis," in *Jazz: A History of America's Music* (Alfred A. Knopf, 2006), 408.

15. Goodman, "Miles Davis," 13. Miles Davis was "unwilling to share that person with the public [at that time]. He express[ed] his conviction that each person has a right and duty to live an independent existence." See Barbara J. Gardner, "The Enigma of Miles Davis," *Down Beat*, January 7, 1960, 23.

16. Gary Giddins, "Miles to Go, Promises to Keep," *Village Voice,* October 15, 1991, 94.

17. "African-American Music," 85.

18. Stanley Crouch, liner notes to Shirley Horn's "You Won't Forget Me" (New York: Clinton Recording Studio, June 12, 14 and August 11, 12, 13, 1990), recording.

19. Ronald Atkins, "A Trumpet Fallen Silent," *The Guardian,* September 30, 1991, 33. Perhaps, Miles Davis's music was based on some mystical or divine, musical revelation. Or maybe his music reflected the glory of God. Davis, of course, was sensitive to such matter, as he played his trumpet with, perhaps, a saintly finesse.

20. Atkins, "A Trumpet Fallen Silent," 33. While it is true that other trumpet players, like Clark Terry or Blue Mitchell or Lee Morgan, had speed and flash; and played with a fire and brimstone way, Davis played with a fierce, silent determination.

21. Richard Williams, *The Man in the Green Shirt: Miles Davis* (New York: Henry Holt and Company, Inc., 1993), 172. Davis could be unbelievably strong during his concerts, always catching the public's ear, no matter when or what he played. It was like a mysterious, unseen force that perhaps guided Davis's trumpet playing in some way.

22. Davis and Sussman, *Dark Magus*, 147.

Chapter 7

Of Spanish Music, Cool Jazz, and Style

Miles Davis oozed sex appeal when he first started out, as a jazz musician, with his conservative fashions. Indeed, he would strut his stuff in classic Italian suits in the beginning of his music career, taking his cue from older jazz men. And during the bebop (jazz) era, Davis dressed the part of a dapper college professor. More importantly, Davis's exotic, dark, good looks made people think of him, perhaps, as Negro *chic*, even with his signature dark glasses and movie-star coolness. As jazz biographer Bill Cole writes: "even in the dress of the [jazz] practitioners, a conservative tendency seemed to have been prominent." He goes on: "Davis during the bebop era was, at the very least, flamboyant, but hard bop brought about bands whose members wore identical dark blue suits, very Ivy-League."[1] Davis dressed no differently. As for his wardrobe at that time, Miles Davis mostly liked to wear solid-colored suits of elegant blue or black, which worked well with his silk or white cotton shirts. But he also wore textured suits in a herringbone or a *Birdseye* pattern. Even pinstripes were in his various wardrobes, which he, no doubt, was able to afford from his savings and the generous stipend from his "well-to-do" father. Davis always thought of himself as being a good dresser. According to his biographer, John Szwed, Davis "was known around the world as much for his hip style as his music."[2] Perhaps Davis was uncomfortably aware of himself. But he prided himself on his style, and sense of taste for fine threads. This was the feral essence of the man, or the *omnipresence* of Miles Davis. He was also influenced by "the fashion [styles] of Hollywood and society, [where] fastidious gentlemen like Cary Grant, Fred Astaire and especially the Duke of Windsor, who was all over the papers in those days . . . were all very well dressed men who were on the smaller side, like him [Davis]."[3] Davis always tried to make a fashion statement; and when he walked into a room, Davis would light it up, so to speak, because he was a sophisticated dresser. In a profound way, his style became his *camouflage* or *armor* more than anything else. Davis usually mesmerized his fans in the way that he dressed, which was a testament to his growing popularity during this time. Also, Davis's sense of style during the bebop era, and after, became a very important thing about him. He certainly set some tongues wagging by the way he looked. Indeed, Davis was perhaps the definition of *coolness*, always shaking things up. John Szwed tells us that "To this day, he [Davis] is revered as the archetype of cool."[4] The clothes Davis wore (on stage), of course, put him in the mood to play his very best; to play his heart out, to use the metaphor.

More importantly, many tried to emulate Davis's mannerisms and sense of style, like the jazz trumpeter Wynton Marsalis, who would later criticize Miles Davis "for abandoning the [so-called] true faith of acoustic [jazz] music,"[5] and the way that Davis would dress later during his fusion period. Nevertheless, Marsalis would dress formally, just like Davis once did, because he firmly believed that "A suit fits his seriousness of purpose and links him sartorially to past jazz masters (and dandies) like Duke Ellington and [Louis] Armstrong."[6] Davis perhaps initially felt this way too, until he would (eventually) change, and start donning the futuristic clothes of a jazz, *judo* master in silk. Prior to this time, John Szwed let us know that "Dexter Gordon pushed him [Davis] to more extremes in fashion later, with the broad-shouldered look, the pads and the lapels,"[7] and processed hair [or straightened locks]. Fortunately, "Miles retreated from [such a way of dressing] almost immediately in the early fifties."[8] To say the least, Davis didn't always care about how he came across to people, or what they thought about how he looked, because he believed that what you see is what you get. Still, Davis relished the attention. Horace Silver once remarked that "being a Gemini," Davis "could be cool, and he could be a little touchy. But he was a [musical] genius."[9] Even the great Duke Ellington compared Davis "to Picasso, in his constant musical reinventions. Yet those reinventions [like his clothes] got him into constant trouble."[10] Davis also didn't care about making unnecessary waves. Indeed, some admirers thought that Davis was unambiguously an evil black man. He was small, but only in physical stature. And there always seemed to be a degree of coldness and detachment in his demeanor, as mentioned. Nevertheless, Davis was resplendent in his clothes. Poet, author, and Davis's biographer, Quincy Troupe, thought of him as an "unreconstructed" black man.[11] Quincy Troup explains:

> By [an] unreconstructed black guy, I meant that Miles [Davis] was a Black man who did not change for anybody. He was an African American man who came out of East St. Louis, and he wasn't going to kiss anybody's behind to get somewhere. He was going to be himself on all occasions. I think that in this country,

because of the fact that we were slaves at one time, the dominant white culture feels that we have to become them. We have to talk in a certain way, dress in a certain way, talk calmly. We do that because we want to get ahead. I understand that. It's that middle-class thing. Miles was that unreconstructed Black man who went on his own path.[12]

So were his fans and audiences just curious about a black trumpeter, who they thought was just weird? Was this the fascination? No doubt, Miles Davis wanted to convey a unique persona, to show his image a certain way. And to be blunt, hip-talking Davis, with his raspy voice, perhaps, exuded sexuality and energy. Or sometimes, Davis would give you a sideways glance that hinted that he had your number; or he didn't give a damn about you. According to Harvard University Professor Henry Louis Gates, Jr., Miles Davis "was the political face of an aesthetic triumvirate," who "expounded and improvised upon resistance to the castration of the Black man."[13] People liked the telltale swagger of Miles Davis, the cool strut of a confident black musician. Professors Richard Mayors and Janet Mancini Billson tell us that

> The performance aspect of being cool means that as a Black performer [who] leaves his house in the morning . . . is "on" and cannot ever completely relax. Even when he is onstage. And African-American males who are not celebrities find it essential nonetheless to perform.[14]

Miles Davis, who had a mysterious, preternatural charisma, seemed always to be "on" it—that is, in terms of how he dressed. Indeed, Davis's style symbolized the rebellious and recalcitrant, cool entertainer, as he embraced "the hipster's credo: individualist, nonconformist, egalitarian, culturally fluid and always one step ahead."[15] And for Miles Davis, being cool meant having "an internal state of calm, almost icy composure,"[16] particularly when he wore his stylish clothes. Moreover, to add credence to this theory of coolness, "the bassist, composer and producer, Marcus Miller, who was part of [Miles] Davis band in 1980,"[17] was quoted as saying, "the clothes were so important back then, particularly in the '40s and '50s, because this was an era when black artists were fighting to be recognized as more than simple entertainers." It was like, "We're going to be as sharp as possible and we're going to command respect."[18] Majors and Billson also succinctly write:

> Cool is critical to the Black male's emerging identity as he develops a distinctive style. This style is highly individualized and is expressed through variations in walk, talk, choice of clothes (threads), and natural or processed hair ("do").[19]

In this regard, the audacious Miles Davis always dressed with style and sophistication, as mentioned, which reflected his personality, and can be categorized as *mercurial*. Toward this end, old photographs taken (onstage) with Charlie "Bird" Parker show a young Miles Davis with a pompadour, and chemically relaxed hair called a process. In the 1940s and 1950s, this "hairdo" was all the rage—that is, until the chemical straightening, greasy *jheri* curl hairstyle took hold briefly in the black community during the 1980s and early 1990s. This is all to say that the classy Miles Davis was unforgettable in his peculiarities, but it seemed everything he did was worthy of comment, especially how he dressed and carried himself. No doubt, a fashion sense was a big part of the debonair life of Davis, as he was always particular about how he looked, because it often affected how he performed onstage during a concert. More significantly, for some, Davis had a serious vibe, or an indefatigable *aura* that was unmatched, as he personified a very cool presence that many liked. Furthermore, Davis's "bad-ass" attitude made people (or fans) want to be around the jazz man, to see him, in all his glory, while experiencing (and appreciating) his music even more than they already did. Indeed, Miles Davis presented an image of what a jazz musician should be during the 1950s and 1960s, as he "set style in demeanor and sartorial elegance as well as in music."[20] Perhaps this was what made Davis so fascinating. Alas, without speaking, Davis could thrill his fans with his custom-designed clothes; and the heart and soul of his music.

To be sure, Davis's cocky insouciance was often imitated, but never perfected by others. Nevertheless, "young men copied his tastes in clothes (then it was very Italian)." Later, it was "(sort of personal mod-ish)." Also, "the stories of his cars (much interest in his white Ferrari), his *amours*, his cursing, his boxing—all were grist for the legend mill."[21] In the 1970s and 1980s, Davis would drastically change his conservative wardrobe for something totally different. Jazz author George R. Crisp explains:

> Betty Mabry [one of Davis's former wives] got Miles listening to the new sounds. She also began to change the way he dressed, making him throw out his Italian-cut suits and sharp brooks brothers and Paul Stuart thread and replacing them with a younger, quasi-African look-Dashikas, bell bottoms, studded belts, and such. Miles looked ridiculous, considering how old he was.[22]

Nonetheless, at this time and from a fashion standpoint, Miles Davis was unique with his fetishistic outfits. For example, the flamboyant Davis wore Napoleonic-looking jackets, with dark silk shirts and Zoo-suit (or baggy) pants, giving him the appearance of a *swashbuckler* of sorts. Davis also wore one-of-a-kind, handmade outfits, with a Spanish dancer's flair, from

"Envelope-pushing Japanese designers like Kohshin Satoh," who sent him stuff."[23] Or Davis wore clothes that reminded you of a matador, or a bullfighter, and his "suit of lights" costume—that is, minus the stockings and tight pants. To get an idea of how Davis looked, go to his live performance on *You Tube*, playing the tune *Hannibal* in 1991. It was a daring look, but proved to be totally Miles. Of course, like a matador, Davis's audiences would judge him based on his skills as a jazz artist. According to Herbie Hancock, "Miles was always the hippest guy around"—that is, "The way he moved, the way he walked, the way he stood when he played, what came out of his horn, and the cars he drove, all of that was stylish."[24] Davis would also wear things (clothes) like a traditional flamenco dancer, who is always accompanied by background music and improvised dancing, very much like Davis improvisations on his trumpet.

Audiences provided the *jaleo*, or hand-clapping and finger snapping, similar to Davis's complex horn playing, which extended "his range further than ever before."[25] The Spanish influences were evident. Richard Cook tells us that "Spanish music and Spanish culture in general had attracted Davis's attention. He went to see a company of Spanish dancers . . . and then went out and bought a stack of flamenco records. He [Davis] and Evans looked through Spanish musical scores, and while in California he had heard a record of Joaquin Rodrigo's *Concierto de Arajuez for Guitar and Orchestra*, a piece which started to haunt him" and would later become the central theme on his famous *Sketches of Spain* album.[26] Also in this regard, *Concierto de Arajuez* (or *Sketches of Spain*) is a modern jazz reimaging of flamenco and other Spanish music as interpreted by Miles Davis, who plays "slowly, methodically, and, for the first time, [used] extensively bent notes."[27] In pursuing his goal to play the music, Davis used his own personal style, while "definitely telling a story," which is what he primarily wanted to do.[28] In the liner notes to "Poetics of Sound," the producers write: "*Concierto de Arajuez* is memorable of Davis's avid ear for music from outside the jazz realm . . . wherein his [Davis's] aching timbre found a new forum for its poetic meditations."[29] Nat Hentoff writes that Davis "performs with a depth of emotion and strength of rhythm that represents a compelling blend of the 'deep song' of flamenco and the cry of the blues."[30] Nevertheless, Cole describes *Sketches of Spain* this way:

> The album was immediately a popular success, but, in actuality, it was lacking the basic ingredient of African-American music, rhythm; the music itself is stunning vertically but it has very little interest horizontally. Nowhere does it have the spiritual power of *Porgy and Bess*. The tempos are purposely kept very slow and many times are free; that is, the music is often moving without pulse, and when there is a pulse, it sounds artificial, like third stream music.[31]

Beyond the impact of his Spanish-influenced music, Miles Davis continued to forge new "social music," or jazz. But it was about Davis's Spanish style. And listeners were rocked on their heels by what he played—that is, his stylish *Sketches of Spain*. Suffice it to say, his hard-core fans loved all of it, as they were, perhaps, faddish devotees; but some grumbled and maybe thought that the music was like a punch in the gut. Whatever the description of his Spanish music, which related to his style, Davis made his mark with what he played on *Sketches of Spain* with his spiritual trumpet. And like with his fabulous clothes, it put him in a unique position or situation. There was just something about Miles Davis and his way of doing things, mainly because his style was at its core different—and cool. To be sure, Davis's style and fashion knew no bounds, as he probably thought about how his music and clothes resonated with some people. In many respects, and later in life, he dressed not so differently than the great black trumpeter William Christopher Handy, who dressed, provocatively, even back in the 1890s, in a sort of Michael Jackson, uniform fashion.[32] Davis would also dress in unexpected ways. For example, he would sometimes greet guests "at his California home in silk harem pants, [with] a flowing silk robe, no shirt, and shades."[33] But Davis wasn't a clown, or a joke, nor was his trumpet playing. This is to say that Miles Davis never limited himself in the clothes that he wore, or what he wanted to do musically; and he never really abided by the traditional rules of jazz. And there was always, it seemed, a spotlight on Miles Davis. Intent on addressing a new sound and music, Davis wanted to create something cool, different, while presenting "a new way of seeing a kind of bruised introspection that was sensitive and volatile."[34] According to music professor Jeremy Yudkin:

> [Davis's] innovative thinking led to . . . new musical styles, including hard bop and his special muted introspective ballads. He also found individuals with whom he could create his performances live and on record. In 1958 and 1959 he led a sextet whose work culminated in the transcendent *Kind of Blue* and the invention of yet another approach to the music (modal).[35]

Ashley Kahn has written: As "modal (or its synonym 'scalar') literally means 'of scales.'" And by definition, "all music, or any sonic system that follows a pattern with one, central "tonic" note, is modal."[36] Along with these same progressive lines, Davis would come to embrace the idea of *modal*, because it took him to another cool place with his music. Ultimately, there were a lot of creative, musical things going on with Miles Davis during the late 1950s and early 1960s. And he "was not afraid to change with the times, either in the [jazz] music he made or in the way he dressed."[37] Davis was often more concerned about how he looked, rather than what people thought about his music, or how he sounded.[38] Nisenson writes: "While tight Italian suits were almost his trademark in the late fifties [when he first started out] and early sixties, colorful shirts and scarfs reflected the more aggressive textures of his music in the middle and late sixties."[39] In this regard, Davis's style was a part of his character, or persona, as he followed his passions. Indeed, the charismatic Davis relied on his intelligence and fashion instincts, to determine how he would play his horn, or wear his clothes over the years. Indeed, the strategy to change his musical style and clothes to *bohemian* chic was by no means a mistake or crazy, as it garnered him even more of a following and burgeoning celebrity, while raising his profile [see Figure 7.1].

Figure 7.1 Miles Davis statue at Ed Dwight's studio in Colorado. *Source*: Author's personal photograph.

NOTES

1. Cole, *A Musical Biography*, 24.
2. "Miles Davis Biographer John Szwed Interview," *Jerry Jazz Musician*, January 27, 2003, 5, http://www.jerryjazzmusician.com/linernotes/miles.
3. "Miles Davis Biographer John Szwed Interview," 5.
4. "Miles Davis Biographer John Szwed Interview," 1.
5. Gabbard, *Hotter Than That*, 203.
6. Marc Silver, "Wynton Marsalis: The Herald of Our Swinging Heritage," *U.S. News & World Report*, October 30, 2006, 63, ww.usnews.com. According to Silver, Marsalis "never considered changing the way he dresses when he performs," as it makes sense to him.
7. "Miles Davis Biographer John Szwed Interview," 6.
8. "Miles Davis Biographer John Szwed Interview," 6. Note that, though Miles Davis began getting "into clothes as an eleven- or twelve-year-old in the late 1930s, his re-education took place at the hands of Dexter Gordon in the early postwar years." See Shane White and Graham White, *Stylin': African American Expressive Culture from its Beginnings to the Zoot Suite* (Ithaca and London: Cornell University Press, 1998), 244.
9. Bob Belden and John Ephland, "Miles . . . What Was That Note?" *Down Beat*, December 1995, vol. 62, issue 12, 16, http://proquest.umi.com/pqdweb?index.
10. John Rockwell, "Miles Davis: Theme with Restless Variations Built In," *The New York Times*, sec. B46, December 27, 2003.
11. Quincy Troupe, *Miles and Me* (Los Angeles, CA: University of California Press, 2000).
12. Douglas Turner, "Miles and Me: An Interview with Quincy Troupe," *African American Review*, vol. 36, issue 3 (Fall 2002): 429, http://web17.epnet.com.
13. Henry Louis Gates, Jr., *100 Amazing Facts about the Negro* (New York: Pantheon Books, 2017), 397.
14. Richard Majors and Janet Mancini Billson, *Cool Pose: The Dilemmas of Black Manhood in America* (New York: Lexington Books, 1992), 4.
15. Thomas Hayden, "Of Hipcats and Cool Dudes," *U.S. News & World Report*, November 1, 2004, 65.
16. Jonah Berger, "Why 'Cool' Is Still Cool," *The New York Times*, November 22, 2015, 10.
17. Michael J. Agoving, "His [Miles Davis] Ensembles Epitomized Cool," *The New York Times*, March 13, 2016, 12.
18. Agoving, "His Ensembles Epitomized Cool," 12.
19. Majors and Billson, *Cool Pose*, 4.
20. "Davis Miles (1926–1991," in *Who's Who in African American History*, ed. Sande Smith (New York: Smithmark Publishers, Inc., 1994), 43.
21. Don Demichael, "Miles Davis," *Rolling Stone*, December 13, 1969, 25.
22. George R. Crisp, *Miles Davis: An Impact Biography* (New York: Franklin Watts, 1997), 110. Coincidentally, Davis's new style seemed to resonate with hard-rockers, or rock and rollers and other fans. And he would dress in a more Mod-like way for the rest of his life, even with his wearing of leather pants sometimes; but he would never go back to wearing Italian suits.

23. Agoving, "His Ensembles Epitomized Cool," 12. According to Agoving, "In 1987, Davis modeled for a Satoh presentation at the *Tunnel* with Andy Warhol. He also wore his designs during a White House visit with Cicely Tyson, his wife at the time."

24. Agoving, "His Ensembles Epitomized Cool," 12.

25. Nisenson, "Round about Midnight." Musically, Miles Davis always wanted to do something different, even playing outside of traditional jazz. This is to say that he wanted to play with a new style, because Davis felt like there was a ticking clock in terms of his longevity; and finally, he knew that he needed young, talented musicians, with fresh musical ideas to accomplish his long-term goals.

26. Richard Cook, *It's About That Time*, 124.

27. Cole, *A Musical Biography*, 87.

28. Cole, *A Musical Biography*, 88.

29. "Poetics of Sound, Miles Davis: 1954–1959," *Hear Music* (2005).

30. Nat Hentoff, "The uniquely creative collaboration between Miles Davis and Gil Evans," original liner notes to *Sketches of Spain* (New York: Sony Music Entertainment, Inc., 1959), recording.

31. Cole, *A Musical Biography*, 87.

32. Mervyn Cook, Photograph of W.C. Handy in *Jazz* (New York: Thames and Hudson, Inc., 1998), 26.

33. Bob Doerschuck, "Miles Davis: The Picasso of Invisible Art," *Keyboard*, October 1987, 69.

34. Adam Shatz, "Cool in Every Way," *The New York Times*, December 29, 2002, https://www.nytimes.com/2002/12/29/books.

35. Yudkin, *Miles Davis, Miles Smiles,* 122–123. It should be noted that Davis "discovered the remarkable effect of playing with Harmon mute (without the central stem) on his trumpet, placed very close to a microphone." See Yudkin, *Miles Davis, Miles Smiles*, 31.

36. Ashley Kahn, *Kind of Blue: The Making of the Miles Davis Masterpiece* (New York: Da Capo Press, 2000) 67. It is important to understand that "young [jazz] musicians followed the lead of Miles Davis into modes," or modal jazz, because "modes were . . . a step toward something new and different." See John Litweiler, "Transition: Miles Davis and Modal Jazz," *The Freedom Principle: Jazz After 1958* (New York: William Morrow and Company, Inc., 1984), 105. According to jazz researcher Eddie S. Meadows, Davis's "switch to modality was the result of a search for a new approach to the harmonic-heavy jazz composition/improvisation styles that existed around 1958." However, "the use of modes as a basis of jazz improvisation was equally as tough as using the sophisticated post Bop harmonies." See Eddie S. Meadows, "The Miles Davis-Wayne Shorter Connection Continuity and Change," *Jazzforschung = Jazz Research* (1988): 56.

37. Agoving, "His Ensembles Epitomized Cool," 12.

38. Nisenson, "Round About Midnight," 146. According to Nisenson, "Miles's love of clothes sometimes almost seemed to supersede his love of music." See same reference and page.

39. Nisenson, "Round About Midnight," 146.

Chapter 8

Of Politics and Civil Rights

In real life, and in Don Cheadle's portrayal of Miles Davis in the movie *Miles Ahead*, Davis was battered by a racist white policeman in 1959 outside of the Birdland jazz club on Broadway in New York, where he was performing at the time. And he had *marquee* billing. But none of that mattered to the unnamed white supremacist cop, because he didn't see Davis as a man or the second-coming of some jazz messiah. Perhaps incensed at seeing the recalcitrant Miles Davis hail a taxi for a beautiful white woman, who probably admired the jazz man and his music, the white policeman harassed Davis by telling Davis to move alone and "stand over (at) the side near the building (Birdland) and not block the sidewalk."[1] Davis, of course, was having none of it, which led to a violent scuffle between the two, as well as a vicious clubbing by the white policeman, with his other white colleagues; and Davis was ultimately placed under arrest. But you could not ignore Davis's joie de vivre, of which there can be no question.

Adoring and loyal fans loved the five-foot-six, whippet-thin Miles Davis; and many were incredibly upset when they learned about his savage beating outside the Birdland jazz club. Though it is commonly understood that black men during the 1950s and even today are sadly looked down upon in our society. Why? Davis, the diminutive black man rightly fought back for his right to stand outside the Birdland, to smoke a cigarette, but the white policeman thought it was necessary to violate Davis's Fourth amendment rights, and to interfere with the *suave* Miles Davis, who he probably thought was an uppity black man. In the end, as journalist Irving Kolodin writes: "Davis was taken to the precinct building where he was attended by an ambulance surgeon . . . and held overnight in jail." When Davis was "released [on] bail the following day, the bandages were on his head, not the arresting officer's."[2] The publicity of this shocking incident, however, probably made Miles Davis even more famous and a hero of the civil rights movement, which gave him more street cred; and later he would be considered a real "bad-ass," because he didn't take crap from anyone, not even New York's so-called *finest*. Nevertheless, Davis was harassed by white cops almost his entire adult life. According to black poet and writer and biographer Quincy Troupe:

> [White] cops and Miles [Davis] have been at odds more than once. He was arrested while sitting in his red Ferrari in a no-standing zone on Fifth Avenue in New York. The cop said he noticed that Miles's car had no inspection sticker and asked him for his driver license. While Miles was looking for it a pair of brass knuckles fell out of his bag and he was arrested. Brass knuckles are illegal under the Sullivan Law.[3]

But in a playboy interview by novelist and writer the late Alex Haley, in 1962, Davis was quoted as saying: "I ain't scared of nothing or nobody, I already been through too much." He (Davis) goes on, "I ought to be dead from just what I went through when I was on dope. . . . I just say what I think, and that bugs people, especially a lot of white people. When they look in my eyes and don't see no fear, they know it's a draw."[4] Civil rights and social activist, as well as bestselling author, the late James Baldwin, who was a friend of Miles Davis, said this about the great jazz trumpeter: "I can see much of myself in Miles. . . . I think it has something to do with extreme vulnerability."[5]

Yet, Davis wasn't afraid of involving himself in the civil rights movement by giving concerts, to support the rights of black people; but he never gave a concert in the Deep South, because of Jim Crow, or racial segregation laws. Furthermore, "in order to raise money for the African Research Foundation in 1962, Miles appeared at *Carnegie Hall*,"[6] in concert, as discussed earlier, even though he didn't particularly like giving concerts because of the limited structured format. Davis preferred playing in small jazz clubs for much of his music career. But later, Davis actually liked playing at large stadiums and rock clubs.[7] Furthermore, according to journalist Greg Granger, Davis gave a highly regarded February 12, 1964 *Lincoln Day* Concert at the newly opened (at that time) Philharmonic Hall in Lincoln Center, now known as Avery Fisher Hall in New York, to commemorate "the birthday of President Abraham Lincoln," and the passing of "the 24 Amendment to the United States Constitution outlawing poll taxes as a voting requirement."[8] But mostly, at the height of the civil rights movement, "it was a fundraiser to benefit projects of the voter Education Project in Louisiana and Mississippi'"[9] that got the attention of people. Many thought that it was a beautiful thing that Davis gave of himself to the civil rights movement, without being paid. It was a selfless act on the part of the infamous Miles Davis. Moreover, "As the civil rights movement became a dominating presence in the public consciousness ... the African-American community increasingly expected Black musicians, entertainers, and celebrities to do their part in the struggle."[10] Davis certainly did his part, especially with his (live) concert performances of the late 1950s and early 1960s. Because of this effort, people can get a little more perspective on who Davis was and what he was all about. Professor of music at Washington University in St. Louis, Monson writes:

> Although benefit concerts generated considerable amounts of money for civil rights organizations, the economic dimension alone cannot explain fully their purpose and popularity. Many of these events offered a dramatic forum in which northern audiences could hear directly from southern activists about day-to-day life on the front lines of the movement. They also gave movement organizations the opportunity to reap the symbolic rewards of celebrity association with the struggle and created social spaces in which musicians and audiences could feel as though they were doing their part to aid the southern struggle.[11]

Although Miles Davis could be unpleasant, mean, uncaring, like a malevolent god, we can definitely define his politics because of his civil rights activism and benefit concerts. In this sense, Davis was genuinely altruistic. After all, he was considered a *jazz god*. As mentioned also, Davis "was to do more concerts, although he preferred the ambience of the nightclub, which had a looseness that befitted the spontaneity of the improvising jazz musician."[12] More importantly, playing such concerts was Davis's way of confronting systemic racism, and the workings of white supremacists. It should be finally pointed out that, black "cultural nationalists perceived jazz to be a self-consciously engaged, economically independent, politically useful art form,"[13] in itself. And this was a good thing for the civil rights movement. Unsurprisingly, "Davis showed that art [or jazz music] could be accessible without sacrificing excellence and rigor." Furthermore, "for Black cultural nationalists, [Miles] Davis projected an image of uncompromising and uncompromised Black identity,"[14] which the civil rights movement was/is all about. And Davis gave voice to black Americans in terms of music and politics during his life, which was quintessentially Miles.

It should be noted here that Miles was never in the trenches (so to speak), or front lines of the African American struggle to combat racism and prejudice, like other black activists and artists, like James Baldwin, a gay black writer, who was "a skilled essayist and thinker and commentator on the racial scene."[15] However, through his music, Davis was able to show his moral conscience and support for the civil rights movement. Davis, of course, shared Baldwin's intractable ideas on race. Baldwin also spoke out eloquently for the freedom and civil rights movements; but Davis did what he could to advance the call for freedom for black people. We only have to listen to Davis's *Filles de Kilimanjaro* to get a sense of Davis's support for black freedom causes—that is, in this recording of his music. Yet, according to jazz writer George R. Crisp, "Miles's optimism about racial progress was short-lived," because of his later involvement with drugs.[16] Nevertheless, prior to him becoming a junkie, as discussed in a later chapter, Davis tried to point the way to a fairer jazz, or social musical environment, where black jazz musicians were paid equitably for their recordings and other artistic endeavors. This is to say that Davis advocated for *profit sharing* for exploited jazz musicians.[17] Finally because of his financial smarts and "business acumen," Davis became "one of the richest men in jazz."[18] And those in the civil rights movement probably accepted this fact about Davis's wealth with a sense of pride and admiration. He certainly knew the critical, economic, and inequitable issues in the jazz music business, particularly when it came to how black jazz musicians were being mistreated, in terms of being paid at lower rates by white record producers; and across the jazz spectrum. In this regard, Davis rejected the "otherness" of being a black musician living in the United States.

NOTES

1. Irving Kolodin, "Miles Ahead or Miles Head?" *Saturday Review*, September 12, 1959, 61. There is no doubt that Miles Davis's small, lithe body was a turn on for some women. And his eyes could be piercing, with a strange intelligence, especially if you made eye contact with him.

2. Kolodin, "Miles Ahead," 61. Perhaps the beating of Miles Davis in the 1950s was the precursor today's unconstitutional "Stop and Frisk" policy, supported and implemented by Mayor Mike Bloomberg (during his administration) where black men were often stopped and harassed by New York police for no apparent reasons. Perhaps Davis didn't understand when he was being offensive, or how people (generally) perceived him. And he probably didn't care either.

3. Quincy Troupe, "Miles Davis: Our 1985 Interview—Cool is as cool does, and in this first of a bitchin' brew on the man with the horn, we discover the birth of the cool. Dig?" *Spin*, September 28, 2019, https://www.spin.com/featured/miles-davis.

4. Alex Haley, interview, "Miles Davis: A Candid Conversation with the jazz World's Premier Iconoclast," *Playboy*, September 1962, http://www.honors.umd.edu/HORN269J.

5. Jacqueline Trescott, "The Poet in Pursuit of Two Legends," *The Washington Post*, November 22, 1989. About his friendship with James Baldwin, whom he (Davis) would visit at his Provencal home in France, Davis stated that they would "get comfy in that beautiful, big house and he would tell . . . all sorts of stories . . . he [Baldwin] was a great man." See Kim Willsher, "€10m Fight to Save James Baldwin's Provencal Home," *The Guardian*, August 6, 2016, 2.

6. "Miles Davis at Carnegie Hall," July 16, 1962, https://www.milesdavis.com/albmusmmiles-davis.

7. Troupe, "Our 1985 Interview."

8. Greg Granger, "Miles Davis and the Civil Rights Movement: The 1964 Lincoln Day Concert," *Something Else*, February 12, 2020, http://somethingelsereviews.com/miles-davis-lincoln.

9. Granger, "Civil Rights Movement."

10. Ingrid Monson, "Monk Meets SNCC," *New Perspectives on Thelonious Monk, Black Music Research Journal*, vol. 19, no. 2 (Autumn 1999): 188.

11. Monson, "Monk Meets SNCC," 188.

12. Eric Nisenson, *Round about Midnight: A Portrait of Miles Davis* (New York: Da Capo Press, 1996), 186.

13. Darlene Clark Hine, William C. Hine, and Stanley Harrold, eds., *African Americans: A Concise History* (New Jersey: Pearson Education, Inc., 2009), 566.

14. Hine, Hine, and Harrold, *African Americans*, 566.

15. Randall Kenan, ed., *James Baldwin: The Cross of Redemption: Uncollected Writings* (New York: Pantheon Books, 2010), xv.

16. George R. Crips, *Miles Davis: An Impact Biography* (New York: Franklin Watts, 1997), 66.

17. Nisenson, *Round About Midnight*, 158.

18. Nisenson, *Round About Midnight*, 158.

Chapter 9

The Meaning of His Blues

Contrary to popular belief, Miles Davis could definitely play the blues. Coincidentally, "anyone wanting to play [jazz] music must first learn to play the blues and then pay [their] dues."[1] And his [Davis's] unorthodox style of playing the blues on his trumpet is magnificently rendered on some of his many albums, like *Kind of Blue* and *Star People*. Indeed, "the roots of African-American music," is most assuredly "church music and the blues."[2] And Davis was knowledgeable about both musical idioms. To be sure, "Preaching the blues—[or] imitating the cadences and the improvisatory spirit of the preacher"[3] was in Davis's blood, so to speak—that is, in terms of him being a jazzy blues musician. Broadly speaking, Davis's blues is buoyant, mature, melodic, broad, and thoughtful, with tantalizing traces of black gospel music. Therefore, his blues is rooted deeply in African American musical history. So does the blues have an original prerequisite? Or is the blues a part of jazz and its aesthetic and artistic sensibilities? According to journalist Kathleen McCleary, "Jazz is a melting pot of musical traditions, including blues, marches, spirituals, popular songs, dance music and military music."[4] Perhaps we should, therefore, recognize, more accurately, that Miles Davis was a master at playing jazz and blues. Jazz, of course, is like a metaphor for blues.

More to the point, Alma Hubner writes: "Jazz . . . is a lot of different things. [And] it doesn't comprise a definite set of rules. [And] a great musician [like Miles Davis] doesn't necessarily have to possess these or those qualities to be a great jazzman."[5] Davis also used good judgment in his blues improvisations, which for some jazz musicians could be a daunting thing. To say the least, "the spirit of jazz is spontaneous invention; the standard form is variations played off the melodies of well-known blues or songs."[6] Davis, in this respect, had a deep understanding of the blues, and played this music on his trumpet in mysterious ways. Indeed, the depth of his blues playing explains his vulnerability. Jazz writer Douglas Clark tells us:

> Miles's [blues] solos have a poetic quality. He speaks not in sentences but in images: short phrases, sudden bursts into the upper register, careful use of dynamics, quarter-tones and staccato passages. His [blues] solos are concise and intense, never verbose or banal. He is not afraid of silence. Miles is not a trumpet virtuoso in the conservatory manner. His tone is comparatively thin, his range limited, and he tends to stumble over fast passages. But his superb musicianship and keen ear allow him to use his facilities fully and to exploit his limitations.[7]

Clearly, Davis was able to construct a bluesy narrative with his horn, as he found that he could play the blues with the best of them, by articulating tunes like the black, jazz singers Nat King Cole or Sammy Davis, Jr. Perhaps in his style or way of playing the blues (through improvisation), Miles Davis was able to express his inner nature fully. In this regard, improvisation, as Ashley Kahn notes, "accurately describes the unique and defining feature of all jazz styles,"[8] including the blues. As jazz critic Whitney Balliett puts it, "Jazz improvisers [of the blues]," like Miles Davis, "tend to re-create their materials in their own image."[9] As mentioned, Davis was a minimalist, as his music and trumpet playing was punctuated by a sort of emptiness. Perhaps he was conditioned to hear what he wanted to hear in the music. More precisely, Davis was well-tuned to pick up on what his band members were playing (onstage), putting his own style to the test. And he was able to live with his shortcomings. It should be borne in mind here that his trumpet playing and blues music had a range of expression. There is a sort of reflective self-awareness in his blues, and he could match the mood at any given moment. This is to say that his (Davis's) blues could excite listeners and make them sad at the same time. Indeed, his music can subtly hypnotize you, "especially on the blues-oriented *Star People* (1983)."[10] To understand Davis's blues, we must also know his motivation for playing certain notes on his trumpet in the first place. Furthermore, it is undoubtedly true that Davis possessed a certain instinct for playing the right notes when it was necessary, because he took his music seriously. Perhaps he had a subliminal or *psychic* gift when he played his deeply moving blues. Or did it all come from his subconscious mind? According to journalist Adam Shatz, "the sound of his trumpet—nearly vibrato-less and often hauntingly filtered through a Harmon mute—was one of the most distinctive and beautiful in 20th-century music,"[11] and must be recognized.

Moreover, Davis's blues, even today, can be a tonic for our tortured souls or psyche. Just listen to his rendition of *I Thought About You*. Perhaps the most important thing about Davis's rendition in playing this brilliant, bluesy music is his authenticity and balance. Moreover, in this regard, his blues is definitely a part of the jazz vocabulary. Pareles writes:

> Although he [Davis] could make his trumpet peal and streak, as he did in his live albums from the 1960s, he had a rarer gift: he could command attention without shouting. His trumpet whispered, its Harmon mute pressed to the microphone, making listeners lean closer to hear the cry at its center.[12]

Alma Hubner offered this anecdote: "Primarily, it's the man that counts. A man," like Miles Davis, "that has a *why* for playing, who expresses feeling in his music, who conveys something of his own to his audience, who, in other words, must have something to say and be able to say it directly, spontaneously and sincerely."[13] Davis was able to show in his renderings of the blues what the music, or jazz made him feel like, especially spiritually, or in terms of his soul; and it wasn't always about pain and suffering either. But jazz critics like Leonard Feather still believed that Miles Davis "could play the blues despite his middle-class upbringing because the black middle-class was not immune from racism,"[14] and suffering. The late musician and writer Albert Murray, however, tells us that the blues is not "inherently concerned with suffering, depression and despair," because it "is a complex and authentic articulation of the nuances of African life in American society."[15] Murray goes on: "Thus, the blues can involve any of a range of emotions and ideas— none of which are necessarily linked with a depressed state of being."[16] No doubt, Miles Davis would have absolutely agreed with Murray, because he (Davis) came from a wealthy family, and he never had to pick cotton to play the blues.[17] Kelley explains it best: "For Miles the blues was a sensibility that comes from an immersion in a culture—cool, hip culture with as much humor as pathos."[18] The reader only has to listen to Davis's *Seven Steps to Heaven* album to attest to Kelley's assertion about Davis's blues renderings.

When Davis played the blues (on his trumpet), it was overwhelmingly beautiful, with phenomenal improvisations that were endlessly evolving. It was unforgettable, idiosyncratic blues and jazz all rolled into one. Nevertheless, Davis once remarked that he "wanted to leave the blues behind. He told [Herbie] Hancock: "We're not going to play the blues anymore. Let the white folks have the blues."[19] But, Davis never really left the blues behind. In this regard, we must never forget the bestselling jazz album of all times, *Kind of Blue*.[20] Jazz reviewer Jim Cheng, in 2000, tells us that "*Kind of Blue* still sells 5,000 copies a week . . . , which is a remarkable feat for a jazz album."[21] *Kind of Blue*, of course, was a musical undertaking that has had a lasting and profound effect on jazz music, as it is unrivaled by any other jazz recording, particularly when it came out in 1959. The tunes on this album are almost perfect. It is, without a doubt, transcended blues, with breathtaking possibilities. The music is otherworldly, with a rhapsody-like inquiry. So was this music inspired by the saints, or the devil? Also, the music on this album sounds alive, as it invokes the nostalgia of the black church. Freelance music journalist Ashley Kahn writes:

> In the [Black] church of jazz, *Kind of Blue* is one of the holy relics. Critics revere it as a stylistic milestone, one of a very few in the long tradition of jazz performance, on equal footing with seminal recordings by Louis Armstrong's *Hot Fives* and Charlie Parker's bebop quintets. Musicians acknowledge its influence and have recorded hundreds of versions of the music on the album. Record producer, composer, and Davis confidant Quincy Jones hails it as the one album (if that were the limit) that would explain jazz.[22]

Davis was seriously concerned about the music on *Kind of Blue*; and he wanted the entire responsibility for its recording. Indeed, Davis came into the recording studio with almost everything already mapped out. In this way, he was able to make headway. He apparently believed that everyone (his musicians) accepted his musical ideas, as his self-assuredness was second to none. Davis just wanted to express his vision of the new music creativity. And he was emphatic about making the music more like what he wanted it to be; and he was passionate about making his recordings work. He especially liked when things happened according to plan, as he was restless, and anxious. In this respect, the blues music on *Kind of Blue* is brilliantly conceived and constructed; and there is/was no ambiguity in Davis's trumpet playing. Perhaps Davis was merely confirming his spiritual, bluesy fervor. He was certainly in the moment during the recording of *Kind of Blue*, in two studio music sessions.[23] To wit, Davis tried to do almost *everything* administratively. The musical/bluesy-jazz tunes came out far better than he had ever thought possible, enabling him to finally reach a certain jazz *plateau*. And the world paid attention, as he broached the *acme* of jazz respectability. When *Kind of Blue* was finally made available to the general public, it was an overwhelming success. More significantly, Davis believed that the music on the album worked out beautifully, as it holds together well enough, even today. In his bid for music immortality, Davis achieved this goal with *Kind of Blue*, as it is still one of his best jazz recordings. Musically speaking, Davis was looking to make a specific album that would be enjoyed and discussed by all jazz fans and musicians. And perhaps some jazz fans became total converts and *true* believers in Miles Davis, and his dazzling piece of supernatural music for the ages: *Kind of Blue*, a recording that musically speaks volumes.

Of course, Davis's incredible trumpet playing comes through best on his ballads, which are soothing, with muted undertones, like with his *Blue In Green* ballad, which "sounds like something which is going in cycles [or circles] around . . . two chord shapes."[24] Furthermore, Davis's horn is especially soulful when he gets a second wind, because he is *all* business with his renowned improvisations. And the slower and harder he plays his trumpet, the listener's heart might skip a beat. It is as if Davis's trumpet sound and music can meld the listeners' *spirit* and *soul* together. He also makes playing the original tunes on *Kind of Blue* seem easy, as if there is nothing to it. Meanwhile, Davis makes his band members shine, too. And this was a feat in itself. So was this just Davis's unparalleled talent as a jazz trumpeter? What is really interesting about Davis's musical approach on *Kind of Blue* is his focused, and offhand, blues permutations. Or more precisely, Davis's nuanced tone, and narcissistic emptiness (or abandonment), stands out, and is particular to his musical aesthetics and conception of the jazz form. Indeed, Davis is, perhaps, thinking deep in his subconscious before blowing a single note, especially as he methodically breaks down the essence of the voluptuous music on *Kind of Blue*. For Davis, it was like having a "back-and-forth" conversation, where he was talking to his respective band members. Journalist Lauran Neergaard writes: "Jazz musicians are famous for their musical conversations—one improvises a few bars and another plays an answer." Neergaard goes on: "That [musical] conversation-like improvisation [activates] brain areas the way that words are put together into phrases and sentences."[25] Furthermore, "even between their turns playing, the brain [isn't] resting, because essentially, the jazz musician is processing what they hear in order to come up with new notes and sounds that fit."[26] And this innovative approach on most of the tunes on *Kind of Blue* is what Davis was trying to accomplish. Davis also had a strong sense of what he played on his sensual ballads, as he wanted the music to sound right, and good, while providing something entirely new and marvelous, with an unusual and lovely ambiance. Maybe it was just meant to be? No matter: the odds were with Miles Davis, with his highly individualized music and authoritative trumpet voice. In terms of Davis's playing of the blues and ballads, African American jazz trumpeter, Lester Bowie tells us that Miles Davis played "completely different from anybody else in his era. The way he plays his intervals, the way he plays through chord changes, that's what made him really different. Everybody else played sort of the same, up and down, musical passages, chord changes, in intervals of seconds, thirds, fourths, fifths, and sixths. But Miles [Davis] plays in between all of that. He plays sideways. He runs through whole tunes sideways."[27] Additionally, Davis played ballads as if he was trying to give or find the absolute meaning to life with his beguiling tunes, which are lyrical and have an unpredictable edge—that is, without a beginning or end.

Moreover, Davis liked playing the lovely ballads on *Kind of Blue*, as if his heart was aching. The music still makes people scratch their heads in wonderment, as if to say: How did Miles play that? Of course, Davis "established himself as one of the outstanding ballad players of this or any period."[28] But was he really satisfied? The brilliant blues ballads on *Kind of Blue* most certainly stay in your head. And by necessity, Davis relied sometimes almost totally on his improvisational skills. The significant thing actually is how Davis played his notes in such a creative way. This sentiment is important to note, because Davis was "no longer . . . interested in harmony for its own sake." Meaning, "His solos [are] a highly distilled version of what is basically a rather complicated musical thought. But since he [Davis] uses only notes that are important to the thought, it becomes direct and to the point."[29] Therefore, it should be understood that Davis's jazz and blues are not mutually exclusive. And *Kind of Blue* represents some of the major themes of his thinking during this period of his musical career. Indeed, Davis's facile improvisations on this album are lush, dark, and mystical sounding, which should be celebrated. The music at times on the incomparable *Kind of Blue* is evocative, serene, and subtle, almost complete, as it seeps over to the mysterious and sacred. The inventive tunes can also be interpreted on many musical levels, perhaps as a challenge. Jazz reporter, Bradly Bambarger summarizes:

> "Kind of Blue" is perhaps the ultimate testament to spontaneity, even in a genre fueled by improvisation. Without rehearsal, the collective created finished music spontaneously from sketches Davis brought fresh into the [recording] studio. Even more remarkable, the classic tunes "So What," "Freddie Freeloader," "Blue In Green," and "All Blues" were each captured in one take. The equally classic "Flamenco Sketches" took just one more try. The Davis conception was intense and evocative, but each of the musicians brought something of himself to the record.[30]

In hindsight, Miles Davis was inordinately pleased with the results of *Kind of Blue*, as mentioned, and himself. This absorbing blues album was, perhaps, the single-most important musical task Davis had taken in his life up to that point, with the possible exception of his *Birth of the Cool* recordings. The music was a breakthrough, as the convergence of musical ideas is unprecedented, *cathartic*. Equally important, the music of *Kind of Blue* helped to define Miles Davis as a jazz man. And interesting enough, the demand for his music is still extraordinarily brisk. *Kind of Blue* finally crystallized to everyone (in the jazz world) what Davis was capable of doing with his "social music." As a matter of fact, his blues and ballad playing brought him international attention and critical acclaim. Finally, *Kind of Blue* is indeed a summary of his blues, and all that he (Davis) had learned about style, melody, cadence, and bluesy-jazz rhythms. To that end, it is Davis's pièce de résistance, and his most significant, enduring *extravagant* jazz masterpiece.

NOTES

1. Cole, *A Musical Biography*, 22.
2. Cole, *A Musical Biography*, 23.
3. Gabbard, *Hotter Than That*, 19.
4. Kathleen McCleary, "Jazz: The Multi-Cultural Beat Goes On," *Parade*, August 2, 2015, 11.
5. Alma Hubner, "Must Jazz Be Progressive?" *The Jazz Record* (April 1944): 8.
6. Kahn, *Kind of Blue*, 66.
7. Douglas Clark, "Miles Into Jazz-Rock Territory," *Jazz Journal* (June 1977): 14.
8. Kahn, *Kind of Blue*, 66. Later, when he recorded *Seven Steps to Heaven*, the listener is convinced that Davis is an incomparable blues man.
9. Whitney Balliet, "Jazz," *The New Yorker*, April 4, 1977, 89.
10. Jon Pareles, "Miles Davis, Trumpeter, Dies: Jazz Genius, 65, Defined Cool," *The New York Times*, September 29, 1991, 5, http://www.nytimes.com/1991/09/29/nyregion/miles.
11. Shatz, "Cool in Every Way," 11.
12. Pareles, "The Alchemist and the Terrorist," 34.
13. Hubner, "Must Jazz Be Progressive?" 8.
14. Robin D. G. Kelley, "Miles Davis: The Chameleon of Cool, A Jazz Genius in the Genius of a Hustler," *The New York Times*, May 13, 2001, 4, http://www.nytimes.com/2001/05/13/arts/miles.
15. Todd Boyd, "The Meaning of the Blues," *Wide Angle*, vol. 13, number 3 & 4 (July–October1991): 57.
16. Boyd, "The Meaning of the Blues," 57.
17. Boyd, "The Meaning of the Blues," 58.
18. Kelly, "The Chameleon of Cool," 4.
19. Kelly, "The Chameleon of Cool," 4.
20. Jerry Shriver, "1959 Saw Jazz Take Giant Steps in Pop Culture," *USA Today*, sec. 3D, June 30, 2009.
21. Jim Cheng, "'Blue' Is a Different Kind of Look at Jazz Legend Davis," *USA Today*, sec. 9D, October 9, 2000.
22. Kahn, *Kind of Blue*, 17.
23. Kahn, *Kind of Blue*, 91–126. According to Ashely Kahn, "If not entirely unrehearsed or of Davis's composition, *Kind of Blue* was still a bold step forward for the trumpeter. He was defining a self-reliant, studio-based approach that in 1959, for the first time in Columbia's studio, allowed him to direct a whole project from composing to band leading and recording (97).
24. Cook, *It's About That Time*, 114–115.
25. Lauran Neergaard, "You Do Say: Brain Scans Show Jazz's Back-and-Forth Works Like Conversation," *Las Vegas Review-Journal*, sec. 6A, February 20, 2014.
26. Neergaard, "You Do Say," 6A. As always, Miles Davis knew what he wanted most on *Kind of Blue*. And everything he did musically took him a step closer to his ultimate goal of reaching the musical *Omega Point*. Finally, the album is an extraordinary accomplishment, solidifying Davis's reputation as one of the finest trumpeter in the history of jazz, especially with his purposeful music.

27. Troupe, "Our 1985 Interview," 19.

28. Cole, *A Musical Biography*, 61.

29. Don Heckman, "Miles Davis Times Three; The Evolution of a Jazz Artist," *Down Beat*, August 30, 1962, 18.

30. Bradly Bambarger, "Miles Davis' True Blue," *Billboard*, August 7, 1999, 74. We should also keep in mind that, "the powerful Davis mystique—still the very definition of "cool"—has obviously long been a popular focal point with "Kind of Blue." To a certain extent, we can only marvel at Davis's playing on *Kind of Blue*, as he assiduously recorded the music with a cool perfection, almost unknown at the time. It defined jazz music and more, as Davis saw a deeper meaning, and theme—besides the blues—in the music. Davis had wanted to create something very high-minded and artistic; and he was successful in accomplishing that.

Chapter 10

Europe or Bust

Concerts and Touring

When Miles Davis toured Europe, he always felt upbeat, because the European people made him feel good, wanted, and appreciated. Indeed, touring and performing in Europe always evoked fond memories for Davis. More importantly, things seemed uncomplicated for Davis in Europe, especially when he described his mood. And for a little while, it seemed like all his little problems (in the United States) were left behind. Playing his horn in Europe also helped Davis with his overall mental well-being; and dispelled his belief that all white people were racists. So Europe was where Davis "understood that all white people weren't the same, that some weren't prejudiced and others were."[1] Davis was also critically respected, and received overwhelming recognition by jazz fans. And while in European countries, Davis encountered very little racism like he faced in the United States in the 1950s and 1960s. Of course, Davis knew that "he still [had to] give [live] performances in noisy, smoke-filled night clubs"[2] in the United States; but he loved performing in countries like Germany, Spain, Sweden, France, or Italy. Therefore, Davis "approache[d] his work [in the U.S.] with the dignity" he thought it deserved.[3] It wasn't that Davis didn't want to be onstage per se; but he was absolutely thrilled to play his trumpet in Europe. It also put things in perspective for him, because it was in Europe that Davis felt a lot more accepted as a black musician.

Perhaps in the back of his mind, Davis recognized the extent to which the Europeans or fans loved him and his recorded music, as he was known as the "Black man" with the golden horn. And they accommodated him famously. Europeans also loved his very presence, because according to Ransom Riggs, Davis "was hailed as a jazz god."[4] Indeed, Davis was worshiped, because his music had gained more than some notice by European jazz fans, and they were fiercely loyal to the man, as if he was a divine figure. As stated already, his very presence fueled the atmosphere during his European engagements. So had Miles Davis "found the divine in [his] music,"⁵ as his former band member, John Coltrane believed he had discovered before his death? Perhaps. Moreover, traveling throughout Europe and performing with his various bands on several occasions were some of the best times in Davis's life, as it presented him with a new musical landscape. Furthermore, the opportunity provided him with a change of scenery from racist America at that time. It also piqued Davis's imagination and musical interests. Additionally, his music carried his European audiences to another place with a soundscape of cool jazz with (often) little recognizable *ghost notes*. All of this seriously reflected Davis's conscious strategy to titillate. Take for example Davis's trumpet playing of the ballad, "I Fall in Love Too Easily," live at Stadhalle, Karlsruhe, Germany on November 7, 1967. Davis played this lovely ballad during numerous European performances; and his level of commitment to this tune was always something to admire, as he had a sneaky ability to catch audiences off guard with his gorgeous trumpet playing.

It was, perhaps, an eye-opening experience for most European fans, or an energizing *jolt* of sound, as Davis unhesitatingly played contradictory notes and different chords, when he thought that they were necessary; and always in the middle register. Also, it should be pointed out that Davis's lyricism and tone modulations on "I Fall in Love Too Easily," is all about his "modal improvisation technique."⁶ To be sure, being onstage anywhere in Europe, Davis was fully present; and his trumpet playing was like defying gravity, to use the metaphor. This is to say that his music seemed outside of time and space. Perhaps his trumpet music was like hearing another sound (or voice) from heaven. And his music played during his first, second, and third visits to Europe worked primarily because of his talented band members, no matter where his band ended up performing. Arts critic Howard Reich puts it this way:

> For his part, [Miles] Davis prove[d] capable of both haunting lyric statements and startlingly wrong notes, of flashes of improvisational virtuosity followed by passages of less than clean and controlled playing. Yet, Davis was shrewd enough to share the microphone generously, placing more attention on his ensemble than on himself, perhaps knowing that it was as leader and visionary that he was at his strongest.⁷

Equally important, Davis was the main draw (or attraction). Or he was considered the (major) musical genius in the room, so to speak. But was he an evil genius? Davis was certainly the musical force that drove Europeans to come hear him play his horn. And no one was able to steal Davis's thunder. Furthermore, as far as his band members were concerned, Davis had a preference not to rehearse while in Europe, except for some rudimentary efforts. Indeed, Davis actually believed that his music didn't need any rehearsal. Was this because he wanted to keep his music fresh? Or was it because Davis liked the spontaneity in his music, which wasn't always perfect? After Davis's death, Herbie Hancock stated: "What I loved was that Miles [Davis] told us that he paid us to work on [musical] things—not to just perfect something in our hotel rooms and play that just to get applause from the audience. He wanted us to constantly work on new things. He stimulated creativity."[8] To say the least, Davis was able to communicate *change* with his music, which some Europeans thought was revolutionary; but he was notoriously inconsistent with his trumpet playing, as mentioned, which was why his music always sounded different, unscripted, and uniquely intense, or musically *risqué*. For Davis, perhaps, it was simply a question of arithmetic—or some social equation, where you don't always get the answer right the first time around; or it (the music) was like a simple computational mistake; but in the end, things all worked out, just like with Miles Davis's music. And listening to his trumpet, even today, dazzles the senses. In this regard, there is little doubt that Davis knew what he was doing, especially performing in Europe, as he was a jazz master. According to Bill Cole, "Miles's music became more beautiful than revolutionary."[9] Cole also correctly explains:

> Miles [Davis] was now the master in the era which ended a tradition, a long, hard struggle through European music theories with European instruments; he [was] a very individualistic [trumpet] player, with a mind that can add long columns of numerals almost instantly. Never relying on extended solos, his whole shaping experience originated in hearing harmonic changes in the music.[10]

Davis's music perhaps lifted the mood of people; and listening to him might have been like hearing the echoes of the ocean, as the waves go back and forward. It was part of Davis's musical "bag of tricks," as he was very much focused while performing, particularly in Europe; and he wielded his horn like a medieval knight who carried a mighty sword, or some awesome weapon; or a protective shield, which created a transformative, music reality. Moreover, Davis's adroitness in playing his trumpet was on full display for his European audiences; and his concerts enhanced his reputation as a jazz musician. Of course, Davis's priority was to play excellent music, like he did with his rendition of *So Near, So Far*. Which is to say that sometimes during his concerts in Europe, Davis's trumpet playing was impossible to explain, as if it had an *ethereal* quality. And such a jazz man as Miles Davis possessed a skill that demanded *god-like* concentration—that is, in terms of him thinking on his feet, blowing his horn, and playing his timeless improvisations. And to say that Davis played well was perhaps an understatement. Furthermore, despite words to the contrary, Davis was usually in complete control of his instrument, as he made unbelievably great jazz music, rightfully called "cool jazz." This is to say that Davis's exquisite music was born in his imagination and outstanding performances. More to the point, Davis's sound during some of his European concerts was much like the human voice in that he could make his trumpet *sing*, or *wail*, and even *talk*, as if he was giving a religious sermon to his mostly white audiences, playing beautiful ballads at every engagement that took their breath away.

Of course, during his concerts in Europe, Davis always tried to make a statement with his clothes and/or outfits and music, while sometimes turning his back to his European audiences. This was strange for the uninitiated, but Davis wasn't necessarily turning away from his various audiences—that is, he was actually focusing his attention on his band, listening to what they were playing with a tuned and critical ear. Hancock explained it this way: "The trumpeter [Davis] often played with his back to the audience simply because he was conducting the band."[11] And the music just clicked with his younger audiences and band members. Moreover, in terms of his music, Miles Davis practiced what he preached in giving back to his European audiences—that is, he played his best. Davis also portrayed himself as one of the greatest jazz men in the world at that time; and Davis always worked with what he had to offer his music. It is perhaps understandable that Davis reciprocated in terms of great jazz, and the love his European audiences gave him. Davis was never caught off guard onstage, either, in Europe, as he was acutely aware of what was going on, despite turning his back on some of his audiences on European stages. Davis was also shy, and he never liked the idea of speaking from these stages, or announcing his specific tunes. As mentioned, Davis was well respected in Europe, and "Despite some superficial complaints, all this secretly [delighted] his audience[s]. They wouldn't want him any other way."[12] Davis was also celebrated because of his "hip" music sounds—and European audiences couldn't get enough of him. For some, Davis's concerts were like a ritualistic event, as his music was like a healing, musical salve, or a divine occasion. One thing is for certain: With Miles Davis, you got the whole musical kit and caboodle, as European fans were often in the *throes* of adoration or admiration, even though they thought that he was delightfully arrogant, but still cool.

Davis usually played a mixture of classical jazz or "social music," blended with popular music and new, seminal tunes. Perhaps the music of Miles Davis did something really powerful to the minds or psyches of different European fans. Indeed, these people were impressed with Davis's odd, but engaging way of playing trumpet. Davis also played the blues during several events; and his basic musical parameters were clear: Play the music as if his life depended on it. And at no time did Davis think that he was wasting his time on the many stages in Europe. It was like his European trips nurtured his confidence and creativity. European audiences would listen to Davis with bated breath, as if he was going to make some kind of mistake, while at the same being taken aback by his unusual sound; especially the different scales and chords he played, in harmony always, with his sophisticated band members, playing in the background. Davis was able to reach deep inside himself to play his music like no other jazz trumpeter of his era. (This is why the music world today still talks about Miles Davis.) Ironically, with his trumpet playing gigs in Europe, even Davis's raspy voice can be heard on some recordings or clearing his throat; and his horn playing became an extension of the man himself. If fans listen to any of his albums, recorded in Europe during his concerts, the music is electrifying, intoxicating, dynamic, and noteworthy. Davis was often pleased with what his bands played, particularly since his trumpet playing is occupied, poetic, pregnant (in a sense) and absolutely divine.

Europeans especially loved Davis's rendition of *My Funny Valentine*. Of course, while often playing this tune in Europe, Davis could make his "trumpet cry and shout, and moan with overpowering effect,"[13] which created spellbinding jazz. Moreover, Davis's soaring trumpet provided a potent voice, "in his first recording" of *My Funny Valentine*, where he "immediately distinguishe[d] himself playing with a Harmon mute into the microphone, an effect he used frequently at that time"[14] in the late 1950s and early 1960s. In this specific way, Davis was prioritizing what he thought was important, as he never acted on musical assumptions. It was as if jazz or "social music," and playing *My Funny Valentine* was (somehow) wired into his brain. Or was it just his *innate* musical ability to play the famous ballad better than anyone else? Davis's conception of *My Funny Valentine* is/was different, because he usually played the tune on the downbeat. And for that reason, Davis was able to reach a new level of concentration and performance, where logic often prevailed, especially with his improvisational skills on *My Funny Valentine*. It was Davis's way of speaking his mind with his horn. Or, as mentioned in an earlier chapter, his trumpet playing was simply another way for him to tell a story, using his instrument as his voice. After Davis's death, it's been reported that the late Cicely Tyson, once Davis's wife, often "[visited] a jazz club" to hear a rendition of *My Funny Valentine*, to honor the jazz man, because "the power of music was a passion Tyson shared with her late ex-husband,"[15] Miles Dewey Davis. Such is the influence Davis still had on jazz music–loving people, particularly with his trumpet solos and ballads. Professor Robin D. G. Kelley explains:

> Miles [Davis] mastered this format, and his use of smears and bent notes gave his playing a vocal quality. This is why his solos are always so hummable. It was never a matter of simply playing "pretty notes" or fewer notes or leaving

more space. Rather, Miles created complete statements with a beginning, a middle and an end, "stories" that possessed a sense of drama.[16]

So Miles Davis is widely lauded for speaking a hurting truth with his trumpet, punctuated by the beautifully conceived logic in his music. To be fair, Davis also worked on his music until he was satisfied with the results that he wanted to achieve, like with his polished ballad, *Someday My Prince Will Come*. It made European fans go wild, as these jazz zealots wanted to hear more, because they were passionate about his music. Even today, Davis's perspective on the connectedness of all music is still relevant; and Europeans, perhaps, understood exactly what he was trying to do. So was it all about what "has been referred to as the Miles magic?"[17] Davis went to extraordinary lengths to make his music absolutely interesting during his touring in European countries, as he fed off the energy of his audiences. Also, in this respect, jazz writer Barbara J. Gardner once asked: "What [were] some of the elements that [formed] the man and the magician in this trumpeter,"[18] who played a blizzard of old and new "social music," or jazz?

Although many European fans thought that Miles Davis also had a peculiar way of doing things, especially when it came to his attitude, many claimed that he was just being different. And the charismatic Miles Davis was able to ride the wave of popularity, even with his famous *hubris*. Davis definitely had a brusque or exuberant disregard for some people. But secretly, as mentioned, Davis liked being admired. For example, he knew that "there [were] women in Sweden in love with his photograph."[19] All in all, "Miles Davis [was] aware of his image and [knew] how to use it."[20] For example, Davis would sometimes arrive late to European events, but he believed that he was worth the wait. And wait they did, sometimes for hours before Davis and his band would show up and take the stage; but he (Davis) was quickly forgiven. Yet, some European fans believed that Davis's style of doing things was awkwardly transgressive, disrespectful, and idiosyncratically strange. But wasn't the "outsider status" what jazz was [or is] all about, in the first place, especially as it pertains to Miles Davis? John Coltrane's biographer Ben Ratliff tells us that the "point of jazz, at least to some degree, is being yourself."[21] And Davis was always true to himself, portraying an image of someone you didn't want to mess with, even in Europe [see Figure 10.1]. Michael James writes:

> Although Davis [maintained] that he [conducted] himself with the best possible intentions and [was] anything but disdainful of the audience,[it] might be forgiven for supposing that he [found] it extremely lucrative to perpetuate this image of himself as an arrogant outsider.[22]

To wit, Davis governed himself accordingly, because he believed that he was mostly right about many things. Also, over the years, Davis said what was on his mind—good or bad—without mincing words. This is to say that Davis wasn't really careful about what he had to say; and sometimes his harsh words were cringe-worthy. Such inner battles gave way to Davis's quirks, as he remained a grudging and angry black man. And no one could defend his worst impulses. To a larger extent, Davis could be an unpleasant man if you tried to approach him, and he didn't know you. Indeed, Davis had a "monumental disdain for the complimentary small talk and instant familiarity that [Black] entertainers are exposed to, and his absolute refusal to indulge in such trivia," unfortunately, "earned him the reputation of being unapproachable."[23] Furthermore, the sometimes disgruntled Miles Davis could be unlikable and argumentative; but he didn't care about whether people saw things his way. And if Davis didn't know

Figure 10.1 Miles Davis statue outside cultural center in Kielce, Poland. *Source*: Author's personal photograph.

you and you showed some kind of familiarity with him, he usually cursed you out, even if you happened to be European. Ron Lorman, "who worked closely with Miles [Davis] and knew him well,"[24] stated that Davis "could be angry . . . he could be razor-sharp bullets between your eyes . . . and you just knew you'd stepped in it" with him, or "you'd said something that had created a monster and you didn't want to have anything to do with [him]—that is, after getting a "fuck you" in that context."[25] So was Miles Davis like a *holy* or *evil* force? Or was his music a worshipful sound, as he entertained his European audiences? Commenting on some of his European performances, which we can now view on *YouTube*, music critic John Lingan writes that:

> Davis is more interesting . . . than the god: I watch him and see someone who styled his hair and wore fine suits and took great care, like all his peers, to present himself exactly as he intended, exactly as he saw himself. His physicality completes the music, grounds it and makes it even more urgent.[26]

It might be a little bit of a stretch to believe that Miles Davis was some music god; but he did have an angelic glow on European stages, with spotlights completely on him while he played his solos in the dark auditoriums. True believers never wavered, as his music was like a *life raft* (of sorts) for some European fans who loved Miles Davis. He was revered because of his mind-boggling jazz music. All that mattered was the music. And when Davis closed his eyes and blew his horn, he was really getting down to business—that is, musically. Europeans tended to listen carefully to him, and with pleasure. It was always a beautiful thing—and jazz at its purist and most entertaining.

NOTES

1. Davis and Troupe, *Miles: The Autobiography*, 129.
2. Chris Albertson, "The Unmasking of Miles Davis," *Saturday Review*, November 27, 1971, 68.
3. Albertson, "The Unmasking of Miles," 68.
4. Riggs, "The Genius of Miles."
5. Malcolm Jones, "Still Chasin' the Trane," *Newsweek*, October 29, 2007, 58.
6. "Miles Davis, the Fifties," 200. Davis's "improvisation technique helped to lay the foundation for the free-jazz movement of the 1960s." (200) It should be noted also that Davis would one day play his own free-jazz (i.e., Bitches Brew), and other such music onstage himself on several European stages.
7. Reich, "Completely Hot," 17.

8. Charles J. Gans, "At 74, Jazz Pianist Hancock Remains Open to Possibilities," *Las Vegas Review-Journal*, sec. 6E, October 30, 2014.

9. Cole, *A Musical Biography*, 96.

10. Cole, *A Musical Biography*, 98. Those who attended his many European concerts and performances, no doubt, were enthusiastic and appreciative, giving his trumpet playing high praise.

11. David Bauder, "Miles Davis Joins Rock 'n' Rollers," *Las Vegas Review-Journal*, sec. 10A, March 14, 2006.

12. David Breskin, "Searching for Miles: Theme and Variations on the Life of a Trumpeter," *Rolling Stone*, September 29, 1983, 49.

13. Howard Brofsky, "Miles Davis and *My Funny Valentine*: The Evolution of a Solo," *Black Music Research Journal*, vol. 3 (1983): 32.

14. Brofsky, "The Evolution of a Solo," 32.

15. Cindy Clark, "Kennedy Center Salutes America's Artists—With a Few Twists," *USA Today*, sec. 4D, December 8, 2015.

16. "The Chameleon of Cool," 3–4.

17. Barbara J. Gardner, "The Enigma of Miles Davis," *Down Beat*, January 7, 1960, 27.

18. Gardner, "The Enigma of Miles," 27. It should be pointed out here that European jazz fans are arguably more serious than almost any other jazz aficionados, save the Japanese.

19. Breskin, "Searching for Miles," 49.

20. Breskin, "Searching for Miles," 49.

21. Jones, "Still Chasin' the Trane," 58. According to Michael James, "Davis . . . made [it] a point of refusing to acknowledge applause," because of the equivocal relationship that [might] exist in an unintegrated society between a [black] performer and a predominantly white audience." See Michael James, *Kings of Jazz: Miles Davis* (New York: A. S. Barnes and Company, Inc., 1961), 74.

22. Michael James, *Kings of Jazz: Miles Davis* (New York: A. S. Barnes and Company, Inc., 1961), 75.

23. Albertson, "The Unmasking of Miles," 68.

24. Chris Murphy, *Miles to Go: Remembering Miles Davis* (New York: Thunder's Mouth Press, 2002), 24.

25. Murphy, *Miles to Go*, 24.

26. John Lingan, "Jazz on European TV," *The New York Times Magazine*, December 2, 2018, 23.

Chapter 11

In Love with Paris

Miles Davis was extremely enthusiastic about the prospect of visiting Paris for the first time, which was outside his terrible reality in the United States. Indeed, Davis was absolutely enamored by the beauty and complexity of Paris, France. Davis was also beginning to gain an international reputation as a jazz trumpeter, and playing his music there (Paris) was a good thing for him. The French, of course, had a unique perspective on the way they saw the world, and black Americans in it, as well as the music black jazz musicians invented and brilliantly played. To be honest, jazz fans in Paris were absolutely appreciative of what Miles Davis had already accomplished as a jazz trumpeter. They especially loved his jazz recordings, which were bestsellers in France; and Davis was glad Parisians got excited about his music. The irascible Miles Davis didn't really know that his music had preceded him; but it put a lot of things in perspective for him. And, it was an auspicious time for the young, angel-faced Davis. Paris also gave him enough time to get a different perspective on life outside of the United States and its institutional racism, particularly the inequality and unfairness blacks had to endure almost every day. But in Paris, the dashing young Miles Davis was the talk of the town, as he was able to hobnob with white Parisians who respected and loved his music. What more could Davis hope for? Paris gave him a tantalizing glimpse of another world, besides racist America. Davis, of course, often told racist Americans to kiss his black *derriere*. Perhaps it was the consequence of his fiery elocution that many white Americans disliked him. In 1957, according to jazz writer Jon Pareles, "Mr. Davis had a throat operation to remove nodes from his vocal cords. Two days later he began shouting at someone," probably a white producer, who "tried to convince [him] to go into a deal [he] didn't want."[1] In this regard, Davis refused to let anyone talk him into something—or some outlandish endeavor—that he didn't want to do. To be

Figure 11.1 Miles Davis statue outside Hotel Negresco in Nice, France. *Source:* Author's personal photograph.

sure, Davis made it known to *anyone* who crossed the line with him, even though it meant that "his voice was permanently damaged, reduced to a raspy whisper."[2] However, Miles Davis knew what was in his own best interests.

Unfortunately, many American *naysayers* thought that Davis was a racist himself and, generally, hated white people. But nothing could have been further from the truth. According to Chris Murphy, a white man, who was once Davis's road manager in the 1970s:

> Miles was definitely *not* a racist. . . . This is simply untrue. Miles understood the differences not only between Black and white culture, but also the differences between French, Italian, Irish, Spanish, WASP, and gay culture. He loved the

richness and variety of different peoples, and the pleasure such richness lent to his life.³

Nevertheless, Miles "was, known for [having] a volatile personality, sometimes making off-the-cuff and arrogant public pronouncements,"⁴ and terse remarks. For example, Davis was quoted as saying, "If I was Black and I turned white, I'd commit suicide."⁵ Such was his (Davis's) feelings about being a proud black man in the United States. But in Paris, Davis was able to let his hair down, so to speak. Being so care free in a beautiful place called Paris was a rare thing for him; but having fun was his priority. It was a kind of freedom at the time that blacks in America could only dream of. Paris was like having a light going on in the dark, metaphorically speaking; and Davis saw the entire city in a different light—that is, in terms of racial equality and race relations, as it was a window to another time and place. To say the least, Davis was enchanted. According to journalist David Breskin, Miles Davis liked traveling "to Paris, where the French iconize[d] him." In this respect, Davis hung "out with Jean-Paul Sartre on the Left Bank,"⁶ and other Parisian intellectuals. Of course, Miles Davis didn't really "understand Sartre, but Sartre [knew an] existentialist trumpet when he [heard] it."⁷ That said, it should be pointed out here that *existentialism* is a "philosophical movement oriented toward two major themes, the analysis of human existence and the centrality of human choice."⁸ And Sartre was the foremost advocate or proponent of this philosophy, as he promulgated these beliefs.

Paris was a very interesting experience for Miles Davis. Interestingly enough, Davis embraced the new nostalgia surrounding jazz and his music at the time, because of his deep feelings for Parisians, in particular. Of course, Davis was treated like some conquering hero, returning from some arduous battle, and having a big party. And he had an adventuresome spirit, and flagrantly and unapologetically did what he wanted to do in Paris. Was it because Davis was extremely motivated because of the way the French revered him—that is, as a man and jazz artist? It was clear to fans in Paris that Davis had that "something," or savoir faire. Again, it was a rare opportunity for Miles Davis. It was *C'est si Bon* all the way, people. But in truth, French fans didn't think it was odd that Davis talked, walked, played, worked, and drank the magnificent French wines with his friends like Sartre, and the black writer James Baldwin, in Paris, as they gathered often together and argued about life and philosophy, and listened to the local black jazz musicians, who had permanently moved to Paris. Some of the older black jazz musicians and *expatriates* respected Davis's trumpet playing and music, but some thought that the young man was a little wet-behind-the-ears whippersnapper. No doubt, Davis expected the best in Paris, and he was not disappointed, as the city was new and wonderful to him. The French people at the time also liked the more dynamic, fun-loving approach to life of black Americans and jazz musicians. Moreover, Parisians thought that Miles Davis was so much in the zeitgeist of jazz music. Indeed, "the improvisational nature of jazz, and the life-style of the jazz musician," like with Miles Davis, "had a special fascination for the French intellectuals."[9] So black music was not that uncommon to Parisian jazz fans, especially when it came to Miles Davis. He had finally exploded into the jazz world and "social music" consciousness, in the early 1950s and 1960s, defining what it meant to play cool jazz; and his fame (as mentioned) had preceded him in Paris. Also, there was no doubt that Davis thought a lot about himself.

Additionally, by this time in the late 1950s, "with the popularity of his sextet and especially of his *Columbia* records, Miles Davis became an international celebrity."[10] Which is to say that after doing his due diligence, Davis never rested on his laurels as a trumpeter and jazz musician. Indeed, "by now he [Davis] was fairly often producing live recordings, in which his trumpet soloing [was] consistently rich and alive."[11] Davis also exuded the confidence of a much older jazz man in full control of his trumpet playing, and his music. Still, his dynamic trumpet was tamed by other *bebop* standards. Davis at this time was also very driven, and wanted nothing more than to be accepted for his ability to play his trumpet, especially for the French people [see Figure 11.1]. Moreover, Davis had an unwavering desire to succeed as a jazz musician. Clearly, Davis didn't know what he would have done if he didn't have the talent to blow his horn. Davis once stated:

> If I didn't play trumpet, I don't know what I would have done. I couldn't stay in an office. . . . I'll never have an easy life. I'll always be in trouble because my nature is to [ask] "why?" to things I don't know anything about. And get in "em" and find out myself.[12]

Therefore, early on in his career, failure was not an option, because he knew fully what he wanted to do in life—that is, play his horn for a living. No doubt, Miles Davis didn't see a place, initially, for him to exist within the conservative American music industry, which was predominantly white. Hence, Davis had to go his own way. Indeed, "Miles decided [that] he was going to do something else,"[13] rather than knuckle under to the wishes of white record executives and producers. In that way, Davis was able to bend them to *his* will, because of the success of his many jazz recordings. He also was a *rascal*, who made people, particularly musicians, do things to make them fit his musical vision. In Paris, Davis took his listeners on a musical adventure, as his band served for new creative grounds. According to jazz writer, producer, and scholar, the late George Avakian, "Miles Davis [was] perhaps the most lyrical and most instantly communicating. [And] in certain contexts, he . . . proved to be an artist of enormous [appeal] to people who know nothing about jazz."[14] Davis was also driven to connect the world to jazz or what he called "social music." But in an interview about the acceptance of jazz in the United States with the late writer Alex Haley, Miles Davis was quoted as saying:

> European audiences [like in Paris, France] are generally more hip about the background of jazz than most of the fans here. Some cats hardly heard here are big record sellers in Europe. In this country [the U.S.], it's more following of personalities.[15]

So as the years passed, Davis was able to use his trumpet talents strategically; and his music had as much originality as it had jazz tradition. To say the least, it (touring in Paris) was a memorable time for Davis, as his music was like a sort of ecstasy in that it stuck in the memory of fans. Indeed, there was a wonderful circus aspect to attending a Miles Davis concert in Paris, because such an event aroused a sense of musical fantasy that intrigued his Parisian fans. Davis's music, in a way, would leave the listener *gob-smacked*, because what he played was sometimes unexpected. Furthermore, many fans wanted a ringside seat, to see and listen to the great music man. In this regard, and making a comparison between jazz and "the church," musician Kurt Elling put it best when he stated that jazz is

> a corrected vision of life, of yourself, of reality, of your divine nature. . . . For a moment, our eyes can see and our ears can hear what there is about us always. That's [the jazz] church. That's music. That's the church of Saturday night, just as much as it is the church of Sunday morning. That's what art does; it alters your perception so that you see the beauty of what is always around you anyway. You just finally get to see it for once.[16]

In his own way, and without sounding *Pollyannaish*, Davis was an advocate for the "Church of Jazz." And for a long time, what moved Miles Davis forward was the great musical unknown. And although Davis's music seemed fairly straightforward and he played his best in Paris, in such a relaxed setting, fans never heard the same *exact* music, played the same way, because Miles Davis often changed his shows every time he gave a sizzling jazz concert in Paris. And even though Davis "was having trouble making an impact as the leader of an innovative band," in the late 1940s, his "reputation as a trumpeter was nevertheless on the upswing,"[17] particularly when he toured Paris in the late 1940s and 1950s. Indeed, jazz writer Steve Pond writes:

> In 1957, Miles Davis was in the middle of turning lots of ears inside out when he went to France for a short tour; while he was there, director Louis

Malle convinced him to write what would be his [first] film score for Malle's *Ascenseur pour l'échafaud* (aka Lift to the Scaffold).[18]

The music score was almost entirely planned by Davis, who had been mulling over it "for a couple of weeks."[19] But it was Juliette Gréco, Sartre's *muse*, who had probably convinced him to do it, as Davis had, by then, fallen in love with her.[20] Perhaps he had been infatuated with the beautiful French woman; and wanted to impress her. Still, Davis had the musical experience, insight, talent, and ability to adapt his music to the big screen. And as far as the film score was concerned, Davis played in a "moody, gentle, post-bop" way, improvising the music that intertwined with a complex, decadent trumpet sound. Indeed, the "unearthly loveliness"[21] of Davis's horn brings the true essence of traditional, cool jazz to the forefront, as it was a creative, musical collaboration that was recorded "in one four-hour session,"[22] showcasing Davis's artistry. Steve Pond, in writing about Davis's trumpet playing on Malle's *Asceseur pour l'echanfaud*, finally tells us that the music is, "more than a film score, it's a document of the restless, searching intelligence of a badass at the top of his game."[23] Davis was playing at a level of consciousness that was unimaginable; and the French or Parisians knew good jazz music when they heard it, as many fans were *connoisseurs*. Furthermore, listening to Miles Davis was perhaps an unforgettable experience that fully satisfied their musical palates. It was definitely a totally new experience for Miles Davis. At least one thing seemed clear, Davis's live performances, in Paris, during his touring were something else.

Moreover, we shouldn't forget Juliette Gréco's "famous romance with" the legendary Miles Davis, "who took Paris by storm."[24] Gréco, a beautiful, petite, white woman was a French celebrity on the rise; and like

> Miles [Davis] was an up-and-coming musical star, and they were immediately drawn to each other. They began an intense affair. [It was] Miles' first real affair since his marriage. Juliette [Gréco] was fascinated by Black music, and Miles was engaged by her lack of prejudice and her European manner.[25]

Juliette Gréco was lovely with a flawless, almost white, translucent complexion, with big, dark eyes, perhaps the envy of every French woman. Of course, Davis initially thought that Gréco was out of his league; but it turned out that the French singer was very much interested in Miles Davis, as she "first saw him while watching from the wings at the *Salle Pleyel* concert hall."[26] It was not so much an unlikely pairing (between the two) as it was the whole idea of a black man and white woman having deep feelings for each other. Interracial relationships, however, were not commonly accepted during this time, at least in the United States in the late 1940s and 1950s. But

Gréco loved jazz music, and would come to love Miles Davis, and wanted to know or experience (in a way) how it might have felt to live the life of a black American, on the so-called wild-side; or on the edge of so-called human existence. Indeed, for some white women at the time, having a relationship with a black man was the ultimate *taboo*, as well as an exciting and novel experience. So was Gréco living out her own fantasies with the dangerous Miles Davis? Also, in those days, some white Europeans were unabashedly racist when it came to interracial relationships; and even thought the French or Parisians were considered *bohemian* and progressive. In other words, no matter how famous the particular jazz artist, black people were still looked down upon, considered inferior, or sub-human by some whites; therefore, many were ostracized from genteel society.

Furthermore, there was a *stigma* for a French woman getting involved with a black jazz musician. But Davis liked the fact that he could stroll down an ordinary street with a white, French woman in Paris and not be persecuted, attacked, or lynched. Or he (Davis) was able to be with Juliette Gréco, in an uninhibited way, without looking over his shoulders, like in the United States. According to Miles Davis, in his autobiography:

> Juliette [Gréco] was probably the first woman that I loved as an equal human being. She was a beautiful person. We had to communicate with each other through expressions and body language. She didn't speak English and I didn't speak French. We talked through our eyes, fingers, stuff like that. When you communicate like that, you know the person is not bullshitting. You have to go on feelings. It was April in Paris. Yeah, and I was in love.[27]

Also, Gréco was more than attracted to the enigmatic Miles Davis, generating a heated and torrid affair. Gréco took Davis to places in Paris that he (Davis) had never been, or wouldn't normally go, which was an experience in itself. It was as if the two were on the same wavelength. Davis was captivated by Gréco's beauty and appreciation for jazz and his music, in particular. Indeed, Gréco's enthusiasm for jazz and adoration of black musicians was unexpected, but appreciated by Davis. She also seemed to really care about the rakish Miles Davis. Additionally, the French woman made him feel good about himself, as a human being, and Davis could (for a time) forget about the rabid racism in America. To be sure, he was able to openly talk or express his feelings to Gréco about *everything*—from music and how blacks were treated (unequally) in the United States. Also, Juliette Gréco hated being objectified, and she got none of that from Davis, as they were learning about each other. Again, Gréco had first observed and studied Miles Davis from afar, as she, no doubt, proudly wanted him. Davis was perhaps overwhelmed. In retrospect, Miles Davis (at first) couldn't wrap his mind around the idea that the stunning French woman wanted him, desired him, especially since he was still in a common-law marriage with his first wife, Irene. Interestingly, Richard Williams tells us that Jean-Paul Sartre eventually suggested that Miles Davis marry Juliette Gréco, which was "a surprisingly mundane suggestion, perhaps, coming from the godfather of existentialism, but one that Davis resisted with the greatest difficulty." Ultimately, "it was a decision he [Davis] lived to regret."[28] Gréco had captured his heart. Perhaps Davis had no idea at the time that Quincy Jones, the great black jazz musician, producer, and conductor, was dating the French woman, too. About his relationship with Juliette Gréco, Quincy stated that the woman was "the Queen of French existentialism." He goes on:

> Juliette [Gréco] was also dating Miles Davis then. She was wonderful. . . . She was brilliant and sweet and would imitate a kitten purring when we made love. Miles was irritated with me for years about it, though it was some time before each of us figured out what the other had been up to.[29]

In spite of everything, Gréco loved Miles Davis in her own way, his music, perversities, peculiarities, and the soul of the man. In turn, he found himself even more infatuated with the French woman. Davis had a connection with Gréco that was deeper than he had ever experienced with a woman. But perhaps such a relationship with Gréco would never have worked, because of the racism and segregation that still existed in the United States—that is, if he brought her there. Among other things, Clive Davis explained:

> The relationship petered out when the trumpeter returned to New York—partly because he was already married; partly, it seems, because, unlike the more naïve Gréco, he knew what complications an interracial relationship could cause in America. But they remained close over the years. It is one of the fairy-tale stories in jazz folklore.[30]

In the end, and predictably, their affair wasn't meant to be; but Gréco always wanted to rekindle her romance and relationship with Miles Davis from time to time, or when she saw him, even before his death. And for a while, Davis was grateful for his brief visits to Paris, and what Gréco had brought to his life. And although he considered it, Davis never believed that he could actually live in Europe or Paris, because his heart was in New York through and through. Gréco, however, might have even followed Davis to New York had he asked, as he (Davis) remained at the forefront of her mind. Perhaps the French woman (Gréco) had found herself utterly obsessed with Miles Davis. Did she even worship him? Perhaps Davis's time in Paris gave him courage for other things in life. And Davis would certainly have pleasant memories of the city later, as he was exhilarated by his time in Paris; and he would visit and perform in the "city of love" on several more occasions.

NOTES

1. Pareles, "Trumpeter, Dies," 3. People particularly didn't want to be on the receiving end of Davis's wrath or unpleasantness.

2. Pareles, "Trumpeter, Dies," 3. According to Bill Cole, Davis's "need to liberate himself from an exploitative situation precipitated the quarrel. Although his voice became gravelly and slightly above a whisper, it didn't affect his playing." See Cole, *A Musical Biography*, 67.

3. Murphy, *Miles to Go,* 219. Meeting different, interesting people in Paris changed Davis's perspectives regarding white people, in general. Back in the United States, unfortunately, black people were still suffering terrible indignities that no human being should have had to face.

4. Pareles, "Trumpeter, Dies," 1.

5. Breskin, "Searching for Miles," 49.

6. Breskin, "Searching for Miles," 49.

7. Breskin, "Searching for Miles," 49.

8. *Merriam-Webster's Collegiate Encyclopedia*, 1st ed., s.v. "existentialism."

9. Nisenson, "Round about Midnight," 69. According to journalist Rebecca Dalzell, "to Black Americans, it was the city of Paris that equaled freedom. Finding it a welcoming refuge from [racism and] the civil rights era, [black] musicians such as Sidney Bechet and Bud Powell [for example] moved [there]." See Rebecca Dalzell, "Paris is for Jazz Lovers," *Las Vegas Review Journal*, sec. 7F, March 22, 2015.

10. John Litweiler, "Transition: Miles Davis and Modal Jazz" in *The Freedom Principle*: *Jazz After 1958* (New York: William Morrow and Company, Inc., 1984), 11.

11. Litweiler, "Transition: Miles Davis,"112. It should be noted here that on Miles Davis's himself firmly in the minds of people who organize concert and [were] general patrons of the arts." See Cole, *A Musical Biography,* 71.

12. Breskin, "Searching for Miles," 49.

13. Troup, "Our 1985 Interview," 9.

14. George Avakian, liner notes to *Miles Ahead, Miles Davis +19* (Columbia Records, 1957), recording.

15. Alex Haley, interviewer, "Miles Davis: A Candid Conversation with the Jazz World's Premier Iconoclast," *Playboy*, September 1962, http://www.honors.uindiedu /HONR 269J. Davis would hobnob with some of the best minds and jazz musicians of his day in Paris. Of course, Davis was a relatively unknown musician at the beginning of his jazz music career. But he would eventually become a well-loved, international jazz man.

16. Joshua Rosenbaum, "Kurt Elling: Keeping the Jazz Faith," *The Wall Street Journal*, sec. W15C, November 13, 1998.

17. Williams, *The Man in the Green Shirt*, 46.
18. Steve Pond, "Soundtracks & Scores: All That Jazz," *Movie line*, December 1996, 36.
19. Pond, "All That Jazz," 36.
20. Rebecca Dalzell, "Paris is for Jazz Lovers," *Las Vegas Review-Journal*, sec. 7F and 8F, March 22, 2015. See also Williams, *The Man in the Green Shirt*, 72.
21. Williams, *The Man in the Green Shirt*, 70.
22. Williams, *The Man in the Green Shirt*, 70.
23. Williams, *The Man in the Green Shirt*, 70. Surely, Miles Davis's music score should have won some kind of award in the United States—that is, for his efforts, like an Oscar for best music score. But that was not to be. Was it because of his so-called race?
24. Clive Davis, "Gypsy of the Left Bank," *The Sunday Times*, July 25, 2010, 13.
25. Nisenson, "Round about Midnight," 70. It should be noted that Miles Davis dealt unflinchingly with the racism in the jazz music world, which was understandably (always) on his mind.
26. Davis, "Gypsy of the Left Bank," 13.
27. Davis and Troupe, *Miles: The Autobiography*, 127.
28. Williams, *The Man in the Green Shirt*, 48.
29. Quincy Jones, *Q: The Autobiography of Quincy Jones* (New York: Broadway Books, 2001), 156–157.
30. Davis, "Gypsy of the Left Bank," 13. Davis was tempted to stay in Paris; but he was profoundly American, so he returned to the United States, without fanfare—but for a while, leaving Paris would almost be his undoing.

Chapter 12

The Twilight of Avant-Garde

Avant-Garde is like an undisciplined approach to jazz, while creating a common musical language through oddly moving rhythms and sounds. But for some jazz fans, avant-garde is an intellectual, musical puzzle; and for the uninitiated, it might be confusing, as it is about music freedom, without complete structure. Of course, during Miles Davis's time, there was the possibility that avant-garde music would ultimately fail with listeners, as some saw it as terribly contrived. Jazz drummer James Marcellus Arthur (Sunny) Murray explained that "Even in [jazz] freedom . . . there should be a certain amount of composition—I mean if you're going out with the emphasis on being a professional musician."[1] It is important to remember that with avant-garde, Davis wasn't enormously impressed (at first), because of the music's lack of control, and the spontaneous nature of the sound. However, according to the late jazz critic Stanley Crouch, in the 1960s:

> At the plugged Nickel he [Miles Davis] and his musicians were staring right in the face of the avant-garde of the period, spontaneously changing tempi and meters, playing common or uncommon notes over the harmonies, pulling in harsh timbers, all the while in a repertoire that was roughly the same as the trumpeter had been using for a decade.[2]

So was avant-garde a subversive jazz music, because it ignored the lyrical melodies and harmonic, traditional jazz foundations? Perhaps for many, the entire notion of playing avant-garde jazz (music) seemed strange, even downright traitorous, or forbidden music. Others were also less than enthusiastic about avant-garde. For example, Davis tried not to waste his time on such insignificant musical objectives. In his infamous 1989 autobiography, Davis "blamed the excesses of avant-garde for the exodus of listeners from jazz—a common opinion, even if Davis himself thought that what variously called 'avant-garde,' 'free jazz,' 'the new thing,' and 'the new black music.' Undoubtedly, Davis felt that it was an attempt by white critics to detour audiences from him."[3] But from a purely musical point of view, avant-garde was indeed significant, even interesting. Perhaps it still is today. Nevertheless, in his "reaction against *Freedom*, Miles Davis was among the many who initially rejected Ornette Coleman's [avant-garde] music." Davis stated that "The man [Coleman] is all screwed up inside,"[4] and he never changed his mind about Coleman. Furthermore, music professor Ronald M. Radano writes:

> From the beginning, virtually all protests by the jazz avant-garde were racially inspired. Regardless of the topic, avant-garde spokesmen who appeared in print in jazz magazines inevitably seemed to base their arguments on racial oppression by a dominant white society. "Racism" became the collective cry, the watchword for the avant-garde jazz community. Any type of opposition, whether directed towards a group or an individual, met with the wrath of the jazz avant-garde, who branded as "racist" the entire jazz establishment.[5]

Perhaps Miles Davis would have agreed with Radano, because after a time thinking about jazz avant-garde, he decided to embrace the music—that is, Davis thought that it was time to change the music again. For whatever reasons, it was widely assumed that Davis would play traditional jazz forever. But much of the traditional musical *shtick* had gotten old, and stale to him. Davis once stated, "When I hear jazz musicians . . . playing all those same licks we used to play so long ago, I feel sad for them." Davis goes on, "I mean, it's like going to bed with a real old person who even smells real old."[6] In other words, the traditional jazz music seemed dated to Davis. He wanted to deconstruct the original jazz sound with avant-garde, and improve upon it, while working out the bugs, so to speak, or smoothing out the rough edge in the music. It was Davis's way of stretching himself artistically, and he became understandably enthusiastic about mixing several musical forms. Avant-garde was/is progressive in the best sense of the term; and Davis wanted definitely to *amp-up* the awkward music, and give it some direction. But for some fans and critics, it was a jazz music world turned upside down. Furthermore, when it came to so-called music *freedom*, Davis was acutely aware of what he wanted to do, or what he wanted to play musically in terms of avant-garde. Moreover, Davis had finally figured out how to get out of his music *lethargy*. In this way, Davis wanted to create a new, all electric, and instrumental-type of sound, because he thought that he knew what people actually wanted to hear. In this regard, and for many, "Jazz is pseudo-democratic in the sense that [it] characterizes the consciousness of the epoch: its attitude of immediacy, which can be defined in terms of a rigid system of tricks, is deceptive when it comes down to class differences,"[7] and how the music is played or interpreted. Also, some jazz critics have even claimed that "jazz is no longer the innovative, and consistently progressive and visionary force in our society."[8] But Davis never believed in such nonsense, because he thought that jazz or "social music" could be the *be-all* and *end-all* in such music, and even if it was challenging.

Almost as noteworthy, Miles Davis was also a very enterprising jazz musician. And he would later have faith in his own conception about avant-garde. Just listen to Davis's "Bitches Brew" album, and some of his other electric-rock-jazz music, like his "Miles in the Sky." Talking about "the radically unorthodox jazz," or avant-garde jazz recording (session) of "Bitches Brew," Wayne Shorter had this to say:

> It was not like: You play, the next person plays, you have a lineup of who was going to solo. There were basically no traditional harmonic chords for the keyboards. It was more an emotional experience. You played off of yourself in a sense. You played off of your sound, rather than a melody. This was where having a sound counted. The sound became the language.[9]

No doubt, avant-garde jazz was a turning point for Davis musically, especially with his incorporation of different electric instruments. Of course, in terms of his new music, Davis often "had to think through [creating different music] for his whole band," because he "had already worked to simplify the harmonic labyrinth of bop as a soloist: he [also] made an art of choosing unlikely yet perfect tempos, and drew on his considerable knowledge of harmony to choose the odd but tellingly right notes."[10] To this end, Davis had a "strong preference for writing [certain music] that [wasn't] overcrowded, especially overcrowded with [specific] chords."[11] More importantly, he didn't care about playing a lot of tiresome chords, and notes. And this attitude and approach to his music didn't change with Davis's embrace of avant-garde, or even his "jazz-rock fusion" music, which ultimately and surprisingly "interested the rock generation in jazz itself."[12] Davis also had to really focus on himself, and write tunes, to grow as a jazz music innovator. And most importantly, Davis would disconnect or disengage himself from musicians that didn't really like what he was trying to accomplish. Eric Nisenson writes:

> Miles' use of complex rock/funk and Afro/Latin rhythms instead of the straight-ahead 4/4 swing, which had dominated jazz for decades, [was] profoundly innovating. [But] playing with such unfamiliar rhythms challenged improvisers, and made them eschew the clichés they had previously relied on. This was very important to Miles; he always wanted his musicians to create fresh new musical ideas, to play something that had never been heard before.[13]

Perhaps Davis was ahead of his time, because he wanted to create a new, authentic jazz-rock sound, with other like-minded musicians backing him up. As the late Joe Zawinul, a white musician, originally from Austria, who thought of Miles Davis as a semi-mythical god,[14] and played piano in his electric band, stated: Davis "wrote simple things to play over, that he could improvise over, which [was] always a blast," and Davis was "the best at that of probably anybody."[15] Furthermore, when Davis played jazz-rock or avant-garde, he played with a purpose, while creating aesthetically challenging music to the ear, as if it was for the gods themselves. Accordingly, "Everything connected with his [Davis's] music has beauty, fire, vitality and grace,"[16] and soul. Also, in a sort of hyperkinetic musical mode, Davis thought that avant-garde could rightly merge or mesh with other musical idioms, which suited him. Inwardly, Davis knew that there was an edgy dimension to avant-garde that he liked. So all things considered, was it his musical *epiphany* to play such music? Moreover, Davis later loved the feeling of freedom and power that avant-garde gave him, as it challenged his sense of being and musical way of thinking. Oddly enough, something clicked within him (Davis) about the freedom and flexibility of avant-garde that he had wanted to seriously explore, with different musical instruments, like the church organ. But his strategy had always been to dive right into the mix of things, and mold the music into his own vision, or proposition. To be sure, Davis wanted to make a surprising, innovative move, when it came to avant-garde. In this way, Davis's aim was to spark the listener to embrace another way, or musical concept. But, by any standard, Davis believed that his musical message was the same as always: Change for the benefit and sake of jazz, or "social music."

Therefore, instead of sticking to the same formulaic jazz music, Davis was willing to stir things up, again, and again, as this is what jazz is all about. Indeed, "jazz [is] an art form, with improvisation and certain harmonic touchstones at its core that constantly evolves as its practitioners search out the new,"[17] and exciting sounds. And at the heyday of avant-garde, it was probably one of the most important changes in jazz music since its inception; and Davis had to make the decision to stay still, as in the status quo, or move forward with his jazz-rock music. To that end, Davis was very self-effacing, but he continued to march to his own musical drum. It has been argued that Davis's later electric rock bands were cutting edge; and even *scary* for some listeners, because of his "use of electric instruments" which allowed for "new [musical] textures," and "popular traditions to the improvisational processes of high art abstraction."[18] Davis certainly understood the implications of avant-garde. But for some, the music didn't make sense at all, as they came away perplexed by his jazz-rock, and particularly the complex jazz rhythms and how Davis played his strange, *wah-wah* trumpet. And "his music was starting to bewilder the buying public, who had been confronted with a stream of 2-LP sets that didn't conform to their expectations of what Miles Davis should be doing (namely, playing lyrical trumpet over a jazz background)."[19] Equally important, Davis's otherworldly trumpet *riffs* proved taxing for some jazz fans, even if avant-garde is actually mind-expanding, and certainly complex. Perhaps Davis chuckled when he recalled the *brouhaha* surrounding avant-garde; but he didn't really care if his rock-jazz music was completely understood by everyone. Critics saw avant-garde as inconsequential; and the many wretched notes and weird sounds didn't have a lot meaning, either. But playing his avant-garde music definitely wasn't boring, mainly because Davis's *triumphant* trumpet sound is what actually caught fans' attention.

More importantly, and despite the withering criticism for Davis's new avant-garde direction, he (Davis) still wanted to express his musical vision, in his own way. For example, jazz writer Philip Freeman explains:

> In the 1980s, Miles was a musician a listener could identify with. He [Davis] had a strong image, with his restless onstage presence and semi-outlandish wardrobe; his band kicked out hard-funk songs with melodies and choruses; and he made showbizzy gestures of inclusion part of the act. All this was at least in part an effort to get himself across to as many people as possible—without ever changing the music into anything he didn't want it to be.[20]

Davis especially liked working out musical things himself, as he was explicit about what he wanted to do. Thus, during some recordings of his avant-garde or jazz rock fusion music, Davis would pass out pieces of paper to his various musicians, that "contained mere sketches of the music with few chord changes, some basslines and minimalist melodic material."[21] Some might have thought that this was a weird thing to do, but such sentiments never stopped his creative musical efforts. Furthermore, Davis did all the little things, behind the scenes, as he was looking for something beyond the basic jazz music idiom. However, it should be noted here that, "Davis's adoption of the electrified sounds of psychedelic rock and the complex rhythm-guitar offbeat of funk is one of the developments in his fusion music most sorely lamented by jazz purists."[22] Nevertheless, Davis was able to expand his musical boundaries, as he was as competitive as any other jazz musician during his day. He also wanted to reach beyond his regular jazz audiences. Indeed, Davis liked the idea of having, and performing before, larger rock audiences. So did he have ulterior motives? No doubt, Davis wanted to make a connection between the younger rock crowd and his jazz or "social music" fans; and he thought that avant-garde or his fusion music would be the ticket, because he wanted to speak their language in terms of the music—and make more money. There were obvious differences in the way that Davis played progressive avant-garde or jazz-rock fusion, but he persisted. So the writing was on the wall for Davis—that is, in terms of him playing his music for white rockers and hipsters, who probably "took delight in accepting Davis as an evil-image cult figure."[23] Davis also liked the music of black pop stars, like Michael Jackson, Prince, and other black Rockers, like Lenny Kravitz, who had this to say about meeting Miles Davis for the last time:

> My godmother was married to Miles, so Miles [Davis] was in my life since I was a baby. I bumped into him on a plane going from New York to LA. He came up to me and told me how proud he was of me, and how he loved my album: "Keep on doing what you're doing." We talked about collaborating on my next album. There was a solo I wanted him to play. But he died, and that was our last conversation. It was a great moment.[24]

So Miles Davis's pragmatic but sometimes awkward music "became a much wider palette as opposed to free-form jazz,"[25] because of the incorporation of rock and electric music. Avant-garde also gave Miles Davis something to feed of, so to speak, especially when he was playing his trumpet, unfiltered. Appropriately enough, avant-garde even allowed for musical exaggeration when it came to his (one-of-a-kind) trumpet improvisations. So is there any jazz that can really be compared to Miles Davis's music? Jazz critic Gary Giddins tells us, "We associate the avant-garde with privation, which Davis [had] never known, and with a specific approach to improvisational freedom, which he [at first rejected]," but later he would make the music his own. Finally, Miles Davis was "a terribly conscientious avant-gardist, continuously remaking jazz in his own image, and often remaking himself in the process."[26] When it was all said and done, Davis sought a type of creative musical *synergy*, because of the chemistry between jazz tradition and a new, musical foundation. In the final analysis, "the rock press [acclaimed] Davis as a daring innovator who [seemed] to be able to get away with any musical experiment, no matter how far out."[27] And although Davis thought, in the beginning, that nothing would ever come of avant-garde, the eclectic, offbeat sound is (today) heard in contemporary music almost everywhere in the world.

NOTES

1. Valerie Wilmer, "Controlled Freedom Is the Thing This Year," *Down Beat*, March 23, 1967, 16.
2. Stanley Crouch, "Play the Right Thing," *The New Republic*, February 12, 1990, 34.

3. Francis Davis, "Jazz-Religious and Circus," *The Atlantic Monthly* (February 2000): 89.

4. John Litweiler, *The Freedom Principle: Jazz After 1958* (New York: William Morrow and Company, Inc., 1984), 105.

5. Ronald M. Radano, "The Jazz Avant-Garde and the Jazz Community: Action and Reaction," *Annual Review of Jazz Studies*, vol. 3 (1985): 74.

6. Sholto Byrnes, "Blowing Up a Storm," *The Independent*, online edition, April 1, 2005, 2, http://enjoyment.independent.co.uk/low_res.

7. Theodor W. Adorno, "On Jazz," *Discourse*, vol. 12, issue 1 (Fall-Winter 1989–90): 50.

8. Eric Nisenson, "Now's the Time!!! 25 Years of Bitches Brew," *Jazziz*, vol. 12, issue 6 (June 1995): 70.

9. Dan Ouellette, "Bitches Brew," *Down Beat*, vol. 66, issue 12 (December 1999): 3, http://proquest.umi.com/pqdweb?index.

10. Gary Giddens, "Miles's Wiles," *The Village Voice*, August 5–12, 1981, 27.

11. Nat Hentoff, "An Afternoon with Miles Davis," *The Jazz Review* (December 1958): 11. Davis didn't like getting involved in conversations with musicians who didn't want to listen to his musical ideas, even if what he wanted to do was off-kilter; or if he wanted to take a new approach to an old music tradition.

12. Douglas Clark, "Miles into Jazz-Rock Territory," *Jazz Journal*, vol. 30 (June 1977): 14. Davis was adaptable and was mostly able to achieve whatever he set out to do with his music; but he was never perfect.

13. Nisenson, "Now's the Time!!!" 72. But to the contrary, Miles Davis was very particular about what he personally wanted to play. It was all about those musical things, which were driven by the beat. Furthermore, his avant-garde music was more than something bizarre and different. And he was proud of his new sound.

14. Brian Glasser, *In a Silent Way: A Portrait of Joe Zawinul* (London: Sanctuary Publishing Limited, 2001), 117. Zawinul also thought that Miles Davis "played like a god." Zawinul also recorded with Davis studio band in the 1960s. His tune "In a Silent Way" served as the title track for the trumpeter's first foray into the electric arena. Zawinul's composition "Pharaoh's Dance" was featured on Davis's groundbreaking 1970 jazz-rock fusion album "Bitches Brew," which won Davis a 1970 Grammy for best jazz performance, large group or soloist with large group. See Veronika Oleksyn, "Jazz Keyboardist Joe Zawinul, 75, dies in Austria," *Las Vegas Review-Journal*, sec. 6B, September 12, 2007.

15. Glasser, *In a Silent Way*, 117. Miles Davis had this to say about Joe Zawinul: "Listen. Zawinul is like Sly [Stone] and [Charles] Mingus. They write things and they fall in love with them. You know what I mean. I don't write things for myself. I write things for my band. When you write things for yourself, your ego take over. I ain't never going to ever damn fool myself into believing that everything, or any one piece I write, is that good—and I ain't going to let my musicians tell me that shit, either. I don't have no yes men around me." See Jimmy Saunders, "An Interview with Miles Davis," *Playboy*, April 1975, 30.

16. Hubert Saal, "Miles of Music," *Newsweek*, March 23, 1970, 99.

17. Byrnes, "Blowing Up a Storm," 1.

18. Michael E. Veal, "Miles Davis's Unfinished Electric Revolution," *Raritan* (EBSCO Publishing, 2002), 163. Davis always believed that there had to be an ending sound to avant-garde, because beginning in an irregular way, as in fits (and starts), the music wasn't always precise and clear cut. And Davis wanted to change all that, to give direction to diverse group of musicians, from classical, rock, pop, blues and jazz, while making a cohesive sound in music.

19. Scott McFarland, "Miles Davis: The 'Electric' Years," *Perfect Sound Forever* (August 1997), 4–5, http://www.furious.com/perfect/miles.html. But the underlying reality was Davis's name carried *cachet* among jazz fans, as they wouldn't just accept any music.

20. Philip Freeman, *Running the Voodoo Down: The Electric Music of Miles Davis* (San Francisco, CA: Backbeat Books, 2005), 170–171.

21. Geoffrey Himes, "Miles Davis: Forty Years of Freedom: The Legacy of Bitches Brew," *Jazz Times*, August 13, 2010, 2, http://jazztimes.com/articles/26369-miles-davis. Davis once stated: "I like the passacaglia form, you know, when you repeat the same bass line and write a simple melody, maybe four bars—it opens up so many possibilities; the rest you can ad-lib." See Leonard Feather, "Miles Davis' Miraculous Recovery from Stroke," *Ebony*, December 1982, 62.

22. Gary Tomlinson, "Miles Davis: Music Dialogician," *Black Music Research Journal*, vol. 11, issue 2 (Fall 1991): 249.

23. Leonard Feather, "Miles Davis' Miraculous Recovery from Stroke," *Ebony*, December 1982, 64.

24. Camille Dodero, "Lenny Kravitz Remembers the Greats who Shaped his Life and Music," *Maxim*, September 2014, 30.

25. Gayle Jo Carters, quote by "Elijah Woods," *USA Weekend*, November 10–12, 2006, 23.

26. Peter Schwendener, Giddens's quote in "Miles Davis: The Loss of Lyricism," *Tri-Quarterly* (Winter 1987): 163–164. What exactly drove Davis's musical thinking? In the end, he undoubtedly came to the realization that he had to explore other musical possibilities.

27. Doug Ramsey, "Miles Davis," in *Jazz Matter: Reflections on the Music & Some of its Makers* (Fayetteville: The University of Arkansas Press, 1989), 52.

Chapter 13

Fusion

The Heart of the Matter

Davis liked the fact that you could also experience his music, as if you were actually at one of his many concerts. Also, when it came to jazz or "social music," Davis was able to discern what was musically possible. By being able to hear in his head what he wanted to play, Davis was able to give (voice or) his grand message in a beautiful sound. In the end, Miles Davis became one of the leading forces in making acoustic jazz acceptable around the world. Some critics, however, would later excoriate Davis's experiment with fusion, or his abandonment of the basic (or traditional) jazz *genre*. According to jazz writers Farah Jasmine Griffin and Salim Washington, "In addition to his contemporary role as chief model for the neo-hard bop school, Davis became the undisputed leader of jazz/rock fusion."[1] In a nutshell, fusion became Davis's connection to the avant-garde movement. Indeed, Davis would eventually become a leading advocate of the avant-garde, or free-jazz movement in the United States and abroad, perhaps to the chagrin of many so-called jazz *purists*, like black jazz trumpeter Wynton Marsalis. But Davis was on another planet with the things he did with his music and trumpet. For perspective, Davis wanted to have a new and different jazz *repertoire*—that is, rather than playing the traditional jazz standards. To say the least, Davis was allergic to the idea of playing the same old music. But jazz purists, like Wynton Marsalis, looked down on jazz fusion. And it was reported that Marsalis was someone who Davis disliked; so he [Davis] was scornful of the young trumpeter, believing that Marsalis hadn't paid his dues. The hard truth was there was a palpable friction between Davis and Marsalis. And it had a lasting negative effect—that is, when it came to jazz. For example, Davis did not like "the younger Marsalis at their first meeting, judging him to be an 'Uncle Tom,' ambitious and self-interested, with a personality that would allow whites to manipulate him."[2] Of course, Davis's greatest asset was that he was constantly changing the music, unlike Marsalis, most of the time. He also thought that the young Marsalis didn't have a musical vision; even with his "legendary technique,"[3] or chops, as he regurgitated a lot of old jazz tunes or music that had already been played and recorded. On the other hand, Davis had a fertile, musical imagination. And jazz fusion gave Davis limitless freedom to play and explore strange chords and notes, creating a different musical frame of reference. Moreover, Davis believed that it was his *holy* task to proceed, full steam ahead, unhindered in an unpredictable musical terrain. According to jazz writer Richard Williams, "Davis's music seemed to have no beginnings and no ends."[4] So was Davis in a state of spiritual grace when he played fusion-jazz music?

Unfortunately, some thought that his jazz fusion made no sense, as it was/ is hard to duplicate Davis's experimental music (exactly). Created in the 1960s, jazz fusion is a combination of modal and harmonic jazz, or "social music," funk, soul, rock, and blues. For many, the music is rhythmically complex. But Davis was up for the challenge in playing this unconventional music. In retrospect, bebop, modal, and acoustic jazz were almost in eclipse, whereas bombastic jazz-rock fusion, new wave, or contemporary jazz and electronic music were on the rise. But, in this regard, many critics thought of Miles Davis as a (musical) demon, even sinister, especially when he broke (ranks or) away from traditional jazz or classical jazz for his electric jazz or fusion music—or another world of music. It was fitting, then, that Davis used his intelligence, imagination, *guile*, and creativity to find another way of making instrumental or small (and large) band music. Indeed, it was an entirely different (or new) view of what made good jazz or "social music." Nevertheless, at that time, jazz critics also saw jazz fusion as a sort of *Trojan Horse*, because of the constant tension and specific way the music manifested itself, with Davis taking the lead and playing great, jazz, fusion music. Meanwhile, other black jazz musicians were wrestling with obscurity. In a profound way, fusion was/is ponderous, even unnerving, but (it is a) necessary music, not some *omnipresent* background sound. And it allowed Davis to play his horn, unencumbered by jazz convention and tradition. Indeed, his fusion music really meant something special to him, particularly because he knew what the impact would be. Davis learned how to really trust his own instincts and his sense of what he thought he should play. Therefore, experimenting with new, musical ideas and techniques was the logical progression for Davis in the music business. And changing the music was in his blood—that is, in terms of jazz, or "social music," and moving forward. Amiri Baraka pointed out that "fusion [could] be seen as a logical motion of Miles' American pop-connected aesthetic, as his solo voice, whether atop, within, or beneath any rhythm, clearly [showed]."[5] Additionally, Davis thought that *fusion* was a necessary and relevant direction in jazz music as it gave him a semblance of controlled freedom. And his "free-form" trumpet playing was also a gift. Was it from God? Or was it like some musical, low-hanging fruit, to use the metaphor, for Davis to stay on top of the jazz recording industry?

With jazz-rock fusion, moreover, Davis "initiated a new phase" in his long and productive or prolific musical career. Of course, by this time, Davis had become more than a jazz *Phenom*. And with the release of the fusion-inspired "Bitches Brew" album, in August 1969, the brash, unusual-sounding music became one of Davis's most important recordings. Indeed, "Bitches Brew" was not only influential, but it was/is a popular LP or CD recording, which is still being imitated by jazz musicians today. And not only jazz enthusiasts bought "Bitches Brew," but also hard-rock fans enjoyed the music of Miles Davis, too. Additionally, it (the "Bitches Brew" album) established Miles Davis as a *bona fide* pop music star,[6] mainly because new, committed, and enthusiastic admirers listened to what he had to play, or say symbolically with his trumpet. But there was a point when Davis thought that people were not listening to his music anymore. Therefore, Davis was poised to raise the music game of "social music," or jazz (again) by performing a new wave sound, or fusion jazz. Stereo review editor, Chris Albertson wrote:

> Miles fans saw him in a different light; they were attracted by his wild look, *outré* clothes and unorthodox demeanor, all of which complement[ed] his intricate musical blend of rock and jazz. These fans generally cared little for the acoustic Miles Davis sound of old, but they knew that he was a giant in the jazz world, a living legend who had moved with changing taste and, indeed, helped to shape it [jazz-rock fusion].[7]

To say the least, many *pooh-poohed* the new fusion music by Miles Davis; but today, it is part of the jazz musical lexicon. To wit, "Bitches Brew" became the building block for the new-wave, jazz-rock fusion movement. At this particular time, Davis's other record sales had been previously slumping in the late 1960s and early 1970s—that is, until the rock-influenced "Bitches Brew" had sold a million copies in its first year and Columbia's public relations office started calling Davis "the Prince of Darkness."[8] Of course, a million copies were quite a hefty number for a jazz album at that time. Indeed, Davis rode the whirlwind of jazz popularity, before the advent of CDs, the internet and (cursed) music downloading. But Miles Davis often moved in a specific direction, or toward musical and political storms of controversy, without batting an eye. According to journalist Atkins, Davis "made excellent copy because . . . he seemed to live in the fast lane . . . to attract controversy,"[9] which was no big deal; or nothing for the brusque trumpet man. Indeed, sometimes Davis's outspokenness (and musical changes) often got him into real trouble with the larger jazz world that rejected his "fresh, new approach" to *social music*, or jazz.

Davis also explained that using "electrical instruments," in his jazz-rock fusion would "break up [his acoustic] band a little later and send [him] into a new kind of music."[10] Musically speaking, Miles Davis believed in what he was doing. Indeed, the legendary Davis had considerable expertise, and years of unique musical experiences. And he was a survivor and fighter for effectively communicating his musical ideas and vision until the bitter end. And this included Davis's embrace of jazz-rock fusion, and even rap, before his death.

NOTES

1. Farah Griffin and Salim Washington, *Clawing at the Limits of Cool* (New York: St. Martin's Press, 2008), 238.
2. Griffin and Washington, *Clawing at the Limits*, 236.
3. Williams, *The Man in the Green Shirt*, 136.
4. Williams, *The Man in the Green Shirt*, 136.
5. Baraka, "Miles after Miles." To be sure, fusion is like an unpredictable situation, where some listeners don't know what's going to happen or what is played next.
6. "Miles Davis: 1964–69 Recordings," *Coda* (May 1976): 8–14. According to Griffin and Washington, "Miles gained new fans as his bands began to be featured at elite rock clubs like the Fillmore. Even though his music remained experimental, the musicians from the rock side of the fusion split related to what Miles was doing." See Griffin and Washington, *Clawing at the Limits of Cool*, 238.
7. Chris Albertson, liner notes to "Miles Smiles—Columbia Jazz, Contemporary Masters" (New York: Sony Music Entertainment, Inc., 1992), recording.
8. Ullman, "Miles Davis in Retrospect," 18. Without doubt, the number of albums sold of "Bitches Brew" was unprecedented for a jazz LP in jazz history. And "Bitches Brew" helped Davis's bottom line—that is, in terms of making money.
9. Atkins, "A Trumpet Fallen Silent," 33. Davis's "Bitches Brew" is a brew of strange sounds and weird musical ideas, played right in your face. Just listen to Davis's *Spanish Key* cut on the aforementioned album, which is like listening to controlled chaos—that is, in term of the *godly* music.
10. Miles Davis and Quincy Troupe, *Miles: The Autobiography* (New York: Simon & Schuster Paperbacks, 1989), 289. To get a feel of this new, electric, rock-fusion music, jazz fans should listen to Davis's 1968 *Miles in the Sky* album.

Chapter 14

Drugs and Retirement

Miles Davis knew that jazz, or "social music" didn't exist in a vacuum, because "in the development of 'modern jazz' during the period following World War II, he had become pre-eminent as one of its masters."[1] Davis would also come to personify the whole idea of jazz. Indeed, it was an opportune time for him, as he was trying to understand the larger jazz music world; and at this period in his life, Davis remained incredibly disciplined, serious, and thoughtful, as there were no shortcuts to his musical accomplishments. Davis was also more determined than many other young jazz musicians at that time, as he had become a catalytic figure. To be sure, Davis was running himself ragged trying to get things done, like recording his music, because he instinctively knew his place, or what he should be doing, and his responsibility regarding his "social music." It was, perhaps, Davis's quest for the jazz "holy grail" of music. Fortunately, his talents and musical vision had finally caught the imagination and attention of grateful jazz fans, especially in Europe, and particularly in Paris. To say the least, his Paris trip was a magical time for Miles Davis, as mentioned in the previous chapter. Equally important, Davis believed that his life up to that point was worth living. He had been particularly taken in by his fervid affair with Juliette Gréco. About his relationship with the French singer during the late 1940s, biographer George R. Crisp writes:

> This perfect, petite vision of beauty, this promise of happiness, would come around to the rehearsals [if he had them] to listen and to focus her attention on Miles [Davis]. Of course, Miles noted this and kept asking anyone around if they knew who she was. Someone said she was an existentialist, to which Miles replied, "I don't care what she is. That girl is beautiful and I want to meet her." Finally, after no one had done the proper thing and made the introductions,

Miles beckoned Juliette [Gréco] over and she told him that while she did not like men she liked him. After that they were inseparable.[2]

But when Miles Davis left Paris and the love of his life, Gréco—things started going steadily downhill for him in the United States; but Davis never wanted *anyone* to feel sorry for him. Then again, perhaps no one understood Davis's psychological scars, pain, and insecurities, as he was filled with *angst* and anxiety at that time. This is to say that life for Miles Davis wasn't exactly easier just because he was living (again) in New York and playing his trumpet at gigs with some of the jazz greats. Essentially, he was still trying to figure things out for himself about life. Some argued that Davis had never really experienced the harsh realities of life, given his family's prosperous background. However, he would eventually learn the necessary attributes for living, accepting things with a *stoicism* all his own. And for a while, Davis was almost willing to do *anything* to get ahead, within limits. In this way, Miles Davis was able to make some decisions about his unfolding life; about how much he wanted to play his famous trumpet, and the music he loved. Furthermore, his position in the jazz scene was strengthened by his political *savvy* and consequential (musical) maneuverings. Davis, at the beginning of his music career, was *only* concerned about the music, and the great black musicians that came before him. He was quoted as saying that he played for himself and other like-minded musicians.[3] What is more, Davis legitimized his standing in the jazz community, because he was always searching for some kind of status. This is to say that he wanted to be noticed, in a hurry, or as quickly as possible in the jazz world. But Davis, even as a youngster, never liked to use the term jazz "to describe his music," because he thought it was "a nigger word."[4] This is to say that Davis believed that the term itself was "used to set aside and diminish the importance of a contribution to the world's music primarily identified with Blacks."[5] Also, Davis firmly believed that credit should be given where it was due—that is, to black musicians.

Perhaps Davis was in a different mindset in those early days—that is, before his drug-haze days, or "drug-fueled period."[6] When Miles Davis was growing up in East St. Louis, he was, no doubt, exposed to drugs; however, he didn't want to mess things up for himself and his burgeoning musical career. Additionally, it would have been a stupid thing to do. Of course, Miles Davis had his own trials and tribulations, but absolutely not indulging in drugs, when he first went to New York, put him in good standing with the elder black jazz musicians who first put the young Davis under their wings. But many of the musicians he eventually played with became drug addicts themselves. And to his detriment, Davis would, unfortunately, connect with jazz musicians that turned him on to drugs; and urged him to do the wrong thing, like partaking in heroin, when he lost his way, after finding his musical niche. Suddenly, Davis became a part of the dark world of jazz. In so many words, Davis jumped regrettably on the *bandwagon* of drugs and fast-track of self-destructiveness. Goodman puts it this way: "Sometime during the late 1940's Mr. Davis succumbed to heroin addiction, which initiated a gradual period of physical decline."[7] While he was on heroin, Davis faced an uncertain musical future, because, in a way, he turned into a neurotic maniac, or a drug fiend. For all that has been written about Miles Davis's drug use, historians, biographers, musicians, and fans alike should know that *apocryphal* stories about his life are not true. For example, many claim that Charlie "Bird" Parker was responsible for Davis's heroin addiction. But nothing can be further from the truth. According to Davis, in his autobiography *Miles*, he stated that "when I first started shooting heroin, I shot up by myself. Then I started hanging out."[8] Therefore, Davis never had a drug-dependent relationship with his mentor, Charlie "Bird" Parker. To be sure, Miles was responsible for his own heroin addiction.

Davis was also considered a rapscallion who had been accused of being a small-time crook and thief. Additionally, some of Davis's friends were nonplused and even annoyed by his change for the worse. To say the least, Davis was facing a situation where he could have lost his life from his heroin addiction. Furthermore, he did almost *anything* to get his next fix, even if it meant pimping women, because he had become a serious drug user and a dirty trickster. Davis even "confessed to pimping during his heroin daze."[9] As a pimp, Davis did what he wanted to do, to get what he wanted: heroin. He also intentionally misled others, particularly women, as he put his personal needs before everything and everyone else. But Davis's destructive behavior couldn't be ignored by some of his associates; nor forgiven. At the very least, Davis's life as a womanizer and abuser of some of his girlfriends, wives, and lovers cannot be overlooked or dismissed; and should serve as a warning to *anyone* today who is indifferent about his (Davis's) dark side and terrible behavior. In other words, we cannot say that Miles Davis was one of the "good guys" when it came to his mistreatment of women. Therefore, understanding his combustible relationships with women shouldn't be *sugarcoated*, to appease those who would inject today's moral and sexual harassment standards into Davis's sordid past. So was Davis a larger-than-life villain—that is, toward some women? Perhaps.

Before his hard drug use period, Davis was a dashing, strikingly good-looking, dark-skinned, young black man; but he became almost unrecognizable, because of his heroin addiction. Perhaps Davis couldn't articulate exactly how he really felt—that is, being an unknown jazz musician, and later rising to international fame—to becoming a drug addict. According to Bill Cole, "Drugs had now taken their toll and pushed him near the point of no return."[10] Maybe Davis started taking drugs because he was bored with life and the old way of playing the music, or the jazz standards. Jackie McLean, an American jazz alto saxophonist, bandleader, and composer, stated before he died, in 2006 that "Miles [Davis] played a very technical, traditional music before 1969, following Ellington and all the great masters,"[11] but he wanted to create or move forward with something different, or a new musical vocabulary, and direction. As mentioned, Davis was also concerned that black musicians were not getting the credit for creating a whole new, jazz musical art form. After all, the United States is where jazz started, "and [today] people love jazz all over the world."[12] Jazz saxophonist and composer Sonny Rollins tells us that jazz is "a peaceful expression of the spirit, of love, of everything."[13] And we should never forget those who were responsible for bringing the music (jazz) to the attention of the world. Davis probably understood this more than most; therefore, he was perhaps bitter about any slight. In the long run, Davis believed that black jazz musicians were not given the proper respect. Nevertheless, jazz writer Salamishah Tillet explains:

> Reflecting the politics of a post-civil-rights-era America, the recognition that African-Americans played a foundational role in creating and innovating in jazz [is] a sign of progress after their often marginal to nonexistent presence in the white jazz biopic.[14]

Therefore, Don Cheadle's *Miles Ahead* jazz biopic (in 2016) is something that Davis might have enjoyed watching had he lived [see Figure 14.1]. Unfortunately, during his narcotics-phased days, Davis was hampered by drugs, mainly because he felt lousy after his eventful trip to Paris, where he was considered "King of the World,"[15] and leaving the beautiful French woman, Mademoiselle Juliette Gréco. Paris had been heaven for Davis, unlike (his poor treatment) in the United States, as mentioned earlier in this book. In Paris, Davis was able to talk endlessly with other freedom-loving people, even with the great painter Pablo Picasso,[16] while soaking up new ideas about art, religion, music, and politics. Davis truly loved this time period in his life. So were all these things the major reasons for Miles Davis's brief downfall? Perhaps. At that point, it probably didn't really matter to Davis, because of his drug-haze period. It was certainly a distressing time for him, particularly being addicted to the *insidious* heroin. But it wasn't supposed to be this way, as his music career had been on a meteoric rise. Appropriately enough, Davis knew and understood that he had hit rock-bottom, after being a burgeoning or new jazz icon. Hence, beating his drug addiction was something he had to do, or die. In essence, Davis had to swallow his pride and stop taking drugs, because he didn't want his life and music career to end in tragedy—or in the proverbial gutter.

Therefore, after locking himself up at his father's farm in Millstadt, East St. Louis, and quitting "cold-turkey," to use the metaphor, Davis was able to fight some of his demons; and finally, "in 1954," he was able to overcome, and "[kick] his heroin addiction and [relaunch] his flagging career."[17] Which is to say that Davis would find his music legs again, pouring himself into his musical work, with a passion and vengeance. Perhaps it was inevitable; and as he got "a grip on his personal life, his music took off again."[18] This is to say that Davis's *gee-whiz* enthusiasm and curiosity about musical things came into play again. Also, during this time, Davis "began his first string of important small-group recordings."[19] In many ways, these were unprecedented times for him. To be honest, Davis knew well enough that there were a lot of musical possibilities for him to rightly tackle. Davis, of course, liked exploring the unfamiliar, and his drive led him (once again) in a new musical direction, with an amazing new band. According to jazz writer Jon Pareles, Davis "made a triumphant appearance at the Newport Jazz Festival and assembled his first important quintet, with John Coltrane on tenor saxophone, Red Garland on piano, Paul Chambers on bass, and Philly Joe Jones on drums."[20] With this new band, Davis had a new sense of dedication, purpose, and determination. Fans were able to attest to the fact that Davis's music sounded so *right* and *good*. It was as if Davis played his trumpet with a calibrated stealth and beauty. Journalist J. Lee writes:

> Largely dormant during the early 1950's under the pressing weight of personal woes, Miles came to the Newport Jazz Festival in July 1955 as one more marcher in a long parade of trumpet players. His terse performance, a happy ending worthy of the wide screen, roused the surfeited thousands gathered in Freebody Park. He strolled off stage as a hero.[21]

The music played at the Newport Jazz Festival, like "Round about Midnight," has become a perennial jazz favorite. On a personal level, Davis's music still lacked the flashy chords and high notes, but it made his trumpet sound more poignant and meaningful. Moreover, Davis became "a more assertive trumpeter, whose bell-like clarity in the high register gave him new authority."[22] In the meantime, Davis's jazz devotees, ultimately, had to come to grips with Davis's ever-changing musical style. It should be noted here that Davis had "that rare gift of being able to give birth and life to new [musical] things which, no matter how startling, always [seemed] natural and logical, and [opened] up new roads for others to travel after he [had] moved on."[23] Accordingly, after his heroin addiction, Davis credited his comeback to "the discipline he observed in the boxer Sugar Ray Robinson,"[24] who became his boxing hero. Jack Johnson, the first black heavyweight champion, was also one of Davis's boxing favorites. Eventually, Miles Davis "took up a boxing program to stay fit";[25] and because it made him feel good, stronger. Throughout it all during this time, Davis did almost everything right because he had faith in himself. Furthermore, he kept doing interesting things in terms of the music until the 1970s. This is to say that his experimental, contemporary work intensified as he grew older, and perhaps wiser. Touring and performing, however, took a toll on his body. And for a long time, Miles Davis was willing to carry the jazz baton to the faithful; but the business of being a modern jazz musician, and "the rigors of world travel [was] necessary to take [black] America's native music to appreciative audiences."[26] However, it took stamina, which was now in short supply for the great jazz trumpeter.

Thus, Miles Davis would eventually lose the fire in his belly for performing his music all the time. Or he just didn't have the energy anymore. Toward this end, Davis had significant health problems, making him sick most of the time. And there was, for the most part, "no music in his head."[27] Davis specifically made the decision to stop playing his trumpet and the music that he loved, because of his many illnesses. Davis suffered from "arthritis, bursitis, stomach ulcers, throat polyps, pneumonia, infections, repeated operations on a disintegrated hip,"[28] and depression. Davis also admitted that he fell off the bandwagon of drugs again, while indulging excessively in cocaine, heroin, barbiturates, marijuana, and alcohol. Perhaps he was trying to medicate himself to death, or drink his pain away with booze, and other intoxicants. An online biography explains Davis's so-called retirement this way: "Troubled by chronic pain from years of physical abuse, a serious kidney complaint, diabetes, a renewed dependence on heroin and cocaine and again at odds with the law, Davis withdrew almost completely from the public eye."[29] He also took up with many loose women for sex and other favors. According to Chris Murphy, Davis "liked his sex kinky";[30] therefore, he was "very active sexually, and his impulsiveness would have probably precluded him from practicing safe sex."[31] Which is to say that Davis did not take *any* vows to a life of piety, as the "jazz religion" does not call for such devotion, or celibacy. Partly for these reasons, Davis left the jazz scene, but not for good. Jazz journalist Scott Yanow writes:

> In 1975 Miles Davis did the unexpected and retired from music, not returning for six years. At 49, he was experiencing bad health and becoming very involved with recreational drugs, including cocaine. His next few years were a complete blur of personal excess while the jazz world speculated about whether he would ever return, and what would happen if he did play trumpet again.[32]

Jazz fans optimistically assumed that Miles Davis would come back to the jazz music world sooner than later. So, perhaps, understandably, people thought that Davis's absence was an *aberration*. But it became clear that he wasn't coming back anytime soon. On his five (or six) years *hiatus*, Davis let the jazz music world pass by, as he sadly watched (the future of) each day

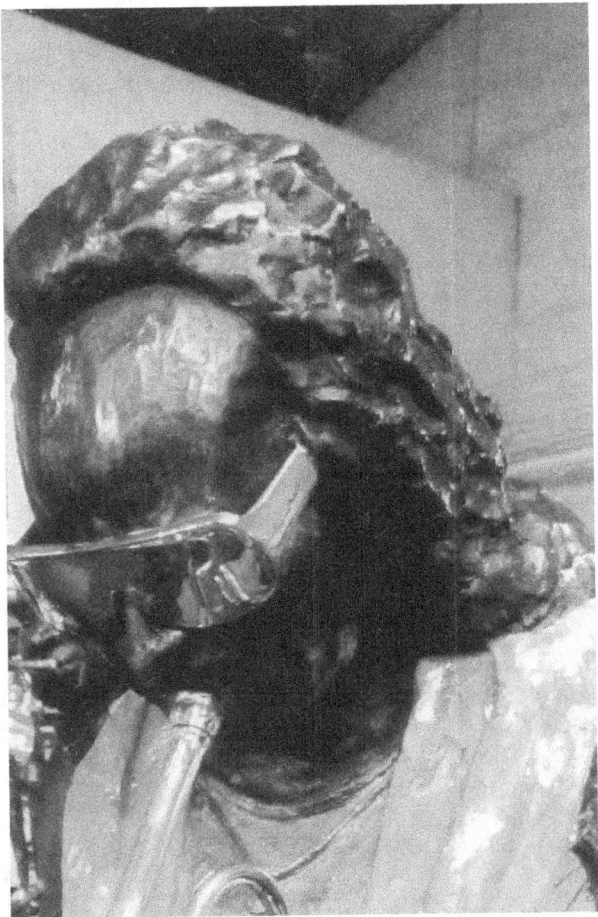

Figure 14.1 **Miles Davis sculpture at Ed Dwight's Studio in Colorado.** *Source*: Author's personal photograph.

unfold; but not in a good way. For jazz fans, it was a frustrating twist to the life of Miles Dewey Davis, as he had been in the jazz music world for a long time. And many jazz devotees sincerely missed him.

NOTES

1. Benjamin Quarles, *The Negro in the Making of America*, revised ed. (New York: Collier books, 1969), 245. Miles Davis, of course, knew in his heart that he had to make his own musical destiny—that is, if he was to be successful as a jazz artist; otherwise, he probably wouldn't have seen the light of day in jazz.

2. George R. Crisp, *An Impact Biography*, 62. Miles Davis turned heads and thrived in Paris, France. And it didn't get any better—that is, until he left Paris, to go back to the United States and New York, and all the racial problems faced by black men.

3. Goodman, "I Just Pick Up My Horn," 1.

4. Goodman, "I Just Pick Up My Horn," 12.

5. Goodman, "I Just Pick Up My Horn," 12.

6. Christina Ianzito, "Interview: Cheadle Channels Miles Davis," *AARP: The Magazine*, April/May 2016, 11.

7. Goodman, "I Just Pick Up My Horn," 12.

8. Miles Davis and Quincy Troupe, *Miles: The Autobiography* (New York: Simon & Schuster Paperbacks, 1989), 132.

9. Kelley, "The Chameleon of Cool," 1.

10. Cole, *A Musical Biography*, 56.

11. Mandel, "Sketches of Miles," 16.

12. Cindy Clark, "The Night Belongs to Kennedy Center Honorees," *USA Today*, sec. 4D, December 5, 2011.

13. Clark, "Kennedy Center Honorees," 4D.

14. Salamishah Tillet, "Hitting the Beat on the Offbeat," *The New York Times*, April 24, 2016, 12.

15. Daryl N. Long, *Miles Davis for Beginners* (New York: Writers and Readers Publishing, Inc., 1992), 57.

16. Long, *Miles Davis for Beginner*, 57.

17. *The Definitive Illustrated Encyclopedia*, s.v. "Miles Davis, the Fifties."

18. Ronald Atkins, "A Trumpet Fallen Silent," *The Guardian*, September 30, 1991, 33.

19. Pareles, "Trumpeter, Dies," 3.

20. Pareles, "Trumpeter, Dies," 3.

21. J. Lee Anderson, "The Musings of Miles," *Saturday Review*, October 11, 1958, 59.

22. Atkins, "A Trumpet Fallen Silent," 33.

23. Dan Morgenstern, "Miles in Motion," *Down Beat*, September 3, 1970, 17.

24. Michael J. Agovino, "His [Davis] Ensembles Epitomized Cool," *The New York Times*, March 13, 2016, 12.

25. Agovino, "His Ensembles," 12.

26. Phil Woods, foreword, in Larry Fisher, *Miles Davis and David Liebman Jazz Connections* (Lewiston, NY: The Edwin Mellen Press, 1996), vi.

27. David Breskin, "Searching for Miles: Theme and Variations on the Life of a Trumpeter," *Rolling Stone*, September 29, 1983, 49.

28. Breskin, "Searching for Miles," 49.

29. "Miles Davis Biography," 8notes.com (2000-2011), 4, http://www.8notes.com/biographies.

30. Murphy, *Miles to Go*, 214.

31. Murphy, *Miles to Go*, 214.

32. Scott Yanow, *Trumpet King: The Players Who Shaped the Sound of Jazz Trumpet* (San Francisco, CA: Backbeat books, 2001), 122.

Chapter 15

The Catalytic Return

Jazz musicians and fans alike didn't know what was going on when Miles Davis left the jazz scene—or what he was actually doing. But they were concerned. And his inaction or lack of performing musically, in public, was disturbing to some jazz fans, as some had become hyper impatient. After all, Davis had been "canonized by the press and respected by his peers,"[1] who loved his trumpet playing. To be sure, "By the time he retired," according to journalist Michael Ullman, "Davis's [trumpet] solos seemed a series of disjointed gestures, dramatic and striking in themselves, but not the patient constructions of earlier years. Nevertheless, during this period he was much praised for his impact on younger musicians."[2] Of course, Miles Davis was already a well-traveled, international jazz star, who tried to surround himself with like-minded people and musicians who lifted him up, or made him feel good, not down, particularly as he was thinking about his place in the music world. And presumably, Davis wasn't thinking about his health either—at least initially. Thus, for a while, Davis was keeping his musical powder dry. Jazz critic Bob Blumenthal writes:

> When he [Davis] quit performing in 1976, rumors immediately began flying about his physical health and state of mind. Apparently he did undergo surgery (although the number and nature of the operations remain unclear), but the most alarming stories suggested that he had become an embittered recluse who no longer cared about music and rarely left his Manhattan brownstone.[3]

Indeed, Davis was living the life of a sort of Trappist Monk, because he was so isolated. Some even believed that Davis was losing his grip on reality, because of his pains, drug use, and various other illnesses. Perhaps at this time, Davis lost his faith in jazz (or social music), as he cut himself off from almost everyone, provoking a storm of criticisms and concern. Still, Davis was influential in persuading many to take up the call and cause of jazz, or his "social music." Many fans just wanted to know when he would return to the pulpit of the "jazz church," so to speak. Jazz lovers wanted so badly for Davis to come back and do his thing, to preserve his legacy. Many felt very strongly about that. But Davis didn't like "social pressure," of any kind, especially from his fans, family, and friends; or *anyone* who had long urged him to return to the jazz music scene. To say the least, Davis was suspicious of *anyone* who tried to push him to do something that he didn't want to do, as he had a "deep distrust of others."[4] Davis also thought that it was extremely rude for people to just show up at his Upper West Side townhouse, or his doorstep, because it had become his retreat and monastery all rolled into one. Therefore, it was the wrong thing to do—that is, to make your presence known before him, particularly if he didn't know you. Davis remained a very private person over the years, and fans had to come to terms with that; but he really didn't want you in his face, "because he was so *shy*."[5] In a January 2021 interview, in *The New York Times Magazine*, Cicely Tyson, an ex-wife of Davis, tells us that "in trying to be kind of [a] tough person that people thought he was, he ruined his life. [But he was] gentle as a lamb. . . . *That's* the Miles Davis I knew."[6] However, Davis could also be bombastic, and more than politically incorrect. And he would address strange visitors with profane language. Or with a few harsh, and *sometimes* choice (curse) words, Davis would put fans and curious people in their place; or he would send them rudely away.

According to journalist Tom Isler, Davis "was shy and vulnerable, arrogant and abusive, more fashionable than he was technically proficient on his horn, exceedingly difficult to work with, and so cool and so secretive that he effectively engineered his own ascension to [a] cultural deity."[7] The truth is: nothing Davis did seemed to hurt his reputation—in the long run—including his heroin addiction, pimping, and womanizing. If anything, it bolstered Davis's reputation even more. In some ways, Davis was often frustrated and angry with whatever or whomever irked him. For example, he thought that his absence from jazz was his own business, and no one else's. Or perhaps Davis just didn't want to get into music again at that time. Additionally, it was hard for Davis to think about playing his horn again, too. However, Davis stated that "you never retire from an instrument if you've been playing it since you were 12 [years old] because it's always in your head."[8] The thing is, Davis got bored with the same old things. Davis was also, as mentioned in the previous chapter, bored with himself, and "bored with the business end of it"—that is, jazz music, which he thought had "always been terrible."[9] But he understood the reality and nature of the music business. Davis once stated, "You know, if you don't watch your money and have somebody who knows about how to invest it, somebody will steal you blind."[10] In this regard, Davis was still definitely a black man, a *badass* with an occasional mean streak. On balance, Miles Davis didn't like the conspicuous politics in jazz music. And "the funny thing is that as disorienting as [this] period was for his old fans, Miles [Davis] stepped into the era of Black power politics and hippie rebellion like he'd had a hand in creating it all along."[11] But Davis was out of the music *spotlight*, or he was no longer on the inside looking out. Still, there were engaged listeners of his music—from Europe to Japan, where Japanese fans equated Davis to the great Japanese actor Toshiro Mifune. So Davis became the Toshiro Mifune of jazz. (Note: this is my own perception/interpretation.)

Another way to put it: The careful listener could, perhaps, understand the philosophical aspect of Davis's jazz music. However, "no one could ever really figure out what was going on inside Davis's head, even as his new way of conceptualizing jazz—holistically, as a process, as a feeling [while making] music history."[12] Admittedly, jazz is an expression and representation of black music, as it is grounded in the realities of pain, and cultural introspection; but jazz is also about *love* and *spirit*. It also tells us of the black experience, while teaching us how to really listen. And by its very nature, jazz is retrospective, and a durable musical force. Therefore, jazz is not an aging musical idiom that will one day be snuffed out. Davis knew this, but he didn't like the term jazz, as discussed in an earlier chapter, because he thought it was "a Black word that [meant] Negro in the white man's eyes."[13] Davis also understood that there would always be a desire for jazz music, because it is a meditative thing, an aesthetic boldness in terms of "social music." Hence, jazz, which is a black music cannot be erased outright by the dominant culture. So Davis's "departure [from the jazz scene] generated as much electricity as his presence."[14] In the final analysis, Davis's music sent ripples of musical influence through our culture and the world, even when he was in musical exile. This is to say that the effervescence of Davis's music is not beyond the human capacity to grasp and learn about black music, as it is another form of communication. Thus, Davis's music aptly conveys and communicates, as well as provides an unavoidable message. Beyond that, Davis's self-imposed retirement from the jazz music world was totally unexpected. Coincidentally, taking off from touring, or performing and recording gave Miles Davis a chance to perhaps reflect on his life, while putting things into perspective. It also allowed him to focus on his poor health. Indeed, Davis tried to make the most of things during his time in musical purgatory. According to David Breskin, "He almost never [left] the apartment." Davis also bragged "about being the best at whatever he chooses," but later, he proved to be "best at doing nothing."[15] Nevertheless, he still lived an extravagant lifestyle, having everything he wanted delivered to him. Davis, in a 1982 interview, stated that "Everything would come to my house. You know, anything you want you can get. All you have to do is ask for it. I [don't] go to the store. I [don't] go anywhere. . . . Try it sometime."[16] As if to underscore what was happening, and what he believed about home delivery, Davis even had "a local pharmacy [send] him drugs without a doctor's prescription."[17] In this respect, Davis was a rebel in every sense of his being. Specifically, Davis didn't care about jeopardizing his reputation, as he seemed more relaxed and comfortable in his own skin, and being on his own. And although he became a notorious recluse, there were times when Davis, perhaps, realized how much pressure he was under to return to performing, and his musical roots.

Unfortunately, Davis simply ignored even some of his jazz elders, like Clark Terry and Dizzy Gillespie,[18] who tried to convince him to play again. Davis was also "spiteful of the [American] press; and when he did grant interviews, he spoke critically and paradoxically of his music, personal life, and friends."[19] Davis even threatened to break Dizzy Gillespie's neck, if the older jazz man didn't leave his house. Dizzy told him, "Man, you're supposed to play *music*,"[20] when he got around to finally visiting Miles Davis at his sanctuary, his brownstone in Manhattan. At first, Davis made it abundantly clear that he wasn't interested in coming back to music. Not yet. But he was still interested in the music; and his commitment to his craft never really waned. So although he was ill and bored, his mind never really stopped working. Davis admitted that when he first retired, he "wasn't hearing any melodies or anything," because he "wouldn't let [himself] hear anything, and all of a sudden these melodies started coming back to [him]."[21] It wasn't like Davis couldn't make up his mind about returning to the jazz music scene; but initially, he made no promises or commitments, because he just wasn't ready. Still, Davis was listening to a lot of different music. He especially liked listening to the German composer Karlheinz Stockhausen, who Davis first heard in the 1960s, and "never stopped talking about him."[22] Journalist Greg Sandow writes:

> Once, on tour in Germany, he [Davis] told his audience to give up on Beethoven: "You've Stockhausen now." Stockhausen, along with James Brown, was a major influence on a dizzying, Miles Davis album, "On the Corner," released in 1972. (Funk and the classical avant-garde, together at last!) Davis and Stockhausen met; they even recorded together, though the results have never been released.[23]

Beethoven, of course, is well known in the United States, unlike *Karlheinz Stockhausen*; but who knows what the future might hold for the German composer (Stockhausen). Perhaps if his recording with Davis is released, Stockhausen might be exposed to a larger music audience. Regardless, Stockhausen gave Miles Davis much to consider, as he did more than a bit of self-reflection about the German composer. And like Davis, Stockhausen, "wanted music to proceed in measureless moments, each without any past, or any future."[24] Interestingly, Davis had a similar distinction and attitude when it came to music, which was possessed by few jazz musicians. And in Davis's own inimitable style, and *nihilistic* vision, his music complimented Stockhausen. For example, Davis seemed "to have had his own notions about performer realization reinforced by Stockhausen's theory of process composition," which creates "space and time for those who play intuitively at the moment of performance."[25] When it is all said and done, music scholar Barry Bergstein succinctly tells us:

> Stockhausen and Davis inspired each other. Stockhausen's use of electric trumpet and *wah-wah* pedal stems from Miles Davis; Davis's incorporation of process and intuition resulted from his knowing Stockhausen's work. They developed similar group conceptions which included new conducting techniques, [which] were affected by cross-cultural and exotic influences, and used improvisation as an integral compositional device.[26]

Even with Stockhausen on his mind, Davis apparently wasn't excited enough, at first, to return to the jazz scene. Nevertheless, there was a lot of speculation in the media and jazz world that Davis would absolutely return. Music promoters were even emphasizing the importance of "setting the stage" for Davis's comeback. Indeed, "when it was announced that Miles Davis was planning a comeback, there was much anticipation in the jazz world."[27] But his return to the jazz scene was more of a rumor than anything else, in the beginning. But some even thought that it was just frivolous talk. Before his retirement, Davis was trying to get things done musically, but it had been a half-hearted attempt, because he didn't want to be fancifully blowing (his horn) in the wind. Therefore, "for more than four years," Davis hardly ever touched his trumpet, "although he would sometimes work on musical ideas at his piano."[28] Inevitably, Miles Davis couldn't escape the music. How could he resist? Davis would eventually emerge from his retirement and health scares ready to play his trumpet again. Mentally, Davis was still there, despite what he would say to the contrary in interviews. Obviously, just playing his trumpet again was a good thing, considering his long absence. And despite periodic announcements of his (Davis's) return, it wasn't that far away. Furthermore, upon returning, Miles Davis became enthusiastic again about his music. In fact, Davis would become steadfast in the pursuit of his "social music," which was a good thing. With timeless elegance, Davis positioned himself again atop the jazz or "social music" world, which he treasured. Moreover, he became diligent and dedicated once more, as he was able to flex his musical muscles. In a sense, Miles Davis was channeling his energy and preparing himself physically, while getting things done in terms of his musical comeback. Of course, Davis was incredibly smart, as "he was never known to make a foolish move."[29] Finally, Davis never wanted to miss out on something that he actually wanted to do. Davis was certainly passionate about what he was doing—that is, before returning to the jazz music scene. And by some stroke of miracle, Davis was back. But was it too soon?

NOTES

1. Cheryl McCall, "Miles Davis," *Musician, Player, and Listener*, vol. 41 (March 1982): 38.
2. Michel Ullman, "Miles Davis in Retrospect," *New Boston Review*, May/June 1981, 20.
3. Bob Blumenthal, "Miles Glorious: The Man with the Brew," *The Boston Phoenix*, July 7, 1981, 1.
4. Kelley, "The Chameleon of Cool," 1. Davis really didn't care about how he came across to others; nor did he care about saying something that he would regret later. Also, Davis never pretended to be something that he was not.
5. David Marchase, interview, "Cicely Tyson on Racial Dynamics in Hollywood," *The New York Times Magazine*, January 17, 2021, 13.
6. Marchase, "Cicely Tyson," 13.
7. Tom Isler, "So What: The Life of Miles Davis Book, by John Szwed," *Yale Review of Books*, March 11, 2020, 2, http://yalereviewofbooks.com/so-what-the-life-of-miles. Davis once admitted: "I was a pimp, I had a lot of girls, I was doin' that . . . I had more money then than I have now. Yeah, I had about seven girls, made a lot of money. Can't call the names, though." See McCall, "Miles Davis," 46.
8. McCall, "Miles Davis," 41.
9. Alkyer, "The Miles Files," 22.
10. Alkyer, "The Miles Files," 22.
11. Greg Tate, "Silence, Exile, and Cunning: Miles Davis in Memoriam," in *Flyboy in the Buttermilk: Essays on Contemporary America* (New York: Fireside books, 1992), 88.
12. Isler, "So What," 2.
13. Pawel Brodowski and Janusz Szprot, "Miles Speaks: I Don't Wana Be Like I Used to Be," *Jazz Forum*, issue 6 (1983): 38.
14. Kelley, "The Chameleon of Cool," 2. Jazz will always remain a mercurial, musical experiment; and there will always be a prevalent assumption that jazz holds the truth unlike any other musical genre.
15. Breskin, "Searching for Miles," 50.
16. McCall, "Miles Davis," 41.
17. Breskin, "Searching for Miles," 50.
18. Breskin, "Searching for Miles," 50.
19. Isler, "So What," 2.
20. Breskin, "Searching for Miles," 50.
21. McCall, "Miles Davis," 41.

22. Greg Sandow, "From Miles Davis to Bjork, They've Loved Stockhausen," *The Wall Street Journal*, sec. D9, December 19, 2007.
23. Sandow, "From Miles Davis to Bjork," D9.
24. Sandow, "From Miles Davis to Bjork," D9.
25. Barry Bergstein, "Miles Davis and Karlheinz Stockhausen: A Reciprocal Relationship," *The Musical Quarterly*, vol. 76 (Winter 1992): 511.
26. Bergstein, "A Reciprocal Relationship," 524.
27. Ron Frankl, *Miles Davis* (New York: Chelsea House Publishers, 1996), 109.
28. Frankl, *Miles Davis*, 106.
29. McCall, "Miles Davis," 41.

Chapter 16

Transformations

It should be noted (once again) that Miles Davis was also criticized early on, in his musical career, for not being a flawless trumpet player. But Davis didn't let his inconsistent trumpet playing stop him from performing and recording, as he was insanely talented and a creative voice. Indeed, jazz critics would often try to chide Davis for his sometimes bad playing and missed notes, as mentioned. But, "the process of learning to play jazz is largely learning how to maneuver a 'mistake' into an unmistakable context, and the split notes [become] more exciting than embarrassing."[1] As we discussed earlier in this book, Davis was a master at making split or missed notes (on his trumpet) work. And even if he "was cracking a lot of notes," what did it matter? Davis once stated: "I always try for more notes than I'm sure I can hit, so I miss some."[2] For his part, Davis probably thought that his various performances and peculiar way of playing his trumpet sprung from the fact that he really didn't have the chops, or lips for higher notes. Jazz writer Howard Mandel writes:

> The trumpeter [Davis] resisted temptations to play high and fast—perhaps because, as Gillespie once remarked to him, he didn't hear that way, or perhaps because Davis figured to set himself off from these musical terrors by playing it cool. Some of his early "mistakes" on [Charlie] Parker sides [or recordings] can be heard as tense attempts to reconcile his simpler desires with bop's will to unbridle virtuosity. Thus began a history of [Davis's] creative reaction, rather than personally embellished imitation, in pursuit of a unique voice.[3]

Furthermore, Davis had a surprising range, even though he played higher notes sparingly. But when he wanted to, Davis could play in the same musical stratosphere as Dizzy Gillespie and others with high-register trumpet playing.

Jazz fans only have to listen to Davis's *Sketches of Spain* album, to test the validity of this assertion. All in all, Davis could play extremely well when his *embouchure* was strengthened. And for some, when Davis played, without making any mistakes, he did "it with such intensity that every note [was] a gem."[4] Apart from this, Davis's real difficulty was the problem (sometimes) with his weak chops, or his *embouchure*, or his lips, where he had a "roll," which is "the imprint of the mouthpiece that [trumpet] players get."[5] In essence, Davis often strained his lips, where calluses would later form. However, Davis's chops (would) improve considerably as he played and practiced—that is, when his *embouchure* was stronger. Of course, Davis's missed notes were sometimes grating on the nerves for some during a live performance, but this was never the case on most of his great recordings. Davis had a warm touch on his horn, but it wasn't always perfect. Also, sometimes critics tended to underestimate Davis's trumpet playing until he would blow them away, so to speak. This is to say that he sometimes confounded the musical expectations of his critics. So if he played a wrong note, Davis would instinctively manage or correct the direction and progression of his sound and music during a live performance, as he was supremely intelligent when it came to music. Also, when Davis became conscientiously faithful to the "jazz church" again, his music seemed "to arouse instant passion."[6] Additionally, jazz critic Dan Morgenstern writes:

> Once he [had] perfected a thing, he [needed] to move on to something new. His music today is in constant motion, ideas bouncing off each other, interaction; many things going on at once; cyclical, unresolved, suspended and full of suspense, electrified and electrifying.[7]

Davis (with his jazz-rock) tried to embody the same bluesy-electronic-psychedelic, fiery music that Jimi Hendrix played before his early death. After all, as mentioned in an earlier chapter, Miles said that "two of his big influences at this time were Jimi Hendrix and James Brown."[8] Equally important, "Miles Davis, like Jimi Hendrix, [oozed] cool whenever he [was] thought of or seen," as he had become "a metaphor for all things hip."[9] Davis would become famous all over again, with his jazz Rock music; but while his "choice of instrumentation was moving toward Hendrix's, he was moving . . . further away from the kind of song-form the [late] guitarist embraced."[10] Nevertheless, Davis was quoted as saying: "I've always liked the sound of the guitar. And of the *sitar*. I [also] like all the strings, except the violin."[11] Davis set out to create a funky, upbeat music that was welcomed and acceptable to jazz-rock fans. It made sense to him. Just listen to Davis's "Miles Run the Voodoo Down" or "Spanish Key" on his *Bitches Brew* album. But jazz critic Stanley Crouch writes: "Before he was intimidated into mining the fool's gold of rock'n'roll, Davis's achievement was large and complex, as a trumpet player and an improviser."[12] Davis, however, wasn't intimidated by *anyone*; and he certainly wasn't alone in his belief that jazz had to constantly change. Moreover, Davis was always striving to connect with new fans and various other people to his electric music.

More importantly, Davis wanted to define himself to a whole different audience. He was certainly trying for something epic when it came to jazz-rock fusion. According to Richard Williams, his *Bitches Brew* and *Live-Evil* albums took Davis "out of the dusty confines of the jazz market and into the rock racks, next to Carlos Santana and the Grateful Dead."[13] Furthermore, Miles Davis knew that he was ushering in a new kind of jazz, or "social music," which would influence the contemporary jazz of today, and in the future, as he engendered a sense of spiritual celebration. But few things troubled Davis more than jazz musicians, who were white, and tried to take credit for creating contemporary jazz, or black music, like Kenny G, a white man, who makes millions playing a sad, repetitive soprano saxophone.[14] As a white musician, Kenny G links "jazz to race and created a myth that Black musicians were [not] the only innovators."[15] For example, in a 1988 *Down Beat* interview, Kenny G stated: "we've gotten terrible reviews from the purist critics who don't know anything about the style of contemporary jazz we play. I live that. I'm one of the creators of it."[16] But Kenny G is really a "copycat," who has "stripped Black [music] and culture of its spirit and got rich on knock-offs."[17] Such matters were always a sore spot with Miles Davis, mainly because he believed that some renowned black jazz musicians had to struggle for acceptance—that is, to a broader jazz world, and audience—like the late "Freddie Hubbard, the Grammy-winning jazz musician whose blazing virtuosity influenced a generation of trumpet players."[18] Hubbard was also influenced by Miles Davis. And to say the least, Davis never thought that Freddie Hubbard got the wider recognition he deserved, or his just due.

Consequently, after returning to the jazz scene, and kicking drugs again, which had been exceedingly difficult, Davis didn't deny the call to his "jazz church," and new music, or his religious, jazz rhetoric. Fans only have to listen to Miles Davis's 1989 *Amandla* album, to get a sense of his commitment and his "uncanny ability to create the perfect context for his improvisation."[19] Davis's music, of course, is exasperating, sometimes impossible, and enormous in every sense of the word when it comes to jazz. Back in 1963, jazz writer Kenneth Tynan had this to say about the trumpeter:

> Miles [Davis] can make his sound; "deathly . . . in its purity"; piercing and orphaned, and so devoid of vibrato that it recalls to one's inner ear the virginal clarity of a Sistine choirboy. With this sound he composes spare, discreet,

elliptical solos, avoiding fast tempi—which are inimical alike to his temperament and technique—as strictly as he avoids flamboyant emotionalism.[20]

Miles Davis also didn't prevent his jazz fans and other rock congregants from expressing their concerns about his trumpet playing—that is, even if he cracked or played some terrible notes on his trumpet. But such criticism sometimes carried a real sting, as Davis was often working on his chops, or his *embouchure*. Ron Carter once wrote that it cracked him up "to hear criticisms about Miles' range on the instrument." Also, to justify or explain Davis's playing, Ron Carter, who once played the bass in Davis's second famous Quintet, stated that "he [Davis] always played the trumpet cold because no warm-up space was ever available."[21] Furthermore, Miles Davis never really worried about jazz critics at that time in the 1980s, because he knew that through God's providence, he would leave a musical legacy. By the way, Davis especially practiced alone when he was working on new music; hence, he was able to control his *embouchure* and what he thought he should play. And before his untimely death, Davis made every effort to be musically relevant, or *evangelical*; and, once again, he presented himself as the *mainstay* in the faith of jazz, sometimes going out of his way to find young jazz converts and devotees, or "musicians whose backgrounds were in the kind of funky music that [he] wanted to be working with, rather than in a jazz tradition."[22] Davis would later recruit Marcus Miller, the talented keyboard, bass player, and composer of new jazz tunes; and alto saxophonist Kenney Garrett, who both played on most of Davis's last recordings, with the exception of his anonymous and final *Doo-Bop*, rap album. There were other young band members—black and white—who brought out the best in Davis when they played in large concert halls, or *gigs* in the United States, Canada, and outdoor jazz festivals (in Europe, Japan, and South America), as well as conventions and other music venues that paid him exorbitant sums of money, while contributing to the cause of "social music" or jazz, and the so-called Church of Miles Davis.

Unfortunately, there were other critics, like James Collier, who believed that Miles Davis was comfortable in odd, musical clichés, and not his exceptional music voice. In essence, Collier wrote that Davis was "a man who possessed only a relatively modest natural gift, but who by dint of intelligence and force of personality made himself one of the major figures of jazz."[23] But if what Collier says is true about his modest gift, why does Miles Davis continue to be considered the most talked about and imitated jazz trumpeter of all time? Davis once summed up his trumpet playing and music this way: "I can't play like anyone else, I can't fight like anyone else. I'm just myself. And I don't fuck around [with] music because I love music."[24] This attitude was Davis's musical reality throughout his life. And Davis's steely, musical resolve was something to be respected. Indeed, listeners can actually feel or hear the bluesy pain in his trumpet and moving, musical renderings [see Figure 16.1]. It should also be noted that Davis's new music (and trumpet playing) is like he took the path of least resistance. Meanwhile, Davis was trying to build his strength and stamina. It was especially important for him to make sure that his health was okay, because little did his fans and audiences know that Davis was still suffering from "an infected leg, an agonizing hip degeneration that led to the implanting of a prosthetic ball-and-socket and withdrawal from the pain-killing drugs necessitated by the hip crisis."[25] Fortunately, the late Cicely Tyson, who was once his wife, in the early 1980s, kept Davis really grounded by helping him with his health; like introducing Davis to "a Chinese

Figure 16.1 Miles Davis statue outside cultural center in Kielce, Poland. *Source:* Author's personal photograph.

acupuncturist,"[26] after he had a minor stroke. Davis's former road manager Chris Murphy writes:

> Soon Miles [Davis] was making visits to Dr. Shin down in Chinatown [in New York]. Whether or not all these efforts had anything to do directly with Miles's medical recovery, I don't know. He probably would have healed by himself in time—but that's irrelevant. What Cicely [Tyson] did was involve Miles in his own healing process. This feeling, that he had some control over his health, improved his mental health immeasurably. By fighting back physically, Miles was able to fight off the depression that was, I felt, the larger problem.[27]

Nevertheless, Davis was doing his best in terms of his physical health, with the help of his soon-to-be-ex-wife Cicely Tyson, whom he had married in 1981. It had gotten to the point that Davis couldn't do much of anything at that time, because of his poor health; but Tyson "had stuck by him through darkness and light," also helping "him quit alcohol."[28] Of course, Tyson had a full-time movie career herself; but they were terribly incompatible, "and . . . went through an ugly divorce in 1988."[29] Also, Davis was still fascinated by other beautiful women, like his first love, Juliette Gréco. However, when she (Gréco) changed her personality (or was it her plastic surgery?); Davis had this to say: "Juliette [Gréco] was the prettiest woman I'd ever seen—since my mother—but when she cut off her nose, her beauty just stopped. How can a man tell a woman she's got to have her nose cut off? It's [probably] about going where you want to go in show business."[30] Finally, at sixty-three years, "Davis's lips [were] now noticeably stronger,"[31] and eventually, he was able to record new albums and perform at various venues, like at the Royal Festival Hall, in England, in 1989, and other places.

NOTES

1. Mike Zwerin, "From Jazz to Pop to Reggae to Jazz," *International Herald Tribune*, July 11, 1989, 1.

2. Zwerin, "From Jazz to Pop," 1. Davis, of course, was his own worst critic. But he was highly criticized for not playing to his potential, or what jazz critics thought he could play.

3. Howard Mandel, "Miles Davis' New Direction is a Family Affair," *Down Beat*, September 1980, 17.

4. Chris Albertson, "The Unmasking of Miles Davis," *Saturday Review*, November 27, 1971, 87.

5. Lance Tooks, *Between the Devil and Miles Davis* (New York: NBM Publishing, Inc., 2004), 41. To be sure, "you can see Miles's' lip roll on his '*Tulu*' Album cover," as well as on the cover of his greatest hits album.

6. Michael Ullman, "Miles Davis in Retrospect," *New Boston Review* (May/June 1981): 18.

7. Dan Morgenstern, "Miles in Motion," *Down Beat*, September 3, 1970, 16.

8. Gary Kamiya, "A Master at Dangerous Play," *Salon Entertainment* (1998): 3, http://www.salon.com/ent/music/feature.

9. Marc Hopkins, "Miles Davis: Selling the Dark Prince," *Jazz Times*, October 2006, 5, http://jazztimes.com/articles/17304-miles.

10. Geoffrey Himes, "Miles Davis: Forty Years of Freedom," *Jazz Times*, September 13, 2010, 2, http://jazztimes.com/articles/26369-miles-davis-freedom. Davis believed that he had come up with a particular musical concept that he thought no one else had done; but it was met with mixed reviews by critics. Listen to his 1989 *Amandla* album.

11. Richard Williams, "On Top of All the Beat," *The Times*, sec. 1A, April 28, 1983.

12. Stanley Crouch, *The All-American Skin Game, or the Decoy of Race: The Long and the Short of It, 1990–1994* (New York: Pantheon Books, 1995), 167. Crouch goes on to derogatorily write that "at one point in the early 1970s, with his wraparound dark glasses and his puffed shoulders, the erstwhile master of cool looked like an extra from a science fiction B movie." See the same reference, p. 179.

13. Williams, "On Top of All," 1A. Davis also "was opening for Lauro Nyro and the Band, among other bands. The younger audiences were grooving with his new, free-form music." To be sure, however, they were unfamiliar with the African rhythms Davis was playing. They were accustomed instead to rock's insistent drum back-beat and a rock-steady bass line elements Miles would incorporate into his later music." See also Quincy Troupe, "Miles Davis: Our 1985 Interview," *SPIN*, September 28, 2019, 42, https://www.spin.com/featured/miles.

14. Stephanie Stein, "Kenny G: Songbird in Full Flight," *Down Beat*, January 1988, 18.

15. John McDonough, "Jazz in Black and White," *The Wall Street Journal*, August 13, 1999, W6.

16. Stein, "Kenny G," 18. "But to even touch [upon such things] today risks jangling politically protected nerves," while "inviting the usual cant of racism and related pieties, all repeated so often they have ceased to be seriously examined." See the same reference, p. 18.

17. Stein, "Kenny G," 18.

18. "Trumpeter Hubbard Dies at 70," *Las Vegas Review Journal*, sec 5B, January 1, 2009.

19. Ullman, "Miles Davis in Retrospect," 18. Davis's new record company, Warner Bros Records, Inc., distributed *Amandla* in 1989, which is a Warner Communications Company, in Burbank, California.

20. Kenneth Tynan, "Miles Apart," *Holiday*, February 1963, 101. George R. Crisp writes that Davis was left "without chops," because he hadn't played his trumpet in five years. And, "it would take time to regain his *embouchure*, and to get back into the physical condition to play as he had," in the past, as Tynan tells us. See George R. Crips, *Miles Davis* (New York: Franklin Watts, 1997), 125.

21. Ron Carter, "Essay about My Funny Valentine" in Liner Notes, *Columbia Records*, September 25, 2004, 12.

22. Scott McFarland, "Miles Davis: The "Electric" Years," *Perfect Sound Forever*, August 1997, 5, http://www.furious.com/perfect/miles. McFarland also tells us that Davis "was not going to outsell the ranks of white boys playing electrified blues guitar which [was] what a lot of people were into at the time. Fortunately, he [Davis] kept at his music anyway (rather than backtracking or waiting for the general populace to catch up with him), because the best was yet to come." See the same reference, p. 5.

23. Ullman, "Miles Davis in Retrospect," 18. James Collier is quoted in his book, *A History of Jazz*.

24. Nat Hentoff, "An Afternoon with Miles Davis," *The Jazz Review*, vol. 1, issue 2 (December 1958): 11.

25. Leonard Feather, "Miles Davis' Miraculous Recovery from Stroke," *Ebony*, December 1982, 64.

26. Feather, "Miles Davis' Miraculous Recovery," 62. In a letter to the editor, Miami Marcel correctly wrote that Cicely Tyson "resurrected Miles faith in himself after he hit rock bottom so that he would go on to create more amazing music," before his death. See "Re: Cicely Tyson," *The New York Times Magazine*, January 31, 2021, 5.

27. Chris Murphy, *Miles to Go: Remembering Miles Davis* (New York: Thunder's Mouth Press, 2002), 174. Murphy also writes, "He [Davis] had several concerts scheduled, which were promptly cancelled. Miles could play his horn with either hand, but performing live in his condition was out of the question. He was crushed emotionally, both by the physical blow and by the cancellation of [several tours.]" See the same reference, p. 174.

28. George R. Crisp, *Miles Davis* (New York: Franklin Watts, 1997), 127.

29. Crisp, *Miles Davis*, 127.

30. Charles S. Murray, "Interview: Miles Davis; Cat who walks by himself," *The Observer*, vol. 40, sec. 5, issue 40 (June 18, 1989): 4.

31. Bob Blumenthal, "Miles Glorious: The Man with the Brew," *The Boston Phoenix*, July 7, 1981, 1.

Chapter 17

The New Music

When Miles Davis returned in 1981 to the jazz music scene, he disappointed "some fans by not suddenly reverting to his 1955 self,"[1] playing acoustic jazz. But Davis re-emerged from his self-imposed retirement with renewed vigor for playing his trumpet and music; and again, he was brilliantly different. Perhaps no one really understood the positive ramifications of Davis's retirement, and how it affected his new music. According to jazz writer Bill Laswell, "Miles Davis was a perfect example of someone who consciously tried to evolve, and by doing that he changed things and confused a great deal of people."[2] Nevertheless, there was an outpouring of support for Davis's music comeback. To be sure, Davis had a profusion of musical ideas; but "he did not pick up where he had left off in 1975; and until his death in 1991 [he] played a hybrid of rock and jazz that was much more approachable and melodic."[3] In other words, a newly determined Miles Davis engendered positivity in moving forward with his new music, because "he was interested in getting out of what he had come to see as the dead end of jazz music: theme/improvisation/theme."[4] Interestingly, Davis was able to adapt, because he thought that people were ready for his new music; but, fans were "dumbfounded by Davis's heady mixture of funk, rock, jazz, electronics, and music that would later be known by such names as ambient, trance, and techno, for which no names existed at the time."[5] This was especially true for those jazz enthusiasts experiencing his music for the first time. Some even called Davis's new music avant-garde. About this name for his music, Davis had this to say: "I don't know what people think and I don't care. Especially that phrase avant-garde—you can look to so many people for that. Just certain people I care [about] what they think."[6] Davis, nevertheless, was concerned about whether people would accept his new music. Also, his actions gave him the opportunity to explore new musical territory.

Therefore, in 1981 he [Davis] returned with an album, "The Man with the Horn,"[7] which is a gorgeous rendering of an infinite, echo trumpet sound; but it was panned by jazz critics, because they didn't understand what Davis was trying to play. Jazz fans, and others, however, liked the "The Man with the Horn" recording, and anxiously awaited his next album. It should be explained that

> Miles [Davis] . . . never stood still. He . . . continually arrived at new concepts, new directions, and then, just as his colleagues in the jazz world have picked up on it, Miles [was] already someplace else. And somewhere else. His career [was] an elusive and tremendously influential path of changes.[8]

This meant that many fans backed what Davis was trying to do musically. Some even found Davis's return a cause to rejoice, or a celebration. In this regard, Davis used his skills as a bandleader to get back into the swing of things. According to the late music producer Teo Macero, in 1980, Davis "was ready, willing and able, it [seemed], and he put together a new group and assembled it together with compositions and [new] arranging ideas."[9] Although Davis didn't want to make any snap decisions, "he saw more than economic possibilities in rock rhythms and electronic sounds." More importantly, "Rock may have piqued his long-time interest in salvaging the banal."[10] His new music could also be traditionally spiritual, while at the same time incompatible, seemingly, with so-called contemporary jazz. Eventually, Davis would play his trumpet with an intensity that was "pushing tonal harmony to its limits," while displaying "a dazzling rhythmic flexibility."[11] It should be remembered that Davis was able to play this way in the 1960s; but with his new music, it was more Rock and electronic jazz. During a concert, in 1982, on Long Island, New York, Davis demonstrated his skills as a jazz trumpeter on the comeback trail. Journalist Lee Jeske explained:

> First and most importantly, at this appearance the featured soloist was Miles Davis. *The We Want Miles* LP revealed that the trumpeter [was] in superb shape and, at this concert, Miles was happy to show off his playing. His first solo was a Harmon-muted beauty—full of the introspection and heartbreak of his finest work. The audience, obviously unprepared for such lyricism early on, gasped with delight. . . . He soloed long and frequently—ranging through some up tempo funk, a bluesy medium tempo, and soft-spoken ballads—and was in control the entire time.[12]

Davis pleased and even surprised a lot of his fans and supporters. But all of his concerts were not as successful. For example, during a Hollywood Bowl concert in 1982, Davis played badly, but he didn't get upset after negative press reports, because his attitude had changed significantly at that time. Davis was quoted as saying, "hell, I was so sick that night I could hardly walk."[13] It was as if his so-called retirement and drug use had taken a tremendous toll physically, mentally, and emotionally on Davis; but within a short time, he was back at playing great, awe-inspiring music, "including Cyndi Lauper's *'Time After Time'* and Michael Jackson's *'Human Nature,'* which he once did with [the classic] 'Bye Bye Blackbird'".[14] A relaxed and confident Miles Davis showed flashes of his old prowess as a jazz trumpeter, with a much bolder and rounder, clear-bell sound. Listeners only have to hear "two albums Davis recorded for the Japanese," which "were both extremely successful. One was *Agharta*, the other *Pangaea*."[15] Davis was extremely excited about playing his trumpet again, even though he was a bit rusty. Davis was once asked if "there [was] ever a time during his absence when he thought he would lose his ability to play?"[16] Davis responded in this way: "It doesn't go like that with me. . . . I never think about not being able to do anything. I just pick up my horn and play the hell out of it."[17] Perhaps the musical voice in Davis's head was something that he more or less developed over the years. Or was it Davis's *eureka* moment, as he bared his soul in his music? Indeed, his lyricism was absorbing and wonderful, leaving fans wanting more. However, *naysayer* and jazz critic Peter Schwendener writes: "Davis's curtailment of the lyrical phase of his career began either in the early sixties, in his pioneering quintet of that time, or . . . in the late sixties, when he started using electric instruments in his groups."[18] Schwendener goes on to write, "Davis was simply not musically adapted to make the switch: his lyricism couldn't survive the electronic onslaught."[19] What Schwendener writes, however, just isn't true, because his *lyricism* was still evident in his new music, which the listener can hear on his 1988 *Siesta* movie score. Another criticism was that Davis's new music overstepped the mark when he mixed the traditional "jazz church" music with other music genres, like Rock and the Bossa Nova music from Brazil, which is beautifully rendered and evident on his *Quiet Nights* album, with Gill Evans's orchestra. Listeners can also hear Davis's lyricism on his electrified music (taken from parts of India) on his *Bitches Brew* album. Miles Davis believed that music shouldn't be put into specific or separate categories, as he felt that all music was eternal, constant, and relatable.

Many critics had stratospheric expectations for Davis and his new music, but it was unreasonable for them to think that he wouldn't experiment with entirely new musical concepts and paradigms, which would later include rap, especially before his death. It was the new reality of jazz music, because Miles Davis believed that jazz, or "social music" would certainly end if it didn't change. In truth, Miles Davis felt that there was a better way of expressing the music, like he was a musical voice of reason. And for some jazz fans, Davis's new music was interesting and enlightening, because they admired his musical zest for life, or his joie de vivre. To be sure, Davis took the esoteric musical path that made the most sense to him. It was Davis's way of staying connected to the larger music world. More importantly, what Davis was trying to do with his new music excited him and brought him joy. Jazz fans had one common and enduring interest in Miles Davis's distinctive artistic viewpoint and musical instincts: His boldness. With that, and as mentioned, Davis was never afraid to do things differently in terms of his music. It seems to give credence to the theory that jazz is essentially about *everything* musical, not some novelty. Davis also believed that once-fervent supporters and fans would stop buying recordings and listening to jazz, or "social music," if it didn't adapt. If that happened, the jazz music game might come to an end, he thought. And, so what if Davis's new, creative musical ideas pushed him in unexpected directions? After all, jazz is jazz, in any form. Furthermore, Davis believed that *he* shouldn't be blamed "for the aesthetic failures of two generations of jazz musicians."[20] Perhaps not surprisingly, Davis was still able to provide jazz fans with a creatively adaptive way to listen to what he was judiciously recording, while achieving his musical vision. In this respect, he spoke articulately with his mournful trumpet.

For some, Davis's new music was unlike anything jazz fans and listeners had ever heard or experienced—that is, the tranquility and peacefulness of his music. Just listen to Davis's 1985 Warner Brothers' recording of *Tutu*: "Suddenly and quite unexpectedly, without any apparent difficulty, a creation [like Tutu] comes into being that's so bang on target that it takes our breath away."[21] It was/is like a gourmet feast of sound; or a musical orgy, with a cherry on top, so to speak. Synthesizer programmer Adam Holzman explained the recording of *Tutu* this way: "There was that creative, magical buzz going on that you get when you know you're really onto something, something that's unique, and that has a really special, new sound. It was a very exciting and charged time,"[22] perhaps, to record such music. It was also particularly true that jazz fans and other listeners were immediately gripped by Davis's new *Tutu* music, and the seductive power of his powerful trumpet sound. In an unprecedented way, Davis's new music can actually transport jazz fans *mentally*, to somewhere beyond the realm of their existence or senses. Carlos Santana, the great Mexican American guitarist, "who worshiped Miles," called Davis's future music—"spiritual orgasm."[23] Santana continued to effusively praise Miles Davis, calling him an instigator and musical revolutionist, who was "a serious brutal artist who would not comply with the plastic [music] system" and "would not tap dance for anybody."[24] Moreover, Davis was able to pull listeners deeper into a direction that was more like some kind of spiritual practice. Was it (listening to Miles Davis's new music) a way of worshiping? Perhaps. Equally important, Davis played and collaborated with musicians like Santana and other jazz, Rock and Roll, and Blues Superstars from around the world and in the United States. When Davis started touring again with his band, Peter Watrous tells us that he (Davis) even opened "rock concerts for Santana." Watrous goes on:

> He [Davis] performed at the Isle of Wight Pop Festival, in front of a crowd estimated at 400,000. Only five years earlier, at the peak of his creative energies, he was still often playing three or four sets a night at hole-in-the wall clubs. Accompanied by Mr. [Wayne] Shorter, Mr. Davis went on to open shows for Crosby, Stills, Nash and Young, the Band, Laura Nyro and others. He [Davis] performed at the home of rock, the Fillmore, and even [recorded] a live album there.[25]

Davis attributed his loyal fan base and new Rock and Roll fans to his championing of all music idioms, because he didn't believe that jazz or "social music" was *monolithic*. But Davis was still trying to wrap his head around being considered a Supreme Being. Movie actress and Davis's last wife, Cicely Tyson, once stated that Davis "was the last one to recognize that millions of people all over the world deem[ed] him a god."[26] Nevertheless, Miles Davis didn't have some kind of god complex. Also, paradoxically, Miles Davis never needed words to communicate his musical message, because he was able to do that with his horn. Furthermore, the very idea of having supporters and jazz fans who loved him was his biggest source of confidence; and no doubt, Davis felt appreciative. Just as important, and ironically, Davis's "sharp electric funk mode" music would become "his longest lasting [musical] idiom."[27] Although Davis didn't know sometimes what shape his new music would take him, he always thought that his sound and music was from a black perspective. Finally, the artistic and lyrical romance of his new music *cannot* be denied or understated. In the final analysis, Davis's new music had a centeredness that was like no other music, as it was the sine qua non of jazz.

NOTES

1. Scott Yanow, Trumpet Kings: *The Players Who Shaped the Sound of Jazz Trumpet* (San Francisco, CA: Backbeat books, 2001), 122. Davis defied expectations. And what made his music interesting was the freshness of his sound, yet again, as he played his trumpet in a magical way.

2. Bill Laswell, "Miles into the Future: Re-Shaping the Music of Miles Davis," *Sound on Sound*, May 1998, 5, http://www.soundonsound.com/sos/may98/articles.

3. Laswell, "Re-Shaping the Music," 1.

4. Marshall Bowden, "The Secret History of Miles Davis in the 1980s," *Jazzitude* (2001): 2, http://www.jazzitude.com/milesdavis.

5. Bowden, "The Secret History," 2.

6. McCall, "Miles Davis," 41.

7. "Miles Davis Obituary," 2.

8. Don DeMichael, "Miles Davis," *Rolling Stone*, December 13, 1969, 25.

9. Max Jones, "The Return of Miles Davis," *Melody Maker*, June 21, 1980, 45.

10. Michael Ullman, "Miles Davis in Retrospect," *New Boston Review* (May/June 1981): 20.

11. Pareles, "Trumpeter, Dies," 4.

12. Lee Jeske, "Miles Davis Felt Forum Interview," in *Down Beat*, April 1983, 46.

13. Leonard Feather, "Miles Davis' Miraculous Recovery from Stroke," *Ebony*, December 1982, 64.

14. Richard Cook, *Richard Cook's Jazz Encyclopedia* (London: Penguin Books, 2005), 153.

15. Jones, "The Return of Miles Davis," 45.

16. Goodman, "I Just Pick Up My Horn," 1.

17. Goodman, "I Just Pick Up My Horn," 1.

18. Peter Schwendener, "Miles Davis: The Loss of Lyricism," *Tri-Quarterly* (Winter 1987): 161. It should be pointed out that, "Miles Davis's ability to dominate the playing of other musicians with his own conception is comparable to [Duke] Ellington's and [Count] Basie's, yet his own trumpet playing, at its best, is as lyrical as the playing of Young, Armstrong, Hodges and the other premodern masters." See same reference.

19. Schwendener, "The Loss of Lyricism," 166.

20. Nisenson, *'Round About Midnight*, 275. Nisenson also rejected the idea of some "Miles Davis curse"— "that one musician's musical direction could have such an enormous effect on two generations of jazzmen."

21. Paul Tingen, "Miles on Target: The Making of Tutu," *Jazz Times*, March 2002, 42.

22. Tingen, "Miles on Target," 42. Spiritually and mentally, Davis's jazz trumpet often got through to the listener, no matter what, as it was like a tearful voice. Note that the album *Tutu* was named for Nobel Peace Prize laureate, Desmond Tutu, the black South African.

23. Jerry Tallmer, "Twenty-Five Years in the Making: Village Resident with New Documentary on Miles Davis," *The Villager*, vol. 74, no. 27 (November 10–16, 2004): 2, http://www.thevillager.com/villager_08.

24. Tallmer, "Twenty-Five Years," 2.

25. Peter Watrous, "Jazz View: A Jazz Generation and the Miles Davis curse," *The New York Times*, October 15, 1995, 2, http://query.nytimes.com/gst/fullpage.

26. Feather, "Miraculous Recovery," 64.

27. Brian Morton, *Miles Davis* (London: Haus Publishing, Limited, 2005), 135. Davis was pleasantly surprised by the chance, once again, to explore new and different avenues of jazz, or "social music."

Chapter 18

Of Critics and Jazz Purists

Miles Davis, no doubt, broke a lot of rules when it came to jazz tradition; but his music was always unique and intriguing. Perhaps Davis always saw things or his music differently. More than anything, Davis was comfortable with his decision to strike out and move forward with his jazz-rock music. And musically, Davis was able to accomplish just about *everything* that he set out to do, especially his ideas of improvisational freedom, because there were no limits in what he could accomplish. According to jazz critic Christopher Smith, "Miles Davis' particular genius was centered in an ability to construct and manipulate improvisational possibilities, selecting and combining compositions, players, musical styles, and other performance parameters."[1] Davis also made pragmatic, musical choices whenever the opportunity presented itself. Moreover, he always wanted to focus on musical things that were important to him. Therefore, Davis didn't worry about what jazz critics said about him. Davis once said: "I don't look at critics. I don't say hello to 'em, I don't care what they're gonna write because I can only do what I can do and that's it. I'm not gonna tell them anything."[2] The main thing that stood between Davis and his music were the so-called jazz purists and critics, who firmly believed that he should always play acoustic jazz. Jazz critic Chris Albertson, however, writes: "it [was] difficult to imagine anyone telling Miles Davis what to do with his music, but he [was] just as receptive to constructive criticism as he [was] ready to give it."[3] Davis finally believed that making music and recordings would be so much easier if he didn't have to deal with white critics and (cursed) promoters.

Obviously, Miles Davis was frequently at odds with those who distributed or put his music out for public consumption. Which is to say, "most jazz critics were (and are) not only white middle-class Americans, but middle-brows as well."[4] Some exceptions were the late Amiri Baraka (aka LeRoi Jones), and the late Stanley Crouch, both black men, and former jazz critics. In this regard, some critics hailed Davis's abilities, as if he were anointed; but some took him to task for his musical innovations and changes, without really understanding what he was trying to do. In other words, Miles Davis would mesmerize and confound critics at the same time.

Furthermore, it seemed like some jazz critics only wanted to hear jazz tunes in their familiar form. Indeed, many thought that experimenting with jazz-rock fusion was Miles Davis's wayward effort to appeal to a wider audience, which included those who didn't know *anything* about the finer points of acoustic jazz. It didn't matter that Davis was an imaginative trumpeter, whose jazz-rock music was harmonically different and complex; the jazz purist viewed his new music with contempt. But jazz and rock fans loved Davis's music all the same. As often happens in jazz, when a new or different musical idea is introduced, critics complain, or are mostly skeptical, thinking that it is a dumb thing to pursue. But what do they know? In a 1962 *Playboy* interview by the late Alex Haley, Davis explained:

> Hell, [there are] plenty great trumpet players [that] don't come after me, or after nobody else! That's what I hate so [much] about critics—how they are always comparing artists . . . always writing that one's better than another. Ten men can have spent all their lives learning technical expertness on their instruments, but just like in any art, one will play one style and the rest nine other ways. And if some critics just don't happen to like a man's style, they will knock the artist. That bugs the hell out of musicians. It's made some damn near mad enough to want to hang up their horns.[5]

Unfortunately, some critics thought that Davis was a lightweight, and were frustrated with his (erratic) trumpet playing and embracing of jazz-rock fusion; but Davis was perhaps inspired by rock music, while aiming for a beautiful sound. Indeed, Davis's jazz-rock was inextricably linked to all phases of modern jazz. Jazz purists, of course, might argue that there is something wrong with *any* change in the traditional method of playing jazz. But such selfish notions are impractical for a music that is always evolving? Some critics, especially the "jazz police," thought that jazz-rock was an end in itself, and Davis served up the *obituary* for traditional jazz music. What rubbish. This sentiment, of course, was a matter of opinion. African American jazz critics like Stanley Crouch thought that Davis's new music, and style on stage, was like a circus act; and his jazz-rock "like jumping out of a plane without a parachute."[6] Jazz trumpeter Wynton Marsalis even told jazz writer Sholto Byrnes that Miles Davis was "a genius who decided to go into rock, and was on the bandstand looking like, basically, a buffoon."[7] The truth is, some jazz critics are particularly daft, because some don't know much about style or the evolution or the progression of jazz. According to jazz scholar Theodor W. Adorno, "a great deal of music is perceived as being jazz or related to jazz only on the basis of its sound, without it being at all interested in the rhythmic principles of jazz."[8] Therefore, there is an understandable impulse to criticize something that people or so-called jazz critics don't like or understand. For some purists, jazz-rock fusion music is a bombshell of sorts. And for others, it has opened up a *Pandora's Box* of musical controversy.

Moreover, from the perspective of jazz purists, there shouldn't be *any* evolutionary, musical experiments, as change is not necessary; and fusion is an affront to jazz *orthodoxy*. This is to say that jazz should never be conceived in uncharted waters. Jazz critics and purists, however, should know that, "the more democratic [or autocratic] jazz is, the worse it becomes."[9] The general point is this: Jazz purists have had only negative things to say about Davis's jazz-rock fusion music. However, "his [Davis's] excursions [in new music] helped keep jazz popular with mainstream audiences."[10] Beyond that, some jazz critics believe that jazz-rock is a *kaleidoscope* of harsh sounds, which is perhaps how some critics considered Davis's new music. Also, jazz purists think that Davis's jazz-rock music is incomprehensible, like jazz critic Ed Brayton, who stated that Miles Davis "had long stretches of his career when his music was virtually unlistenable to me. His [Davis's] experimental jazz recordings were simply horrid, though I recognize that I think that only because I tend to regard the entire *genre* as horrid."[11] It is wildly unfair for critics to put Davis's music down when most can't carry a tune, or even play a musical instrument. In other words, despite what critics had to say, Davis had the talent to back up his boasts. And he certainly could carry a tune, unlike some tone-deaf critics and *naysayers*. Indeed, the ability to carry a tune is an art in itself. Stanley Crouch's scathing criticism of Davis's music isn't interesting or profound, because it crosses the line. Writing about Davis's new music, Crouch once noted: Davis's sound on his *In a Silent Way* is "long, maudlin, boasting," and "lost among electronic instruments," which is "no more than droning wallpaper music." He goes on: "Davis was [also] firmly on the path of the sellout" with his *Bitches Brew* album, which "fully launched jazz-rock with its multiple keyboards, electronic guitars, static beats, and clutter. Davis's music became progressively trendy and dismal," proving "beyond any doubt that he [had] lost all interest in music of quality."[12] All this is to say: jazz purists mostly hated to hear Davis's new music. Or perhaps they saw jazz-rock as so much noise; or just no good. But it should be pointed out that, if Davis didn't like something he did [musically], "it [was] usually because it didn't capture [for him] the right feeling."[13] The magnitude of criticism and negativism about Davis's new music was lengthy and brutal, as the reader can perhaps ascertain. But such criticisms didn't hurt his fame.

Hence, we should be disappointed or disgusted with the plethora of harsh criticism of Davis's new music in some quarters, particularly their jaundiced analysis. Jazz purists even belittled and misrepresented Miles Davis as a musician. Equally important, some jazz critics virtually wrote Davis off, like Wynton Marsalis, who was quoted as saying: "They call Miles's stuff jazz. That stuff is not jazz, man. Just because somebody played jazz at one time, that doesn't mean they're still playing it."[14] Clearly, some critics of Miles Davis's new music didn't care enough to even educate themselves on the subject of jazz itself. Indeed, Marsalis and others should have known what John Gennari writes:

> The central role in Jazz performance of the improvised solo both puts a premium on individual style and makes it necessary for soloists constantly to seek fresh approaches to familiar material. By modifying timbre, reworking phrasing, adjusting dynamics, rethinking harmonic and rhythmic relationship, and reinventing melodies, jazz improvisers [should] constantly seek to establish difference—to distinguish their voices from those of other performers, and to mark each performance as a distinct statement within their own oeuvre.[15]

And even though jazz-rock became the consistent thread in Davis's later music, he was the perfect example of perseverance. On top of that, Davis was a no-nonsense musician, who was serious about his craft, as music was his priority. Nevertheless, for some critics, Davis's music seemed hard to square, particularly since many admired his early work. Moreover, Davis had earned millions of devoted jazz and rock fans for his jazz-rock music and recordings. Jazz writer Douglas Clark tells us that Miles Davis "opened up new possibilities for jazz but never lost touch with its roots: individual improvisation, melody, blues, and that rhythmic buoyancy once called swing."[16] But we must also ask the question: Was Davis "sacrificing the grace and power of his music at the altar of show biz?"[17] Fortunately, Davis's continuing preoccupation with change in his music did not diminish him. Indeed, he encouraged musical change and adaptation, although jazz purists thought that he had "sold out." Bassist Phil Raney tells us that when Miles Davis "started to experiment with electronics," the jazz purists "were like that's not jazz. Miles sold out. He's not doing jazz anymore. But you know what, jazz is a little bit of all that—it's big band, it's trios, it's fusion." Raney goes on:

> You have so many different elements. You've got the smooth jazz. You've got the straight ahead. You've got the R&B. You've got people mixing jazz and hip-hop and all that. I just think it has evolved into a whole bunch of different things . . . it depends on what you want to call jazz.[18]

With Davis's mixture of rock and jazz elements, his music was instantly appealing, but jazz purists thought that jazz rock fusion was some kind of protest to the orthodox jazz tradition. But nothing could have been further from the truth. Davis's jazz fusion music wasn't just about restructuring jazz, it was/is also about trying to mix and combine different ways to make a pleasing sound, or music that turned your head, making people listen. So this was Davis's way of getting out of a musical rut, while pushing the music forward. And Davis understood the enormity of what he was doing creatively and musically, while having no misgivings. But the jazz purists still hated jazz-rock, because many believed that the music was an atrocity. Indeed, Davis's later or new music rubbed some jazz critics, like Marsalis and Stanley Crouch, the wrong way. Their criticisms even morphed into an all-out feud, which continues to this day, and even in Davis's death. Perhaps it started when Marsalis was embarrassed and humiliated by Miles Davis during "the Vancouver Jazz Festival in 1986," where an uninformed "producer apparently tried to orchestrate a poignant intergenerational moment, by having Wynton come up on stage to jam with Miles's band;" but Miles would have none of it, stopping his band and crudely telling Wynton to "get the fuck off the stage."[19] Perhaps this incident left a lasting scar on Wynton Marsalis's *psyche* and bitter taste in his mouth. Who knows exactly? Instead of respecting the elder jazz trumpeter, Marsalis continued to disparage Miles Davis, "for abandoning acoustic jazz in favor of jazz-rock fusion, and Davis sniped that Marsalis was spending too much time playing classical music and not developing his own improvisational voice."[20] The feud was a contradiction between the jazz critics (like Marsalis) and what jazz fans expected from Davis and his need to change the direction of his new, authentically constructed music. Miles Davis often dismissed the criticism from Marsalis and others, but he had this to say about the young trumpeter:

> He [Marsalis] started saying things—nasty, disrespectful things—about me, things I've never said about musicians who influenced me and who I had great respect for. A lot of people thought I was getting jealous of Wynton. I wasn't jealous. I just didn't think he was playing as good as people said he was playing.[21]

Davis could dish it out, as well as take the flak from critics, and jazz purists. In this regard, journalist Kenneth Tynan claimed that "Miles had an innate grasp of the basic English art of One Upmanship."[22] Also, according to Tynan, the great Lena Horne, in 1963, told him that: "Miles is a potentate. He's also a puritan, and the combination can be pretty sadistic."[23] Wynton Marsalis should have celebrated Davis's musical differences and innovations; but, perhaps, he was never able to reconcile his jealousy and anger about the older jazz man. Marsalis even said: "Miles was never my idol. I resent what he's doing [musically] because it gives the whole scene such a letdown. I think Bird would roll over in his grave if he knew what was going on."[24] But who exactly made Wynton Marsalis the guardian of jazz? More importantly, if Davis wasn't Marsalis's trumpet idol, why did he try to play like him? According to Marsalis's biographer, Leslie Gourse, "the elder trumpeter's influence was particularly obvious in 1981 on Wynton's first and second albums, recorded in 1983."[25] And before Davis died, there was still a dark history between the two men. Additionally, what Marsalis should have known and recognized is: Miles Davis is still a musical role model for many jazz trumpeters, even today. Popular jazz trumpeter, Chris Botti, a white man, for example, confessed: "The reason I play music is because of the first statement I ever heard on the trumpet by Miles Davis, 'My Funny Valentine.' That's how powerful his sound was to my heart."[26] Marsalis might argue that Davis's 'My Funny Valentine' is straight-ahead, acoustic jazz, not rock fusion. But it is also important to also understand that "A lot of [Davis's] later experimentation is slighted in the neo-conservative critical climate of jazz today, and particularly by the jazz orthodoxy promulgated by Wynton Marsalis (another Juilliard trumpeter) and the brain trust surrounding him at jazz at Lincoln Center."[27] Of course, jazz critics and purists should offer constructive suggestions, rather than sermonizing about what jazz (is or) should be. In this respect, the black musician Anthony Jackson succinctly writes:

> The innovators, upon whom the music has always depended for its incontrovertible spiritual strength, *would not* destroy it. Why, then, do we now find Mr. Marsalis and his congress of simple-minded wanna-bes extolling the virtues of "pure" jazz, taking upon themselves the twin mantles of protector and rejuvenator? Inasmuch as the form has shown itself to be more than capable of withstanding the vicissitudes of neglect, corruption, revision, and outright attack, I maintain that this latest crop of "redeemers" is more artistically bankrupt, morally hypocritical, and historically irrelevant than any that has come before.[28]

Jackson is absolutely right in his assessment about jazz purists and critics, especially when it comes to comments made by Stanley Crouch and Wynton Marsalis. But most significantly, "it must be said that nobody [can] usurp Miles Davis's place in the pantheon of jazz stars."[29] Furthermore, we should discuss "the persistence of the critical divide [that] is evident in recent appraisals of fusion music and its place within the broader scope of jazz history."[30] For Miles Davis, playing jazz-rock fusion was the instinctive thing for him to do, as he moved forward with the music. Not surprisingly, Davis embraced jazz-rock fusion with a lot of optimism and enthusiasm. And his choices in changing his "social music" were more

Figure 18.1 Miles Davis statue outside Montreux Music & Convention Center, Switzerland. *Source*: Author's personal photograph.

than a political one. For some, it was the right move, while others pooh-poohed him. But what jazz critics, and the like, should finally know is that Davis's younger band members (throughout the years) completely understood where he was coming from with his music, as they wanted to contribute, and advance the "jazz church" [see Figure 18.1]. Nevertheless, no matter what Miles did, in terms of his new music, some critics and jazz purists will always say that he (Davis) sold out.

NOTES

1. Christopher Smith, "A Sense of the Possible: Miles Davis and the Semiotics of Improvised Performance," *The Drama Review*, vol. 39, issue 3 (Fall 1995): 41.

2. Cheryl McCall, "Miles Davis," *Musician, Player, and Listener*, vol. 41 (1982): 41.

3. Chris Albertson, "The Unmasking of Miles Davis," *Saturday Review*, November 27, 1971, 87.

4. John Gennari, "Jazz Criticism: Its Development and Ideologies," *Black American Literature Forum*, vol. 25, issue 3 (Fall 1991): 23, http://webliks2.epnet.com/DeliveryPrintSave.asp?tb. (3/29/05). While signed at Columbia Records Company, Davis thought of himself as the "company nigger," who expressed a belief that his "label was not affording black artists equal opportunities in terms of exposure." And for this reason and other disagreements, he would leave Columbia Records for Warner Bros. See Chris Albertson, "The Unmasking of Miles Davis," *Saturday Review*, November 27, 1971, 68.

5. Alex Haley, interviewer, "Miles Davis: A Candid Conversation with the Jazz World's Premier Iconoclast," *Playboy*, September 1962, 6, http://www.honors.umd.edu/HONR269J/archive/Miles. (5/10/2005). In this statement, Miles Davis was never afraid to share his thoughts and opinions, as he became more used to speaking to the media in terms of (many) interviews over the years.

6. Jerry Tallmer, "Twenty-Five Years in the Making: Village Resident with a New Documentary on Miles Davis," *The Villager*, vol. 74, no. 27 (November 10-16, 2004): 1, http://www.thevillager.com/villager_80/twentyfive (6/11/2005).

7. Sholto Byrnes, "Blowing Up a Storm," *The Independent*, April 1, 2005, 1, http://enjoyment.independent.co.uk. (6/11/2005).

8. Theodor W. Adorno, "On Jazz," *Discourse*, vol. 12, no.1 (Fall/Winter 1989–90): 47.

9. Adorno, "On Jazz," 50.

10. "Miles Davis Biography in Full: Miles Dewey Davis III," *Biography.com* (1994–2010), 3, http://www.biography.com/articles/Miles (4/25/2011).

11. Ed Brayton, "Miles Davis Redux," *Dispatches from the Culture Wares*, May 27, 2004, 1, http://www.stcynic.com/blog/archives/2004/05/miles.

12. Stanley Crouch, "Play the Right Thing," *The New Republic*, February 12, 1990, 35. Some jazz purists thought that Davis went too far in his musical creativity, like with his recording of *In a Silent Way* album. Many thought it was vague, abrasive and just random sounds. However, the listener can hear threads of sound that would eventually lead to his later fusion work, in earnest. Also, it takes only a moment's reflection, while listening to this album to know that Miles Davis was on to something in terms of jazz, or the music.

13. Albertson, "The Unmasking of Miles Davis," 87. As mentioned, jazz-rock fusion allowed for the real possibility for expanding jazz, or "social music," as it wasn't some kind of musical *hijinks*.

14. Byrnes, "Blowing Up A Storm," 2.

15. Gennari, "Jazz Criticism," 1.
16. Douglas Clark, "Miles into Jazz-Rock Territory," *Jazz Journal*, June 1977, 12.
17. Neil Tesser, "Blowing on Empty: Miles Davis at the Altar of Show Biz," *Reader*, sec. 1, February 18, 1983, 40. Jazz-rock was a new musical way; but some critics thought that it was nothing but a stratagem by Miles Davis to make more money. But his new music was always popular with many jazz audiences and fans.
18. Jerry Fink, "All That Jazz—And More," *Las Vegas Sun*, April 17, 2007, 7.
19. Michael Holman, "Miles Davis v. Wynton Marsalis: Jack Johnson in Jazz," *All about Jazz*, March 8, 2005, 2, http//:www.allaboutjazz.com/php/article (6/11/2005). See also Miles Davis and Quincy Troup, *Miles: The Autobiography* (New York: Simon & Schuster Paperbacks, 1989), 374.
20. Holman, "Miles Davis v. Wynton Marsalis," 2. The criticism of Miles Davis by Marsalis smacked of pure narcissism and jealousy, because he refused to acknowledge that Miles didn't want to be straitjacketed by some old, musical, jazz concepts.
21. Ron Frankl, *Miles Davis* (New York: Chelsea House Publishers, 1996), 112.
22. Kenneth Tynan, "Miles Apart," *Holiday*, February 1963, 103.
23. Tynan, "Miles Apart," 103.
24. Byrnes, "Blowing Up A Storm," 2. No matter what was said to the contrary, Miles Davis was able to bridge the worlds of jazz, rock and blues with enormous skill and aplomb while never compromising his ability to produce his own sound.
25. Leslie Gourse, *Wynton Marsalis: Skain's Domain, A Biography* (New York: Schirmer Books, 1999), 159.
26. Tiffany McGee, "Chris Botti: My Favorite Jazz Albums," *People Magazine*, October 8, 2007, 48.
27. John Rockwell, "Miles Davis: Theme with Restless Variations Built In," *The New York Times*, sec. B46, December 27, 2002. Marsalis is still not as popular as Miles Davis, even in death. It has been argued that Wynton Marsalis is single-handedly destroying jazz with his total embrace of old jazz music.
28. Anthony Jackson, "The New Dark Age," *Bass Player*, vol. 9 (Mar/April 1991): 78.
29. Gourse, *Wynton Marsalis*, 159.
30. Michael E. Veal, "Miles Davis's Unfinished Electric Revolution," *Raritan* (EBSCO Publishing), 2002, 154.

Chapter 19

Montreux and Death

Aesthetically, Davis's new music wasn't as straightforward as his old music had been, like his recordings with Gil Evans's orchestrated *Birth of the Cool*, *Porgy and Bess*, *Sketches of Spain* and *Miles Ahead*.[1] Still, listening to Davis's *Amandla* album is nothing short of exceptional. According to black author and jazz writer Charles Murray, Davis's *Amandla* "is richly imbued with [Gil] Evans-derived textures and colors; a musky, intoxicating distillation of [Duke] Ellington and Debussy."[2] And although *Amandla* is not a *tete-a-tetes* approach at playing traditional jazz, the sound is like a musical overture, or it is more like an avalanche of Davis's new trumpet sound. It should be noted that at this point in his life and career, Davis didn't care about what other jazz musicians were doing in creating new jazz, as he was focused on what he was doing, his "social music," and what he could do.

Moreover, Davis seemingly had it all as a jazz trumpeter. It was later during this time (in 1991) that Davis received a phone call from the great black musician and composer Quincy Jones, asking him to perform at the Montreux Jazz Festival, as he (Jones) was a co-producer, along with the founder of the festival, Claude Nobs. They had the unenviable task of convincing Davis to participate. In other words, Nobs and Jones wanted Davis to play at the event, and recreate "some of the incredible music he had made with the [late] arranger Gil Evans."[3] In his autobiography, Quincy Jones put it this way:

> Claude [Nobs] and I had been in Miles's apartment in New York negotiating the contract with several lawyers while the man himself was upstairs.... Eventually Miles eased down and inched further and further to the center of the room. Before we knew it, he had gotten exactly the deal he wanted, for video and TV rights, and control of his image on the [later] poster. "This is gonna be

Figure 19.1 Miles Davis gravesite, The Woodlawn Cemetery in Bronx, NY. *Source*: Author's personal photograph.

real expensive," he told us. I said, "But Dewey, all we need is a large orchestra." To my great amusement, he insisted, "Q, *you* understand—this shit is hard to play."[4]

Before Miles Davis played anywhere he looked at the *pros* and *cons*; and he did whatever he thought was best for him. Perhaps Davis fretted in private that he wouldn't be able to do it, or couldn't make the prestigious jazz event, as he was perhaps *allergic* to the idea of playing the old music. After all, when Davis wasn't feeling well because of various illnesses and ailments, he didn't always follow through with his commitments and lucrative concert dates. Also, Davis didn't like *anyone* putting pressure on him, even Quincy Jones. In other words, Davis needed to be comfortable with the timing, the logistics, and everything else, as he was agitated and exasperated, having once lost his mental bearing, because of his drug use. The main challenge was actually getting Davis to the event itself. Davis probably uttered many expletives, because he really didn't like the idea of performing at Montreux, and playing his old music. Therefore, much to the chagrin of Quincy Jones, the event remained in a state of flux. Hence, Quincy Jones brought on the young black trumpeter Wallace Roney, who was "a leading disciple of the Davis sound and style,"[5] to play if Davis didn't show up; and to play the hard parts in the upper register, if Davis couldn't. Roney had always drawn comparison to Davis, but he had his own unique style and trumpet voice, which is wholly his own. But Roney once stated: "I think I was the first of the young trumpet players who really tried to embrace Miles's complete style. And I did it based on my own quest for knowledge and my personal relationship with Miles. That's what makes me different."[6] Miles Davis really liked (the late) Wallace Roney, who was like his *doppelganger*, because Roney, perhaps, reminded Davis of himself—that is, when he (Davis) was young, passionate, and musically ambitious. And Davis passed the musical baton to Wallace Roney, so to speak, before his own death, by presenting him with two of his *Martin Committee* trumpets and a flugelhorn.[7] Furthermore, despite Quincy Jones's concerns and precautions, Davis was on the brink of being seriously paid more money than any other jazz musicians (at that time) for one single jazz performance. But, of course, "Davis wanted to make [even] more money," because he had "one of the most flamboyant lifestyles in the [music] business, buying expensive sports cars, it [seemed], only to crack them up."[8] Davis also had to maintain his posh new home in Malibu, California.

It had taken a while for Davis to regain a semblance of his health; but he wanted to prove his *marquee* power—once again. What was also remarkable about performing at the Montreux Jazz Festival was Davis would revisit the music of his past. Davis also knew that he couldn't *side-step* the Montreux event, because it had been advertised widely, worldwide, in fact. So grudgingly he finally accepted Quincy Jones's invitation; but Davis was still reluctant to look back at his old music. Davis was teased by even the black writer Quincy Troupe who had helped Davis with his bestselling autobiography. When Troupe reminded the elder jazz man that "he [promised to] never play that old music again," Davis didn't like the playful ribbing and needling from the *tactless* Troupe, and ultimately told him to "shut the fuck up."[9] As Davis's last female companion, Jo Gelbard tells us: "Miles didn't like doing Montreux, he was very unhappy there.... [Additionally,] Miles was tired, and he was dying, but Montreux gave good money and it was supposed to be his retirement money."[10] Davis also said: "If I ever look back I'll die."[11] No one wanted to believe it, however. Another major concern that Quincy Jones had (before the Montreux event) was Davis didn't like rehearsing, because strangely, he wasn't always interested in getting the music perfect. Jones stated: "I started to get nervous about Miles being able to play all of this stuff without coming to a rehearsal, because it's a hell of a lot of music. It's like classical music. You have to play it with the orchestra."[12] But in the end, everything worked out, and came together famously. Also, Davis showed his bravado by just showing up at the Montreux Jazz Festival.

It was a rare opportunity to see and hear the great Miles Davis play his horn. The Montreux audience seemed to be excited and mesmerized by what Davis was playing, as if in a trance. Or, as jazz writer Bill Milkowski puts it, "The crowd was transported to jazz heaven."[13] Meanwhile, that night, Davis gave one soulful rendition after another of his old music. It might have been like listening to Davis's music (as if) in a dream, or where the listener could take off in flight from the edge of a great chasm, without harm. Davis played on his trumpet like he was on a mission, or like there was no tomorrow, almost exclusively in the lower register, with a bonanza of soul-stirring music. Ron Frankl writes: "On the night of the performance, 47 musicians [including Quincy Jones as conductor] joined Davis on the stage. Despite his poor health, Davis performed splendidly, seldom faltering."[14] As for some, and unexpectedly, Davis played his legendary horn magnificently. If fans watch the documented recording of this event, called *Miles & Quincy Live at Montreux*, they can see that Davis had a visible glow, as if there was an aura surrounding him, even with his stylish reading glasses and unique wardrobe—or adorning his very cool clothes.

Milkowski tells us: "For jazz purists, it was a monumental comeback. . . . Miles showed up and delivered the goods, blowing with the kind of confidence, soulful phrasing, and dramatic power that few critics thought he still had in him."[15] One thing was abundantly clear: The Montreux Jazz Festival concert was a success. Wallace Roney, who "was taken under his idol's wing" had this to say: "That [Montreux Jazz Festival] concert was so beyond criticism. Miles was making a statement. It was his last testament, the music that he wanted to leave us with. I didn't realize he was that sick, but he must have known."[16] Finally, for Quincy Jones, "conducting Gil's orchestrations for Miles was one of the most gratifying experiences in [his music] career."[17] All this is to say: It was a night to remember, an event that Quincy Jones had dreamed about, as it had been an unprecedented occasion, or an unbelievable breathtaking concert. Quincy Jones probably saw that the appreciative jazz fans (at Montreux) were at the edge of their seats the entire time, as it might have been a little bit surreal, because again, Davis had been present in the moment.

No doubt, Miles Davis was a crowd-pleaser, and it had become obvious that the Montreux jazz fans were enamored with the aging trumpeter. But Davis's trumpet playing had been less about the old music than about his confidence, because, in a way, he had magically tricked out his trumpet sound. Davis was also mindful of his Montreux audience, and "had been 'blown away' by revisiting his large-ensemble music.[18] Afterward, Davis's energy had been drained, because he didn't look like he was in good health; but he was not defeated. Davis knew that he had an undetermined time on earth, but he felt like he still had things to do. Indeed, Davis thought that he would be able to play his horn forever, or longer, with more incredible music down the road; but it was not to be. So when Davis returned to his Malibu home in California, he was extremely tired, but looking forward to what would come next—that is, his next move in his music ventures, like working on his jazz-rap (Doobop) album. He also wanted to put another band together and focus more on his painting. In other words, Davis didn't want to stand still, but "he checked into a Los Angeles hospital, as he had done so many times before,"[19] to have himself checked out. Davis was trying to get his life back in order, while making some positive changes. He also knew that having a healthier lifestyle would help him control his impulses, and, perhaps, fix some of his other medical problems. Unfortunately, Davis still had some hurdles to overcome, but he never cried— "except through his horn."[20] According to Frankl, Davis's condition deteriorated, and he developed another serious case of pneumonia," and "died on September 28, 1991" when he was "65 years old"[21] [see Figure 19.1 and 19.2]. The hardest part for many fans was to accept the fact that the *jazz god*, Miles Dewey Davis, was dead. Many thought that Miles Davis had plenty of more miles to go in terms of his musical journey; but this wasn't meant to be. Others had no idea that Davis didn't have much time left, and many were crushed when they heard the news of his passing.

Figure 19.2 Sir Miles Davis's headstone, The Woodlawn Cemetery in Bronx, NY.
Source: Author's personal photograph.

NOTES

1. Charles S. Murray, "Interview: Miles Davis; Cat Who Walks by himself," *The Observer*, vol. 40, sec. 5, issue 40 (June 18, 1989): 6.
2. Murray, "Interview: Miles Davis," 6.
3. Quincy Jones, *Q: The Autobiography of Quincy Jones* (New York: Doubleday, 2001), 293. It was quite evident that Miles Davis would not convert back to always playing traditional jazz, or embrace the so-called orthodoxy of jazz music again.
4. Jones, *Q: The Autobiography*, 293.
5. Nate Chinen, "Recalling Miles Davis by Crossing Cultures," *The New York Times*, May 12, 2008, 1, http://www.nytimes.com/2008/05/12/arts.
6. David Adler, "The Man with the Golden Horn," *Jazz Times*, September 2004, 62.
7. Adler, "The Man with the Golden Horn," 63.
8. Michael Ullman, "Miles Davis in Retrospect," *New Boston Review*, May/June 1981, 20. Davis, of course, wanted to do things musically that would boost his earning potential while protecting his money, assets, and financial future.
9. Quincy Troupe, *Miles and Me* (Los Angeles, CA: University of California Press, 2000), 106.
10. Marshall Bowden, "The Secret History of Miles Davis in the 1980s," *Jazzitude*, 2001, 1, http://ww.jazzitude.com/milesdavis.
11. Bowden, "The Secret History," 1. See also Troupe, "Miles and Me," 106.
12. Bill Milkowski, "Miles Plays Gil," *Down Beat*, October 1991, 26.
13. Milkowski, "Miles Plays Gil," 26.
14. Ron Frankl, *Miles Davis* (New York: Chelsea House Publishers, 1996), 116.
15. Milkowski, "Miles Plays Gil," 26.
16. Dan Queliett, "Dark Prince in Twilight," *Down Beat*, vol. 68, issue 5 (May 2001), 4, http://proquest.umi.com/pqdweb. In the late Cicely Tyson's 2021 book, *Just as I Am*, she writes: "The Miles [Davis] I knew was sensitive and ailing, bruised by the hurts this life metes out. With trembling lips, he told me of the years, during his childhood in East St. Louis, when he'd been called Blackie by his friends and even some of his families gazed down upon as nobody, rendered invisible by his dark hue." See David Marchese, "Cicely Tyson on racial dynamics and Hollywood," *The New York Times Magazine*, January 17, 2021, 13.
17. Jones, *Q: The Autobiography*, 293.
18. Adler, "The Man with the Golden Horn," 63.
19. Frankl, *Miles Davis*, 116.
20. Murray, "Interview: Miles Davis," 6.
21. Frankl, *Miles Davis*, 116.

Chapter 20

After an Ending

There is no doubt that Miles Davis was an indomitable spirit and musical visionary in terms of jazz or "social music." He was also a genius when it came to playing his horn. More importantly, Davis constantly pushed the outer boundaries of the jazz world, mainly because he could. Furthermore, Davis had the talent to back up what he musically wanted to do. Indeed, Davis challenged ordinary notions of jazz, and influenced the jazz world longer than any other jazz musician during his time, or era. This is to say that Davis changed the game and vision of his music, as well as the dimensions of jazz; and he presented his accentuated music in a dramatic and almost sacred, or consecrated way. According to jazz critic Kenneth Tynan, "the modern movement in jazz has many mansions, but only four architects: the late Charlie Parker, Thelonious Monk, Dizzy Gillespie and Miles [Davis].... These were the four horsemen of the jazz apocalypse that began in the 1940s and ended by transforming the music; new complexities replaced old naivetés, and in the process jazz grew up."[1] Therefore, Miles Davis was a musical *iconoclast*, who challenged the orthodoxy of the jazz music world. In this regard, Miles Davis was able to see the jazz music world, perhaps, more clearly and objectively. It has also been argued that Davis changed jazz music out of necessity. In addition, he shattered jazz conventions with his smarts and ingenuity. Which is to say that Davis's music clicked with people; and he quickly adapted his sound, to reflect his taste, the times, and what he wanted to play. To be sure, "Miles Davis was also beyond the music, like few jazz artists ever have been. He was [also] outspoken and controversial at a time when Afro-Americans were demanding to be heard and insisting on social change."[2] Of course, Davis didn't like the insidious nature of racism in the jazz music world. But he never really cared about winning some kind of acceptance from white people. Was this because Davis didn't want to answer to anyone? Perhaps. Davis also had a feeling that his music was more significant, even more important than himself.

Miles Davis predictably became the voice of jazz, because "he wanted his music to be better than humans are—in effect to make music too good for this world."[3] In this way, Davis became a devout priest of jazz. And his genius is obvious to those willing to listen to just some of his music. Accordingly, "for more than 50 years," Miles Davis "was a central figure in several of the most prominent movements in jazz. He recorded with Charlie Parker, set the standards for "cool jazz" and hard bop in the [1950s], led the jazz excursion into modal playing and won new fans—while alienating old ones—by inspiring the fusion revolution."[4] Davis, of course, was the most celebrated jazz musician of his generation. And he became the epitome of contemporary jazz trumpeters, as he was a jazz master in his own right. In fact, Miles Davis "charted the direction of jazz for more years than perhaps any other musician."[5] In this respect, many musicians have called him one of the most important voices in jazz. In large part, Miles Davis seemed almost superhuman, because he had impeccable judgment about jazz music. Which is to say that Davis continually made changes in his music, without batting an eyelid. To that end, he was able to upset the jazz apple cart again and again, integrating contemporary jazz with popular music and other musical idioms. It should be remembered that there were just a handful of jazz musicians who dared to challenge jazz orthodoxy. Davis also made a name for himself throughout the world by his talented trumpet playing, and his musical innovations and improvisations. Of course, "Jazz is by its very nature a music of improvisation. . . . Therefore of invention. . . . Therefore of ongoing change."[6] Equally important, improvisation is the absolute key to jazz.

Needless to say, a jazz musician's confidence in his improvisations is a foundational element of the music, particularly the eruption of sounds, exaggerations and new ways of visiting or interpreting the music (jazz), while imparting a sort of musical dialogue. Miles Davis was a master of improvisation, as he imparted a progressive, rapturous music with his horn, while embracing something like the improvisational music of the *Holy Ghost*. Perhaps Davis's music makes the very *gods* take notice. So was Davis a black jazz messiah, because of his improvisations? Professor of music at Duke University, Frank Tirro writes: "Improvisation, the somewhat mystical art of performing music as an immediate reproduction of simultaneous mental processes, is but the daily fare of the practicing jazz musician."[7] Professor Tirro goes on:

> Jazz [improvisation] can be perceived on many levels, but to comprehend fully those jazz creations which transcend the ordinary, those which are works of art,

one must grasp the information supplied by the rhythm section to put syntactical order to the language, statement, and grammar of the jazz solo.

The minimum professional requirement of the improvising jazzman is that he plays everything correctly. Technical mastery of an instrument is assumed. Then he has the task of constructing an unusually clever solution, of accomplishing an unusually difficult feat, or of completing a process in such a manner that it expands the very framework of the original task.[8]

In retrospect, Miles Davis was all about changing the music and expanding the framework of jazz. He could have played it safe, and continued to play the old, traditional jazz music; but Davis was not about that. Or he didn't want to be a part of the *lethargic* jazz tradition. Davis was also able to let go of the past, because he wanted to embrace the future when it came to jazz. This is to say that Davis never wanted to look back in regard to his music. Indeed, he was open to almost *anything* musically except returning to his past. To be sure, Davis was *never* content to play the same jazz tunes or the same clichés (or gigues) as when he first started out. The late black jazz critic Stanley Crouch wrote: "Always interested in ways to improvise that would get past clichés, Miles Davis was a bandleader expected to develop styles to high points, then either to abandon them or to alter the approach so radically that the result would almost be the same."[9] But Davis's beautifully improvisational music and style did not diminish the jazz idiom in anyway. Jazz, after all, can make complex musical tasks easier, as it can actually stimulate a listener's brain, allowing them the opportunity to focus (on something), while playing the music in the background. Perhaps most of all, listening to jazz is uplifting and a very spiritual experience, especially when listening to Miles Davis's "powerful melodies and persistent, innovative drive,"[10] and improvisations. Davis approached playing his music as if it was a sacred duty or religious activity; and his admirers continually sang his praise. According to jazz singer Cassandra Wilson, "there's something in his [Davis's] sound [that] is so strong, so masculine. But at the same time there's another thing so intimate that [it] seems almost feminine."[11] Equally important, his musical compositions served to embellish the worshiping of jazz. The reality is: The spirit of his (Davis's) improvising (and music) soars; and because of this, Davis became more than a jazz myth.

In general, and on the whole, Miles Davis was able to conceptualize and put in place his irresistible musical ideas, thoughts, impressions, and artistic views, which went beyond, perhaps, a person's normal appreciation. Furthermore, science writer J. R. Minkel writes, "Jazz greats [like Davis] have said that spinning off an improvised tune is like entering another world." Moreover, "improvising a jazz tune puts the brain in an altered state."[12] Davis also knew that Jazz could also be a galvanizing reminder that music is for *everyone*. This assertion is one specific thing that people should all understand about the jazz music lexicon. As for his music, Miles Davis "was fond of saying, [it] speaks for itself."[13] Perhaps we need reminding that Davis (while he lived) was like a violent storm, blowing his horn beautifully across the jazz landscape. The dynamics in his music of several jazz styles was absolutely amazing, as his trumpet playing rightfully commanded attention. And as discussed earlier in this book, Davis "was a pioneer, innovator and trendsetter, all the while producing constantly changing styles and consistently outstanding work," which was "always moving forward and changing;" and "unparalleled in music."[14] For example, Davis's no-holds barred jazz is demonstrated in his 1972 *On the Corner* album, which "was derided as if it threatened the very fabric of jazz, or possibly music in general."[15] Nothing, however, could have been further from the truth, as Davis's *On the Corner* album is real *funky* while remaining hard-hitting; and presenting an off-beat and densely textured sound. Davis was at the height of jazz *funkatude*, as he used "loops, overdubs, [backbeats], and splices, creating "a captivating sound collage."[16] Critics and jazz purists (in 1972) hated the album, but *On the Corner* has become a consistent sound in terms of electronic music, and "hailed as one of Davis's most important works." Music writer Spencer Patterson puts it this way:

> In a way, the LP's dense sonic stew is more akin to modern electronic music than jazz, though it features traditional jazz instruments, such as saxophone and trumpet. [But] "On the Corner" presents a rather formidable listening experience for newcomers.[17]

Davis, of course, never believed that his *On the Corner* musical ideas would be a flop or rejected, because he thought deeply about what he was doing, particularly on this album. Notably, Davis always thought through musical things in a provocative way. This is to say that Davis put things together musically far better than, perhaps, any other jazz musician at the time. If nothing else, this accolade might have seemed "strange considering that Davis made a career of defying the expectations of critics and audiences alike, but it [was] just one more paradox associated with this mercurial [jazz] artist."[18] Also, according to music critic Larry Kart, everything Miles Davis played came "down to the blues; and despite the electronic-funk trappings of his [bands], Davis's blues [was] always the jazz blues."[19] To be fair, his music always had a kind of rough edge, bluesy swing to it, because "the music of Miles Davis is the music of a deep thinker on the African-American experience."[20] More importantly, "Miles [Davis] was a true master of restraint with regard to the creative process of his improvised lines."[21] Which is to say that Davis's innovative "lines are more varied and original than any other trumpeter, of his time."[22] In many ways, Davis's music was a metaphor for black manhood. As professor of American studies at Yale, John Szwed explained: "Davis embodied a new style of Black identity, a stance that was existential rather than ideological in nature, and therefore all the more unnerving to white racists."[23] Additionally, Davis had a notorious love-hate relationship with white Americans.

And those whites who recorded or produced his music could be infuriated with him. But Davis couldn't stand whites who were racists. As such, Davis was often rebuked for making insensitive remarks about white people; but he didn't give a damn. It is not farfetched or overreaching to say that Miles Davis disliked some whites, especially white cops. In other words, "Davis [was] by no means indiscriminate in his hostility to whites."[24] When asked in an overseas interview in 1985 about what he wanted to be remembered for, Davis quipped: "I don't know. I can't think of anything I'd want them to say. Oh, yeah. One thing: I'm not white. 'He wasn't white.' That's what I'd want them to say."[25] Moreover, Miles Davis didn't care about the stench of jealousy and racial hatred; otherwise, he never would have been able to perform. And aside from his feelings about some white people, Davis was "a complex, stubborn, proud [black] man, but curiously without an excessively inflated ego for one who [had] achieved so much."[26] Many were acutely aware of Davis's personal, negative baggage during his entire music career. And he (Davis) *did* have an ego, despite words to the contrary. For example, in 1963, Tynan wrote: "Miles [Davis] in the flesh [was] not always as dependably superb as he [was] on his records. In public, he sometimes [displayed] the kind of diffidence that [concealed] (and often [protected]) enormous private egotism."[27] After all, Davis never shared his *real*, inner thoughts with *anyone*, even the many—black and white—women that he was involved with over the years.

Some saw Miles Davis as a wretched person. Many even felt he was obnoxious, a villain, despicable, and a conceited man, as he did things sometimes for shock value, especially bad things committed during his life, from his drug use, to the pimping and abuse of women (including his three wives). Perhaps we can forgive and offer our absolution to one of the greatest jazz musician the world has ever known, as Miles Davis left an irreducible impression on his jazz fans, and others who knew of him. Davis definitely left his mark on the jazz world. As mentioned, Davis was very serious about his music craft, and in a way, he became the musical preacher of jazz, or a *beacon* for jazz. Equally important, Miles Davis "is one of very few artists whose work transcends time and generations."[28] Perhaps Davis believed that God, or some spiritual being, was on his side, or was guiding him. Characteristically spiritual in his own way, Miles Davis literally became the voice of jazz, like a god. Indeed, "his individuality and constant desire to stretch himself symbolized jazz."[29] He certainly had a god-like wisdom when it came to jazz, or the future of his "social music." Also, despite words to the contrary, Davis was a pioneer of sorts when it came to electric, new wave, and contemporary jazz; but he wasn't given a lot of credit or recognition (at least, what he thought he deserved) for laying the groundwork for such impactful music.

It was as if Miles Davis absolutely disrupted musical expectations the entire time he played jazz and recorded his music. Was this ability his godly gift? Richard Cook writes:

> Perhaps his [Davis's] two great gifts were his ability to lead and focus [musical] groups thick with talent but lacking a collective persona; and his charisma as a soloist, employing an uncanny knack of turning a musical situation in the direction he chose and using his own instrumental voice to personify it. As an icon, both in the music and at the high end of popular culture, he has no jazz rivals: even Armstrong and Ellington have to bow to him in that regard.[30]

So was Miles Davis able to succeed because he was in the right place at the right time? Above all, Davis made musical changes that made a significant difference with the incomparable jazz, or "social music." Jazz, of course, is also a state of being; and Davis understood this fact better than most, even though he didn't like the term (jazz) itself. The late Max Roach, who was a great jazz drummer, and a friend of Miles Davis came to embrace his way of thinking about the term; because "late in his [sterling] career," (Roach also) "rejected the term "jazz" altogether, saying it relegated his music to second-rate venues and low pay."[31] With perhaps a wink of an eye, Miles Davis had changed the direction and progression of jazz. Therefore, he couldn't escape the criticism from a *phalanx* of jazz purists, and the jazz press, who didn't like Davis's venturing into electronic, jazz-funk, or jazz rock fusion music. But Davis didn't care, as he ploughed ahead with his music and creativeness. Davis, of course, needed to explore new musical territory, to produce jazz that was meaningful to him, and overwhelming to people who loved his music. Indeed, what Miles Davis did musically was something interesting, precious, and curious in itself, because when other jazz musicians were trying to figure out what Davis was doing, or playing—to change his sound—he had already moved on to the next thing, like leaving acoustic jazz in the dust. After his death, Davis was even inducted into the Rock and Roll Hall of Fame, as mentioned, on November 28, 2005, where the Foundation board members of this esteemed music organization announced:

> Miles Davis was one of the 20th century's most creative artists changing the sound of popular music many times in his six decade career. His music

experimentation beginning in the late 60's created a fusion of jazz with Rock and Roll, soul, funk and hip hop.[32]

Unfortunately, jazz purists and critics, perhaps, didn't like that Miles Davis was given this prestigious Rock and Roll Hall of Fame honor/award. Some also felt that it was deeply offensive and degrading for Davis to later serve as the opening act to young, white rock, and rollers. Why? It was as if the critics thought that Davis should have been excommunicated from the "Jazz Church," for his jazz-rock fusion transformation, and break-away from the traditional jazz platform. But what exactly did they know? To be sure, some jazz critics saw Miles Davis in a negative light, like the late Stanley Crouch, who *never* liked Davis's electric music. Perhaps it was painful for Crouch to witness Davis's musical metamorphosis from acoustic jazz to jazz-rock. Or perhaps Crouch thought that Davis's new sound was like listening to a perfect bugler gone wrong, with his harebrained musical ideas. But we should also wonder if Crouch had even listened to all of the jazz trumpeter's electric music? Probably not. Another jazz critic, Greg Tate, has unfairly written that Davis's electric *Live-Evil* album "tracks like a gonzo invasion of the ghetto by technically advanced booty snatches from a parallel universe."[33] What exactly does Tate mean by such an asinine comment? It should be noted that some jazz critics don't have a clue about what it means to be an innovative jazz musician like the late Miles Davis, as they are stuck or hampered by living in the stagnate, jazz past.

No matter how often jazz critics panned Davis's music, he rose from the ashes, so to speak, again and again, while showing his skills at playing his horn. Davis is still talked about today, and he will always be missed for some time to come. Perhaps the reason that Miles Davis remains revered by jazz fans, even after his death, is because he never begged for forgiveness to *anyone* for his actions, even when he was wrong. Also, as mentioned previously in this book, Davis really didn't have *any* regrets, because his peculiar behavior and style is what made him who he was, especially in regard to his odd or eccentric choices in life. Before Miles Davis died at St. John's Hospital and Health Center in Santa Monica, California, he had been contemplating the future and discussing new musical ideas, for his next album, with talented young musicians like Marcus Miller, Prince, and others. Indeed, his "final studio project, *Doo Bop*, found him collaborating with Brooklyn rapper Easy Mo Bee on a synthesis of hip-hop, doo-wop and be-bop. Unsurprisingly," Miles Davis "was still forging new connections and avenues of [musical] expression until the very end of his life."[34] Had Davis lived, we can only imagine what his jazz-rock, funk, and Hip-Hop music would have evolved into. For many admirers and jazz fans, the music is just not the same, because Miles Davis is not in our presence today. Finally, it should be understood that a lot of melancholy exists in the landscape of jazz, because of the absence of the god-like musician at the forefront of jazz or "social music" for so many years. But in the years since his death in 1991, Davis's music continues to capture the listener's ear, as he "is still the future. [Davis] is for damn sure a glorious [music] past."[35] Unfortunately, we have to live in a world without Miles Dewey Davis. And it is hard to shake knowing that the great jazz man is not with us anymore, but his music goes on.

NOTES

1. Kenneth Tynan, "Miles Apart," *Holiday*, February 1963, 101. Miles Davis wasn't swayed by anyone when it came to his music, with the possible exception of the late Gil Evans. Furthermore, Davis wasn't locked into jazz tradition, nor living in the jazz music past.

2. R. J. De Luke, "Miles: Ever Changing, Ever Perplexing," *All About Jazz*, 1996–2005, 1, http://www.allaoutjazz.com/php/article.

3. "Miles Davis Biographer John Szwed Interview," *Jerry Jazz Musician*, January 27, 2003, 17, http://www.jerryjazzmusician.com/mainHTML.cfm.

4. "Cassandra Wilson Pays Homage to Miles Davis March 31 Concert," March 12, 1999, http://www.uiowa.edu/-ournews/1999.

5. "Miles by the Box," *BMG Jazz Club*, November 2004, 4.

6. Francis Davis, "Jazz–Religious and Circus," *The Atlantic Monthly*, February 2000, 90.

7. Frank Tirro, "Constructive Elements in Jazz Improvisation," *American Musicological Society*, vol. 25, no. 2 (Summer 1974): 285.

8. Tirro, "Constructive Elements," 288.

9. "Cassandra Wilson Pays Homage," 2.

10. Jeremy Goodman, "Miles Davis," Silver Chips Online, February 16, 2005, 1, http://silverchips.mbhs.edu.

11. "Cassandra Wilson Pays Homage," 2.

12. J. R. Minkel, "The Roots of Creativity," *Scientific American Mind*, June/July 2008, 8.

13. De Luke, "Miles: Ever Changing," 1.

14. De Luke, "Miles: Ever Changing," 1.

15. Spencer Patterson, "Davis' 'On the Corner' is No Pedestrian Effort," *Las Vegas Sun*, sec. 16E, April 8, 2005.

16. Patterson, "Davis' 'On the Corner' Is," 16E. The collective musical energy of Miles Davis on his album, *On the Corner* (1972), shows "a seemingly effortless grasp of *funk* without sacrificing the rhythmic, melodic and harmonic nuance that had been present throughout his entire career." See "Miles Davis Biography," *8notes.com*, 2000–2011, 4, http://www.8notes.com/biographies/davis.

17. Patterson, "Davis' 'On the Corner' Is," 16E. "On The Corner" actually captures the public and cultural imagination when it comes to jazz. Many felt that Davis,

at one time, was disconnected from the greater jazz community; but Miles Davis thought that such matters and picayune things were totally and utterly irrelevant.

18. Marshall Bowden, "Miles Davis Biography," *Jazzitude*, 2001/2002, 1, http://www.jazzitude.com/milesbio.htm.

19. Larry Kart, *Jazz in Search of Itself* (New Haven: Yale University Press, 2004), 213.

20. Greg Tate, "Silence, Exile, and Cunning: Miles Davis in Memoriam," in *Flyboy in the Buttermilk: Essay on Contemporary America* (New York: Fireside, 1992), 86.

21. "Biography of Miles Dewey Davis, 1926–1991" the official Davis web site, 1, http://www.milesdavis.com/bio.

22. "Biography of Miles," 1.

23. Adam Shatz, "Cool in Every Way," *The New York Times*, sec. 7, December 29, 2002.

24. Hubert Saal, "Miles of Music," *Newsweek*, March 23, 1970, 100. According to Richard Cook, Davis was "consumed by the corrosive consequences of racism, which obsessed him, and drugs, which shadowed him for most of his adult life, he could be a despicable character, even to friends and lovers; yet he was equally beloved by most of those who knew him." See Richard Cook, *Richard Cook's Jazz Encyclopedia* (London: Penguin books, 2005), 153.

25. George Varga, "The Miles Davis Interview," *Overseas*, July 1985, 34.

26. Saal, "Miles of Music," 100.

27. Tynan, "Miles Apart," 101.

28. Edna Gundersen, "Miles Davis: The Complete Columbia Album Collection," *USA Today*, sec, 14D, November 27, 2009.

29. Scott Yanow, "Miles Davis," *Jazz Heritage Society*, 2005, 15.

30. Richard Cook, *Richard Cook's Jazz Encyclopedia* (London: Penguin Books, 2005), 153. To be sure, Miles Davis "possessed one of the most gifted and curious minds in music history; and compromise was not in his blood." See "Miles Davis Biography," *The Rock and Roll Hall of Fame and Museum*, 1, http://rockhall.com/inductees/miles.

31. Matt Schudel, "Jazz Drummer Roach Dies," *Las Vegas Review-Journal*, sec. 5B, August 17, 2007.

32. "Rock and Roll Hall of Fame and Museum: Programs: Public Programs," *Press Room*, November 28, 2005, 2, http://www.rockhall.com/museum/releases.

33. Greg Tate, "The Electric Miles," *Down Beat*, part two, August 1983, 22. It should be noted that Davis's "career-long example of pushing the boundaries has influenced many of rock's leading lights, particularly those who eschewed the status quo for musical explorations on rock's more experimental tip." See "Miles Davis Biography," *The Rock and Roll Hall of Fame and Museum*, June 9, 2011, 1.

34. "Miles Davis Biography," *The Rock and Roll Hall of Fame and Museum*, 2, http://rockhall. com/inductees/miles. Therefore, Davis was trying to embrace his musical future with strength and optimism, as he tried to get things done.

35. Gary Giddins, "Miles to Go, Promises to Keep," *Village Voice*, October 15, 1991, 83, 94–95.

Chapter 21

In a Quiet Way

In many ways, we can argue that Miles Davis was one of the best jazz trumpeters of all time. But this is still subject to debate by the jazz purists and others who criticized Davis, even at the height of his popularity, because some didn't like his creative and different musical path. Davis was able to reimagine his performance music, but jazz critics especially didn't like that he "moved into the larger, more lucrative, rock venues of his younger contemporaries."[1] Davis was also particularly adept at traveling the world and playing his horn. Indeed, before his death, and "throughout his last decade he toured and recorded prodigiously,"[2] spreading his jazz, or "social music" message. Additionally, Davis performed "regularly through the last years of his life," despite his poor and deteriorating health.[3] Most importantly, Davis was not a jazz charlatan, just because of his jazz-rock fusion music, as discussed already in this book; or because he (Davis) wanted to embrace and play pop tunes, like with some of the songs of Michael Jackson, Cindi Lauper, and Prince. In regard to Miles Davis and Prince, jazz critic Paul Tingen writes:

> Although the planned collaboration between Miles [Davis] and Prince came to nothing, Prince did send Miles eight instrumental compositions in the beginning of 1991. Miles played three of these, "Jail Bait," "A Girl and Her Puppy," and "Penetration," during his 1991 tour. Some of these live performances found their way onto [music] bootlegs, but what was hitherto unknown is that Miles went into the recording studio during the German leg of his 1991 tour, and laid down these three tunes with his live band.[4]

For such efforts, Davis was admired and widely celebrated in the larger, musical scheme of things, because he became a worldwide jazz-rock *Phenom*. But it was something that Davis hadn't thought much about, all things considering. Or perhaps he didn't care. Of course, Davis had a dark, brooding, self-effacing personality that sometimes matched his music. Nevertheless, jazz purists claimed that Davis relied too much on his various bands, rather than strong or powerful trumpet playing. During his last performance at the JVC Jazz Festival in New York in 1991, for example, Davis "was incapable of sustaining more than a few notes at a time,"[5] but it was more because of his serious medical problems and other physical ailments, more than anything else. Moreover, Jazz writer Mike Zwerin stated that "People say that his [new] musicians [were] not up to [his] sidemen of the past." But Miles Davis played "just enough," and "his [young] musicians [were] just right for the [overall] textures" of his sound. Therefore, Davis often stood "in the middle of his [sometimes] seven" piece bands, "signaling with a wave of his [trumpet] bell or a pointed finger."[6] And even though Davis, an elder jazz statesman, was never considered the best trumpeter in terms of his technique; in all other aspects, he was more than brilliant, as he inspired, as mentioned, the next generation of jazz musicians. But whether Davis was the greatest jazz trumpeter remains to be determined for some music critics. All in all, the music and "work of [Miles Davis] the trumpeter" makes "the most important single figure in the history of jazz, and one of the great cultural icons of the 20th century."[7] Furthermore, the jury is still out in terms of *any* musician taking over Davis's reign as the world's greatest jazz man, because he was the most successful, accomplished, and versatile black jazz musician during his era; and even after his untimely death.

Davis spent years perfecting his trumpet sound, creating his musical voice like no other musician. But when it was all said and done, Davis simply thought of himself as just a different or special trumpet man; because he never felt inadequate compared to his peers. Moreover, Davis wasn't ashamed of the publicity he sought for himself, because he thrived on self-promotion, becoming sort of the *epicenter* of jazz or the "social music" world. No one would argue that Miles Davis, during his remarkable life, had been anything less than phenomenal, as he reached the pantheon of jazz *gods*. Also, his music today appeals to a wide range of listeners, or people from different backgrounds, especially the newly proclaimed jazz fans. Davis also got a tremendous response from his jazz fans all over the world, but most especially in Japan, South America, and Europe, because his music was never underrated by those who knew him and his work. Davis's exemplary music even today sounds new and fresh. More than any other jazz musician, Davis earned his place in American music history; and many jazz fans who supported Davis were glad to see him finally be given his due. But consider: Davis sometimes felt under-appreciated. Furthermore, critics should not downplay Davis's role in jazz music with their controversial and specious rhetoric about his uneven trumpet playing, which they thought was like so much noise, because he

(Davis) was still (or always) looking for different ways of musical expression. To say the least, Davis never abandoned his quest to create new, spiritual music, no matter the odds or circumstances—and criticism. Of course, Davis's unerring judgment about jazz and/or his "social music" set him apart from other jazz musicians. Also, in this respect, we are still wondering who will be the breakout jazz trumpeter, like a Miles-Davisesque jazz star. Indeed, jazz trumpeters today struggle to compete with Davis's body of work, style, and musical output. Additionally, many jazz musicians still have a problem with just being jazz artists or entertainers, like Miles Davis. About entertainers, the late jazz bandleader of the swing era, Artie Shaw once stated that "An entertainer is out primarily to please people." However, "the role of an artist is essentially to please himself," to actually "stretch out the boundaries of the medium to put sounds on silence that weren't there,"[8] which jazz musicians always strive for with their improvisations. Davis, perhaps, understood what Artie Shaw believed, because he considered himself a musician, an artist, and an entertainer.

In the end, things have changed considerably for the better when it comes to jazz, mainly because Miles Davis made a personal statement with his music. And regardless of a person's musical taste, *he* or *she* can find something that they like about Miles Davis's music. Also, listeners don't have to be intellectuals to enjoy his music; but they have to be willing to be musically challenged, because of the complexity of his trumpet sound. It is also reasonable to conclude that listeners are rarely disappointed or bored by his recordings. Davis's music must also be understood against the collective ideas and theory of jazz. In so many words, jazz is quintessentially American, or African American; and no one should forget this historical fact. But what exactly defines the jazz experience? Davis realized that he had to play his music from his own frame of reference—that is, as a black man living in a divided, fractured nation. Wayne Shorter called Davis "an original Batman," because

> He was a crusader for justice and for value. He'd be Miles Dewey Davis III by day, the son of Dr. Davis, and at night in the nightclubs [he'd be] in his lizard skin suits with the dark shades and [he would be] doing his Batman-fighting for truth and justice.[9]

Essentially, Shorter was telling us that jazz could be political, and so could Miles Davis. So was it his own pride and self-importance that made Davis so engaging and political? Admirers are no closer to knowing the *real* Miles Davis, and what exactly made him tick. We might know something of Davis's politics—that is, in terms of who gets *what*, *when*, and *how* in the jazz community; but fans and musicians are still trying to learn all of his secrets. After all, Davis was a (music) rebel to the very end. Marcus Miller explained: Davis "was acclaimed and criticized and nothing that was ever said to him made him change what he felt he had to do. That's very important for a musician to learn, because [we] can be so easily swayed by [some] people who have nothing to do with what you're about. They only know what you've already done; [but] they have no idea of your [musical] goals."[10] Without a doubt, Davis is still the "sound of jazz," because his music is incredibly important to musicians, students, and jazz fans alike—and the rest is history, as they say. In the final analysis, Davis represented "restlessness and querulous doubt rather than riot and open [musical] rebellion, just as the [great] lyricism of his [outstanding ballads] and solos."[11] In many ways, Davis should have been considered the savior of jazz while he lived. Which is to say that Miles Davis created a music that will be hard to forget in the future. Indeed, the fact that jazz or "social music" matters at all is a testament to Miles Davis. In this way, he is *immortal*. And when the final story is written about Miles Davis's genius and the fact that he made music—more than just the same old jazz—is commendable. With an analytical eye, we must also understand the purpose, or the zeitgeist of jazz and how this musical genre is far from dead. This is to say that jazz and Davis's music will be played and studied, even at major universities, long after his critics have left this world. Professor Christopher Harlos writes: "In the five decades since Miles Davis's brief encounter with institutionalized music history at Julliard, the gradual acceptance of jazz studies on the American campus is indicative of a more general call for research in areas of popular culture previously considered beyond the purview of traditional scholarship."[12] Indeed, jazz and the music of Miles Davis is a fixture now in music programs on college campuses across the United States.

Music students and jazz majors in higher education exist subconsciously in Miles Davis's universe, as his "social music" continues to shape the music world across our planet. Therefore, Davis's "influence was enormous when he was alive and has only increased in the [decades] since his death."[13] Moreover, Davis's accessible legacy is perhaps the magnificent music he created, making him one of the most studied jazz musicians, with the possible exceptions of the great Duke Ellington or Charlie "Bird" Parker. Thus, Davis was one of the greatest contributors to modern jazz. So where exactly does jazz go from here? Well, the *jazz faith* will last forever, and nothing says this more strongly than Miles Davis's recorded music, because it gives us an understanding of jazz itself. Miles Davis's influence in our concept of the "Jazz Church," or jazz religion, is not limited to his one-of-a-kind trumpet sound, and improvisations, as he took up the paintbrush later in life, creating large, beautiful, complex canvases. In this respect, Davis indulged his inner Picasso. With his painting, Davis was also influenced by the famous and late black artist Jean-Michel Basquiat as he was a true renaissance man. Hence, in

1980, Davis had "been seeking expression not just through music but through visual art," too. Therefore, "what began as a simple outlet for his creativity—developed into an obsession."[14] Before Miles Davis died in 1991, at the twilight of his career, he spent "several hours a day sketching and painting. His [excellent] art, like his music, [was] characterized by a commitment to true expression and change,"[15] which was another new thing for the jazz man. Davis once explained: When "I'm usually doing this [drawing or painting], and when I do this I don't do anything else. I can hardly get to [my] horn."[16] Davis, of course was extremely proud of his artistic accomplishments, same as his indelible mark on the jazz music world. According to Mike Zwerin, "It is not unusual for musicians," like Miles Davis, "to come to painting. This private and silent work can be a relief for someone who makes his living in [such] an endeavor," like with jazz or *social music*, "that requires collective effort [and] demands applause."[17] Zwerin goes on to write:

> It may be that musicians start to paint because there is something about music that no longer satisfies them. Stylistic curiosity might very well wane after leading the way through bebop, modality, Rock, [Doobop] and funk.[18]

Davis never tried to hide behind *anything*, even his art. Perhaps most important: Fans and others should admire the almost magic and singularity of his artistic vision and artwork. Davis's delicate and thought-provoking paintings are "mostly *abstract*, on canvas and paper," which are dense, sexy, and dark, evoking a sense of Pablo Picasso's great works, or of African imagery and mysticism. Davis used "acrylic paints, pencil and pastels," and worked ardently with Jo Gelbard, a white woman, and New York artist, who lived with Davis "for the last five years of his life."[19] Unfortunately, after Miles Davis's death, Jo Gelbard tried, in November 13, 2001, to sue the Miles Davis estate, claiming that "she was, by reason of the purported business relationship, entitled to certain estate assets." However, the State Supreme Court of New York disagreed, and dismissed the case (unanimously), "without cost."[20] There will probably be others who might lay claim to Miles Davis's legacy in the future, as he was triumphant in his music and artwork. So will these unnamed individuals be successful in their pursuits? Probably not. Through it all, Davis, as an artist and painter remains wildly popular—worldwide. Some of Davis's drawings and paintings, after his death, have even been exhibited in London "at The Gallery in Cork Street" in 2005.[21] And some of his artwork was displayed "at the New York's Nerlino Gallery in [the] early spring of 1990."[22] To be clear, Miles Davis was a self-taught artist, and his stunning artwork today is exhibited in galleries throughout the world. Of course, Davis followed "no school of thought and [sought] no consensus of opinion [about his art]; rather, he [pursued] his work separately—absorbing impulses and influences from the world around him, interpreting them visually, and trusting the results."[23] In this regard, Davis became a painter of some note, and his artwork will always be with us, and remembered. About Davis's artwork, Paul Tingen writes:

> Aside from Picasso in painting, there is no popular 20th century artist who has been able to remain modern until his death, and to hit the target in so many different styles. Miles [Davis] was able to achieve this because he constantly moved forward while never losing touch with his musical roots, and because he fully trusted his own musical judgements and never waited for others before making a move.[24]

With his numerous artworks, Miles Davis inevitably spoke to the entire world, so to speak, not just to his own jazz, or "social music" congregation. In a 1988 interview, Davis jokingly commented: "Fortunately, I have something to fall back on [as an artist]. I [also] make enough royalties so that I'll be 95 before I spend all the money and wear all my clothes."[25] We can only speculate about what Miles Davis would have been able to further achieve as a painter had he lived long enough, to further his craft as an artist and musician. Unfortunately, Davis died at the age of 65, never reaching the age of 95. But his aforementioned statement suggests that he finally felt, perhaps, that he was on firmer ground as an artist, even more so when he painted his sophisticated canvases. Just look at Davis's artwork (or his own self-portrait) on the cover of his *Amandla* album, to know that he could actually paint. Indeed, Davis's artwork and oil-paintings (as well as his music) have cemented his legacy. As a bandleader, Miles Davis was very tough and demanding; although he was mostly, "an introvert who combated his shyness by creating a forbidding image . . . frequently [appearing] angry in public, not only generally ignoring his audience but acting as if he despised them,"[26] or wanted to punch them, perhaps. In this respect, Davis's approach to life was like boxing, which he was also devoted to. He especially had an admiration for Jack Johnson, the first black man to win and hold the World Heavyweight Boxing championship. Miles Davis, of course, "drew parallels between [Jack] Johnson, whose career had been defined by the fruitless search for a great White Hope to dethrone him, and Davis's own career, in which he felt the establishment had prevented him from receiving the acclaim and rewards that were due him."[27] In addition, Davis felt that jazz or "social music" had never gotten the audience it truly deserved; and what black jazz musicians in particular, wanted. In 1970, Davis contributed "extensively to the soundtrack of a documentary"[28] about Jack Johnson "by filmmaker and fight promoter William Cayton (later famous for managing a young Mike Tyson)."[29] On this particular soundtrack, Miles Davis "plays some intense and adventurous solos," and most importantly, the music "comes across, in its style and attitude and rhythmic drive, like rock and roll—[because] no doubt Miles [Davis] felt that the free-spirited, rebellious image [or sound] of rock would communicate Johnson's own iconoclastic personality."[30] To that end, Davis on this unusual album gives us a template for the future of jazz; and it is unlike any other music in jazz history. This is to say that Davis's *Jack Johnson* music is much larger in theme and scope. Davis was a prolific talent and put a spotlight on the jazz music movement, particularly with another complete scoring of the 1987 film *Street Smart*, starring Morgan Freeman, Kathy Baker, and the late Christopher Reeve. The music on this film shows the deliberateness of Davis's musical process, as he kicks butt and takes names, so to speak, on this remarkable soundtrack. That said, Davis's abrasive trumpet sound probably felt right to him; and what he set out to do musically on *Street Smart* was extremely fruitful and relatable.

In no uncertain terms, Miles Davis was acutely aware of such serious music matters. Equally important, Davis's attitude about the racist America of the 1940s and 1950s had somewhat mellowed later in his life, especially in the late 1980s and early 1990s, as he was more appreciative of his audiences and fans, who really liked that Davis even took up acting, like his major role in the 1991 *Dingo* film, where he plays an aging jazz man; or his appearance on a Miami Vice episode in 1985, where Davis played a convincing drug dealer and a pimp, by the name of Ivory Jones. In this regard, Davis was able to show his acting chops. Davis was also able to energize his audiences' spiritual potential, perhaps, by his inspiring, soaring music, like on Davis's *Siesta* album with Marcus Miller. This Spanish-flavored music is the soundtrack for the film of the same name. Listen particularly to the track, *Los Felis*, which is close to a *godly* music. Jazz fans will be positively astonished or amazed by Davis's effervescent music on this *Siesta* album. Miles Davis also rightly acknowledged some of the other jazz greats that came before him, like Louis Armstrong, who had been successful as a popular jazz musician, movie actor, and public figure. Armstrong was also noted for being "the first *scat* singer, improving nonsense syllables in the manner of a horn."[31] Davis absolutely loved Louis "Satchmo" Armstrong. He also adored the great Duke Ellington, who once asked Davis, at the height of his fame to play in his Big Band, which he politely declined. Miles Davis's fame is still showing up in all sorts of ways, today, as jazz musicians maintain their prayers and devotion to his "social music," in the Church of the Holy Jazz Sepulcher, to use the metaphor. Jazz clubs and concert venues all over the world are the "brick and mortar" places for worshiping jazz.

More significantly, Davis was honored with numerous awards during his career and life, receiving several Down Beat, and Billboard awards for his music and trumpet playing. Before his death, Davis received twenty-four

Grammys; and was also given a Grammy Award for lifetime achievement in March 1990. He also received, in November 1984, "the Sonning Music Award for lifetime achievement in music."[32] Furthermore, Miles Davis, on July 16, 1991, was honored with Knighthood in France's Legion of Honor, which is the highest cultural honor in that jazz-loving country. Moreover, Davis was bestowed the title of "Sir" and inducted into "the Knights of Malta (by the Order of St. John) in November 1988, who was cited for being not only a [great visionary] musician, but in other [creative] realms," too, like his amazing "artistic impressions in oil-paintings and sketches, [which] have drawn critical acclaim [as already mentioned] and have been shown in [art] galleries around the world,"[33] like in Spain, Germany, France, Japan, Switzerland, the United States, and other countries. Then, there are statues of Miles Davis in his birthplace of Alton, Illinois; Nice, France, at the *Hotel Negresco on La Promenade des Anglais*, which shows Davis as a portly jazz trumpeter, in colorful, outrageous clothes. Additionally, there is a statue of Miles Davis in Kielce, Poland; and there is a bronze statue of the jazz man in Montreux, Switzerland, on the lake waterfront at Geneva. As of this writing, however, there is no wax figure of Miles Davis at Madame Tussaud's Museum of Wax Figures in London, which contains contemporary and historical individuals; but there is a wax statue of Miles Davis at the Griot Museum in St. Louis Missouri, whose original name was the Black World History Wax Museum. Finally, there was (at the time of this writing) a larger-than-life bronze sculpture of Miles Davis (shown in this book) and taken at Ed Dwight's Studio in Denver, Colorado. Ed Dwight is a black sculptor and artist, and former black test pilot and first black astronaut trainee in the NASA program. There are also beautiful bronze busts of Miles Davis taken at Ed Dwight's Studio and presented in this book. Bear in mind that all of these tributes to the foremost and legendary trumpeter, Miles Davis, are well deserved. And Miles Dewey Davis will never be a coincidental footnote in history. Even in death, Davis is still an enormously popular figure, who took the music and artistic path that suited him. According to jazz critic Ben Ratliff, for example, Miles Davis once declared "that he was no longer interested in music with a clear beginning or end, [and] the shock waves [in jazz] began."[34] So was what Miles Davis did in jazz a cardinal sin? The answer is no. And why did his success as a jazz man engender such envy? Even today, Miles Davis means so much to the jazz world. So what can we learn from this black man, this late, jazz trumpeter? Probably *everything* when it comes to jazz, or "social music." Davis is buried at The Woodlawn Cemetery in the Bronx, New York, where many jazz enthusiasts also wish or desire to be buried—that is, next to [Miles] Davis, or Duke Ellington, and Lionel Hampton,[35] and other jazz greats.

NOTES

1. "Miles Davis Biography," *8notes.com* (2000–2011), 4, http://www.8notes.com/biographies/davis.asp.
2. Howard Mandel, "Sketches of Miles," *Down Beat*, December 1991, 18.
3. "Miles Davis Biography," 5.
4. Paul Tingen, "Miles Beyond," *The Last Word Original Liner Notes*, April 2001, 18, http://www.miles-beyond-com/last.
5. "Miles Davis Obituary," *Race Matters.org*, 2001, 2, http://www.racematters.org/milesdavisobituary.htm (4/27/2011), 1–2. Davis's last concert events produced "sell-out" crowds, especially in Europe, as if he was a religious televangelist; with thunderous applauses and unbelievable feelings of excitement, even if he (Davis) was sometimes in bad form, or put on a bad show.
6. Miles Davis, "The Moveable Feast," *Jazz Forum*, issue 3 (1983): 49.
7. Sholto Byrnes, "Blowing Up a Storm," *The Independent*, online edition, April 1, 2005, 1, http://enjoyment.independent.co.uk.
8. Claudia Luther, "Bandleader Artie Shaw Dies," *Las Vegas Review-Journal*, sec. 1A & 10A, December 31, 2004.
9. Krystian Brodacki, "Wayne Shorter Remembers Miles Davis," *Jazz Forum*, January 1992, 26.
10. Mandel, "Sketches of Miles," 20.
11. Leonard Feather, "Miles and the Fifties," *Down Beat*, July 2, 1964, 98.
12. Christopher Harlos, "Jazz Autobiography: Theory, Practice, Politics," in Krin Gabbard, *Representing Jazz* (Durham: Duke University Press, 1995), 131.
13. Joe Goldberg, "Miles at 75," *Billboard*, vol. 113, issue 23 (June 9, 2001): 2 & 52, http://web17.epnet.com.
14. Miles Davis and Scott Gutterman, *The Art of Miles Davis* (New York: Prentice Hall Press, 1991), 1. Accordingly, "the hallmarks of Miles developing visual style are a bold, uninhibited use of color; a loose, improvisatory, yet definite sense of structure; and a delight in the expressive possibilities of the face." See the same reference.
15. Davis and Gutterman, *The Art of Miles Davis*, 1.
16. Davis and Gutterman, *The Art of Miles Davis*, 1.
17. Mike Zwerin, "Rio Women and Colorful Squares by Miles Davis, the Painter," *International Herald Tribune*, July 11, 1988, 1.
18. Zwerin, "Rio Women," 6. Davis it seemed had a natural ability to paint, even at his advanced age. Talking about painting, Miles Davis once asked an interviewer, "Do you [or should you] approach a canvas like a musical composition, with some form in mind? Or do you figure it out as you go along?" Perhaps Davis already knew the answers to his questions, because nothing stopped him from drawing and painting. See the same reference and page number.
19. Byrnes, "Blowing Up a Storm," 1.
20. "Jo Gelbard, Appellant, v. Peter Shukat *et al*, Respondents – New York," *Case Law Full Display*, November 13, 2001, 1–2, http://www.lexisone.com/lxl/caselaw/freecaselaw.

21. Byrnes, "Blowing Up a Storm," 1.
22. Davis and Gutterman, *The Art of Miles Davis*, 2.
23. Davis and Gutterman, *The Art of Miles Davis*, 3.
24. Tingen, "Miles Beyond," 20. According to Art and Entertainment writer Kristen Peterson, Picasso once said that a picture "is not conceived and determined in advance." Instead, "while you're doing it, it follows the change ability of the idea." Davis, of course, had the same attitude with his artwork. See Kristen Peterson, "Take Five: Picasso Ceramics Exhibit," *Las Vegas Sun*, June 14, 2007, 7. But when asked what his drawings and paintings had to do with his music, Davis replied: "They don't have anything to do with the music." See: Gary Giddins, "Miles Davis at 60," *The Village Voice*, August 1986, 5.
25. Zwerin, "Rio Women," 6. It has been reported that Miles Davis's wealth at the time of his death was nineteen million dollars. His estate is worth considerably more today.
26. Scott Yanow, *Trumpet King: The Players who Shaped the Sound of Jazz Trumpet* (San Francisco, CA: Backbeat Books, 2001), 117. Although Davis had several interviews during his life, he was still a man of few words.
27. "Miles Davis Biography," 5. See also Jack Johnson, *My Life in the Ring & Out* (New York: Dover Publications, Inc., 2018).
28. "Miles Davis Biography," 5.
29. Michael Holman, "Miles Davis v. Wynton Marsalis: Jack Johnson in Jazz," *All About Jazz*, March 8, 2005, 1, http://www.allaboutjazz.com/php/article.
30. Holman, "Miles Davis v. Wynton Marsalis," 2.
31. *Merriam-Webster's Collegiate Encyclopedia*, 1st ed., s.v. "Armstrong, Louis."
32. "Miles D. Davis III," *Movers and Shakers of the Sovereign Military Order of Malta*, September 2, 2008, 3, http://moversandshakersofthesmom.blogspot.com.
33. "Miles D. Davis III." Miles Davis was enormously touched and honored when he was granted knighthood by the Knights of Malta. He wanted people to call him Sir Miles Davis, because of this honor; and even his gravestone shows this honorific.
34. Ben Ratliff, "A Jazz Innovator During His Late, Funky Phase," *The New York Times*, August 3, 1997, 1–3, http://www.nytimes.com/1997/08/03/arts.
35. "Cemetery plot buyers stay close to jazz greats," *Las Vegas Review-Journal*, sec. 3A, July 11, 2014. See also Davis Gonzales, "A Knight of Jazz Enters It's Royal Cemetery; Sir Miles Joins the Duke, a King, and a Patriarch and Kindred spirits in Woodlawn, the Bronx," http://www.nytimes.com/1992/06/09.

Conclusion

Before his untimely death, Miles Davis felt a spiritual obligation to play his music and heavenly tunes. Indeed, Davis's music today still lifts up our collective heads to the sky or heavens, while his jazz or "social music" continues to burst into our thoughtful minds and imagination. To say the least, Davis has become part of *jazz lore*. It seemed God or the *Supreme Being* had a greater purpose for Miles Davis before he died, because of his insatiable appetite for jazz, or "social music." So is jazz indeed a religion? Perhaps. Moreover, did Miles Davis hear some *godly* message to play his trumpet the way that he did? Or was it Davis's singular musical voice that spoke to people? Equally important, did he speak with a musical voice that touched upon the *Holy Spirit*? Or was Davis's music close to the heavenly angels? Indeed, was he a jazz messenger of God? It should be noted that Miles Davis's "music always conveyed a certain depth, as if it came from some mystical place that only precious few 'tuned-in' individuals have access to."[1] Just listen to *any* of his recorded ballads. This is to say that Davis "carried a certain spirituality in his music." However, "he was not at all religious."[2] According to jazz writer Eric Nisenson, Davis "had no use for religion ever since he discovered as a boy that churches were [racially] segregated."[3] This was understandable (on the part of Miles Davis) given that God is supposed to be equal for all so-called races of people. So did Davis give credit to the *almighty* or himself? To be fair, Davis was preternaturally gifted as a musician. Therefore, "it's difficult to have a discussion of religion and spirituality regarding Miles Davis and not mention his music."[4] Obviously, there will always be a microscope on why and how Davis did things, especially musically. Additionally, jazz writer Julie Coryell explained that Miles Davis revealed "an almost supernatural, uncanny ability to read the thoughts, hopes, wishes, and fears of those around him."[5] Furthermore, Davis's inexplicable music still gives listeners food for musical thought, as his sound aptly symbolizes a sort of virtue and spirit. Beyond that Miles Davis's trumpet playing took commitment, talent, musical ability, and (most of all) timing. Furthermore, Davis proved his jazzy mettle over the years while he lived. But "he proclaimed no cosmic *evangel*, as did [John] Coltrane, and he [Davis] was neither a [blackish] visionary like Albert Ayler nor a mad scientist-poet like Ornette Coleman."[6] As for jazz spiritualism, a former (jazz) band member of Davis, Sonny Rollins had this to say: Davis had "more an amalgamation of . . . religious convictions, including [the] belief in reincarnation . . . [and] the blessings of the great Spirit."[7] In this way, Davis was unfailingly true to himself, rather than to some god.

Furthermore, in terms of jazz being a faith, Davis "always considered jazz to be a possession of Black America, and he resented what he perceived to be a sort of co-opting of jazz by white people."[8] To say the least, jazz is fundamentally a black music. And when it is viewed through the dynamics and prism of Miles Davis's musical career and background, it makes more than a lot of sense to bring this fact about jazz to the forefront. Professor of music at the University of Virginia, Scott De Veaux writes:

> Jazz is strongly identified with African-American culture, both in the narrow sense that its particular techniques ultimately derive from Black American folk traditions, and in the broader sense that it is expressive of and uniquely rooted in, the experience of Black Americans.[9]

The real faith in jazz, however, is essentially based on the belief that it is firmly a musical conviction. Or is jazz a fulfillment of a certain musical reality? More importantly, is jazz the root of the spirit in music generally? Clearly, "Jazz can amount to a religion for those fans whose dedication to it becomes a ruling passion in their lives, often to the amusement of their unconverted family and friends."[10] But as far as Davis's music is concerned, it is as if the discerning jazz listener can hear his thoughts through his horn, which is uniquely soothing and spiritual. Davis literally gave us another way to listen to jazz or "social music," without compromising or making any excuses. In this way, his music is like it came down from the brightest star in the heavens. Even jazz saxophonist and brother to jazz critic and trumpeter Wynton, Branford Marsalis, who once played in Davis's band and appears on his *Decoy* album, "credits the trumpeter [Davis] with teaching him how to listen, [or] how to say more with less."[11] For a jazz musician, Miles Davis garnered an inordinate amount of attention—that is, in terms of other jazz men. Of course, Davis had attained a level of cultural and musical *ubiquity* during his life that was unmatched, unless you compare him to Louis Armstrong or Duke Ellington. Nevertheless, many critics and jazz purists thought that Miles Davis (later) played in an amateurish way. But Eric Nisenson writes:

"Miles's music deeply [affected] people; he [was] able to reach a part of us that other musicians, no matter how accomplished their technique, cannot touch."[12] Indeed, with Davis's music, the listener can rejoice in the Majesty of God, as he was a spiritual force that rippled throughout the jazz community, with his angelic horn. Jazz enthusiasts were captivated by his recordings and performances, as his music (even today) speaks for itself. As prizewinning science-fiction writer Lucius Shepard tells us:

> He [Davis] turned his back on the audience and muttered into his horn as if pronouncing a curse he didn't want anyone to understand. He played mean, he played nasty, he played coolly sneering blurts of sound, and even when he played beautifully, it seemed he was commenting on beauty rather than lending it voice, that at the core of every melody was a disaffection that rendered beauty irrelevant, an attitude increasingly informed by a politics compounded of anger and heroin and egomania.[13]

Regardless, Miles Davis was considered a kind of music saint or prophet by popular acclaim. So did Davis strike a *Faustian* bargain in order to play his trumpet so beautifully; and while making lasting recordings? Or did he make the ultimate deal with the devil to play the way that he did? According to bestselling author Edward Hirsch, the mysterious trumpet sound of Miles Davis has "an aching, near-deathly purity." Hirsch goes on: Davis also had "a restless gift for innovation, a rock bed integrity, and something else ineffable,"[14] perhaps, like a sulky intelligence, close to the *Omega Point*. So should Davis be canonized by the so-called Church of Jazz, because he belongs to the whole world, like the Dalai Lama?[15] After all, there is no absoluteness in jazz; nor is there absurdity. Jazz, of course, at its essence, suggests a way of devotion in that we can seriously think about and listen to what is being musically imparted, with no misgivings or regrets. While he lived, Miles Davis understood these fundamental things, as well as the fact that jazz or "social music" was hard to play excellently or beautifully. But for the *uninitiated*, Davis's music might still fall on death ears, to use the pun. Still, in many respects, Davis *was* like the Dalai Lama, because he was an inspiring, spiritual/musical leader; and he got *unstinting* support from his young band members and others who played or worked with him over the years.

Equally important, it should be remembered that many of Davis's former band members have had nothing but great things to say about Miles Davis. For example, electric bassist Dave Holland stated: "Miles [Davis] was a great band leader. He liked to incorporate ideas of those involved in his [music] projects. He'd ask for suggestions. If he liked what he heard and felt it was appropriate to the tune, he'd say, *Let's do it*. It was a very organic process. Of course, Miles was at the center with a guiding hand."[16] Through it all,

Miles Davis, in terms of his music, had a forward-looking state of mind; and a remarkable sense of purpose. Which is to say that Davis followed his gut feelings when he made his music, which was paramount above all other things. But as a "jazz bandleader," Davis "discovered and nurtured as many young, gifted and previously unknown musical talent" as anyone, such as Miles's alumni: "John Coltrane, Sonny Rollins, Bill Evans, Herbie Hancock, Tony Williams and John McLaughlin,"[17] to name a few jazz men. So can we emphatically say that Miles Davis was one of the best jazz bandleaders ever? Perhaps. Beyond the sheer scale of the music Davis produced/recorded, he paved the way for many young jazz musicians. Thus, it wasn't true that Davis believed *only* in himself; but he did follow his own *North Star* when it came to his music, which was deeply emotional and timeless. Indeed, Davis put his heart and soul into playing his horn, sometimes concentrating to the point of exhaustion.

Davis was also hard on himself when it came to his music, but he never felt guilty for what he had accomplished. In this regard, Davis wouldn't let others marginalize him as a jazz musician, because his music was what defined him. As for his "social music," Davis's "musical thinking might be summed up succinctly as follows: the amalgamation of musical cultures . . . which combined classical, jazz, [rock], and ethnic elements."[18] Davis's jazz perspectives and groundbreaking musical innovations, and different paths of jazz (or "social music") continue to reverberate, even after his death. Nevertheless, Davis was sometimes underestimated, but he changed the sound of jazz as we know it. This is to say that Davis created new music that was beyond some of our own jazz experiences. And fans and other musicians looked to Davis for guidance when it came to jazz. Indeed, some listeners had something like a *god-like* affection for him, despite his reclusive nature, which only added to his (Davis's) mystique. Subsequently, the jazz community found many loyal fans over the years, because of the incomparable Miles Davis. Yet, some jazz purists and critics posthumously pooh-poohed Davis's jazz-rock fusion music, even when he was inducted in the *Rock and Roll Hall of Fame*. Some felt also that even the way that he dressed later in life was vaudevillian, or comical. But Davis's wardrobe style should have never been mistaken as being cartoonish or unprofessional, as it was all about being incontrovertibly cool. So was Davis's ability to change his style and music every five years (or so) the secret to his success and longevity as a jazz musician? Perhaps. Needless to say, we are still celebrating Davis's music, which is a testament to his universal appeal in the jazz and rock worlds.

In so many words, "Davis played jazz, period. But his forward-thinking sensibility, insatiably curious muse and eagerness to move music into uncharted realms made him a contemporary musician, irrespective of genre."[19] To be abundantly clear, Davis's music was not some kind of "one-trick pony," so to speak, because he was flexible (musically) and creative when it came to playing his impressive horn, particularly with hard rockers. Davis also built his legacy on the idea that his music should change, and become more accessible to *everyone*—or to *all* music lovers—not just a few jazz fans. And more than anything, Davis wanted to be remembered. So did Miles Davis really sell his soul to rock 'n' roll? Absolutely not. Davis's jazz-rock fusion music, of course, reflected something more in the genre; but it didn't diminish him in the eyes of his die-hard, jazz admirers, much to the chagrin of jazz purists, like Wynton Marsalis, who believed that Davis gave up "a large portion of his integrity."[20] But what Marsalis probably doesn't understand is that to remain pertinent, jazz must not be stagnant; and Davis's music captures the true essence of this belief. The point is, even though some people didn't like Miles Davis's amalgamation of jazz or "social music," and rock, they still didn't put him down for trying something musically different and new. Davis made himself plain: "Well, my main thing is to create and not to compare. You understand that? I don't wanna be like I used to be years ago, you know what I mean? I hope I've advanced through all the years in the sound and composition. Stravinsky never wrote anything the same way."[21] Davis's comments are important to understand, because he was highly intelligent, as mentioned, and always tried to follow through on his ideas, while putting a lot of thought into his music. However, some of his musical ideas, like jazz-rock, were rejected by some, even with his unflinching approach to playing his horn. But few of his jazz-rock fans forgot Davis, his music, and the way that he jammed with his *"bad-ass"* horn. Jon Pareles explained that Davis was "always looking for a next frontier. Not content with mastery, determined not to repeat himself, he kept looking ahead—chasing, and often seizing, that idea on the horizon."[22] In this particular way, Davis attained the most exalted position in jazz. He is even more popular and respected today than when he was alive; and *all* of his music is unforgettable, and etched in jazz history. On top of that, Davis gained both wealth and prestige from his music. Upon Miles Davis's death, Keith Jarrett, the great jazz pianist, who once played keyboards in Miles's electric band, reflected:

> Miles, while he was alive, was a resonating object. Everyone's playing resonated, somehow, off him. When [Davis died], there's no object there. Players are, all of a sudden, alone. . . . Everyone dies, but I think Miles was the strongest jazz presence that many people will ever see in their lifetimes, whether anyone thinks he was playing jazz at all in the last 20 years. It doesn't matter. He was still there. You can hear that he was capable of doing that if he wanted to.[23]

Jarrett is absolutely right in his brilliant assessment of Miles Davis, because he [Jarrett] knows that the late jazz man actually defied expectations and the musical imagination. To be sure, Davis tried to redefine jazz, as he was always in motion musically. More importantly, according to the late jazz drummer Max Roach, Davis was "*never* going to play anything banal." And he was always going "to play [music] his way."[24] In a large sense, Miles Davis ended jazz history with his music. Or did he? Furthermore, in no uncertain terms, Davis's music will remain important as each generation (in the future) discovers his recordings, which are still fresh as when he first made them. And whether we believe it or not, Miles Davis *was* political about most things, and to a certain degree, even with his music; although it's been argued that he wasn't necessarily political.[25] This notion, however, wasn't true. Indeed, Davis was about more than just his music. For example, "Throughout his life, Davis [had] been an outspoken critic of discrimination,"[26] and white racism. And he never apologized for speaking out. Moreover, being outspoken about racial politics never hurt his music career. Davis also took political stands against Jim Crow Laws, and white rule, especially when he had run-ins with white police. Moreover, Davis stood up for what he believed; and no one can take away from his political activism, or his skills as a bandleader and jazz trumpeter, particularly as he strove to influence the jazz music world. According to Ron Frankl, Miles Davis's "exquisite trumpet sound will always be one of the most distinctive voices in the history of jazz."[27] To say the least, Davis is still heard loud and clear throughout the music world. And the bravery of his work is significant, because Davis's brand of jazz runs deep.

Some believed that Miles Davis was proof of the existence of God, because of his immaculate trumpet playing, and electric music. To be honest, Davis was the *real* deal. After Davis's death in 1991, the Reverend Jesse L. Jackson, "at a memorial service, at St. Peter's Church on the East Side," in New York, stated: "I hope for [the archangel] Gabriel's sake, now that Miles Davis is on the scene [in heaven], that there is more than one seat in the trumpet section."[28] In regard to Jackson's comments, we must not deny the "colossus" spirit of Miles Davis, as he was iconic, legendary, and seemed to be in the jazz *limelight* for almost his entire adult life. And this was, perhaps, what separated Davis from other jazz musicians. Indeed, he was lauded by fans and jazz musicians alike, as earlier discussed. And like the jazz pianist Oscar Peterson, Miles Davis could "play so hot and so deep and earthly" that "it just shook you when you heard such musicians play."[29] Furthermore, even in death, Davis's legacy has grown; and his contributions to jazz cannot be overstated. Therefore, "Miles Davis [was] more than just a jazz musician; he [was] a cultural icon, known even to people who can't tell bebop from fusion."[30] Fortunately, the world still has an appetite for jazz. And this is always worth considering, given that Miles Davis was never a musical slouch; and no one has deflected from his jazz dominance. Perhaps Davis had wanted to die before a large audience, playing a lovely note. Or did he want to let go entirely, because he was too tired to continue his battle with death? Also, did Davis feel the weight of the entire jazz world? Or perhaps David felt like he had done enough—that is, he had made all the musical statements that he had wanted to make in life. No doubt, there is still a lot to learn about Miles Davis. Was he even from our world? To be honest, Davis remains a mystery, and "a deity unto himself."[31] Finally, his illustrious jazz and music acumen will never be forgotten, as he has been transformed into jazz *royalty*, and sainthood. Miles Davis was not an angel, but he was touched by greatness; and his death made him a great loss to the music world. It is difficult to imagine a time or place without his righteous "social music," or lovely sound. Consequently, there might never be another jazz man quite like Miles Dewey Davis.

NOTES

1. Tom Kershaw, "Miles Davis's Religion and Political Views," *The Hollowverse*, March 15, 2013, 1, https://hollowverse.com/miles-davis.

2. Kershaw, "Religion and Political Views," 1.

3. Eric Nisenson, *'Round About Midnight: A Portrait of Miles Davis*, updated edition (New York: Da Capo Press, 1996), 282.

4. Kershaw, "Religion and Political Views," 1.

5. Julie Coryell and Laura Friedman, "Miles Davis," in *Jazz-Rock Fusion: The People-Music* (New York: Delacorte Press, 1978), 42.

6. Lucius Shepard, "Miles Davis: He Was a Hero Descending, Never Flinching from the Experience," *Nation*, vol. 277, issue 3 (July 21/28, 2003): 2 & 22, http://web17.epnet.com/deliveryprintsave.

7. George W. Goodman, "Sonny Rollins at Sixty-Eight," *The Atlantic Monthly*, July 1999, 88.

8. Kershaw, "Religion and Political Views," 1.

9. Scott DeVeaux, "Constructing the Jazz Tradition: Jazz Historiography," *Black American Literature Forum*, vol. 25, issue 3 (Fall 1991):528.

10. Francis Davis, "Jazz-Religious and Circus," *The Atlantic Monthly*, February 2000, 90.

11. George Varga, "The Miles Davis Interview," *Overseas*, July 1985, 34.

12. Eric Nisenson, *The Making of Kind of Blue: Miles Davis and His Masterpiece* (New York: St. Martin's Press, 2000), 21.

13. Shepard, "He was a Hero," 2 & 22.

14. Edward Hirsch, *The Demon and the Angel: Searching for the Source of Artistic Inspiration* (New York: Harcourt, Inc., 2002), 204.

15. Richard Gere, "Dalai Lama: He Belongs to the World," *Time*, April 18, 2005, 17.

16. Dan Ouellette, "Bitches Brew," *Down Beat*, vol. 66, issue 12 (December 1999):32, http://proquest.umi.com/web?index.

17. Varga, "The Miles Davis Interview," 34.

18. Leonard Feather, "Miles and the Fifties," *Down Beat*, July 2, 1964, 98.

19. "Miles Davis Biography," *The Rock and Roll Hall of Fame and Museum*, 1, http://rockhall.com/inductee/miles.

20. Peter Culshaw, "A Talent for Making Music and Enemies: Hard Not to Like Him," *Brothers Judd Blog*, 1, http://www.brothersjudd.com/blog/archives.

21. Pawel Brodowski & Janusz Szprot, "Miles Speaks: I Don't Wanna be Like I Used To Be," *Jazz Forum*, vol. 6 (1983): 39.

22. Jon Pareles, "Miles Davis: The Alchemist and the Terrorist," *The New York Times*, October 6, 1991, 34.

23. Hank Bordowitz, "The Zen of Jazz Moves Keith Jarret," *Jazziz Magazine*, April/May 1993, 60.

24. Max Roach, comments in "Sonny: Memories of Miles," *Musician, Player, and Listen*, vol. 41, March 1982, 44. As far as Davis's jazz-rock fusion was concerned, Max Roach noted that the trumpeter was "good at marketing and if [that was] what the public will buy and accept, then [he would] play that too." In this respect, Davis was a self-promotional genius. See the same reference.

25. Kershaw, "Religion and Political Views," 2.

26. Varga, "The Miles Davis Interview," 34. "Such [political] matters," according to Leonard Feather, were "mild irritants but [politics didn't] seem to bother him deeply." Feather goes on to explain: "after [several] years of discrimination . . . [Davis] developed a protective armor heavy enough to inure him against solecisms." But Davis never tried to skirt political issues, particularly when they negatively affected him. See Leonard Feather, "Miles and the Fifties," *Down Beat*, July 2, 1964, 98.

27. Ron Frankl, *Miles Davis* (New York: Chelsea House Publishers, 1996), 117.

28. Paula Span, "Musicians, Friends Honor Jazz Legend Miles Davis," *The Washington Post*, sec. A26, October 6, 1991.

29. Marya Hornbacher, "Return of a Virtuoso," *Smithsonian*, January 2006, 60.

30. Marshall Bowden, "Miles Davis Biography," *Jazzitude*, http://www.jazzitude.com/milesbio. Davis's jazz hasn't waned. In fact, the rest of the world is catching up, as they begin to play his music. Devotees are likely to mention how Miles Davis touched them in some (spiritual) way. But you can't pigeonhole his music into just one category.

31. Francis Davis, "Jazz-Religious and Circus," *The Atlantic Month*, February 2000, 90. Davis's mellifluous music today deserves applause, as he still has a global audience, as jazz fans are still fascinated, to no end, with the jazz man.

Bibliography

"3 Jazz Profiles-Miles Davis." *BBC Radio*, February 16, 2006. http://www.bbc.co.uk/radio3/jazz/profiles/.

"African-American Music: The blues Had a Baby." *The Economist*, March 30, 2019.

"Armstrong, Louis." In *Merriam-Webster's Collegiate Encyclopedia*, edited by Mark A. Stevens, 91. Springfield, MA: Merriam-Webster, Inc., 2000.

"Biography of Miles Dewey Davis, 1926–1991." The Official Davis Website. http://www.milesdavis.com/bio (3/10/2005).

"Cassandra Wilson Pays Homage to Miles Davis March 31 Concert." March 12, 1999. http://www.uiowa.edu/-ournews/1999.

"Cemetery Plot Buyers Stay Close to Jazz Greats." *Las Vegas Review-Journal*, July 11, 2014.

"Davis Miles (1926–1991)." In *Who's Who in African American History*, edited by Sande Smith, 43. New York: Smithmark Publishers, Inc., 1994.

"Existentialism." In *Merriam-Webster's Collegiate Encyclopedia*, edited by Mark A. Stevens, 55. Springfield, MA: Merriam-Webster, Inc., 2000.

"Jazz." In *Merriam-Webster's Collegiate Encyclopedia*, edited by Mark A. Stevens, 841. Springfield, MA: Merriam-Webster, Inc., 2000.

"Jo Gelbard, Appellant, v. Peter Shukat et al, Respondents—New York." *Case Law Full Display*, November 13, 2001. http://www.lexisone.com/lxl/caselaw/freecaselaw.

"Miles (Dewey) Davis." In *Merriam-Webster's Collegiate Encyclopedia*, edited by Mark A, Stevens, 44. Springfield, MA: Merriam-Webster, Inc., 2000.

"Miles by the Box." *BMG Jazz Club*, November 2004, 4.

"Miles D. Davis III." *Movers and Shakers of the Sovereign Military Order of Malta*, September 2, 2008. http://moversandshakersofthesmom.blogspot.com.

"Miles Davis at Carnegie Hall." July 16, 1962. https://www.milesdavis.com/albmusmmilesdavis.

"Miles Davis Biographer John Szwed Interview." *Jerry Jazz Musician*, January 27, 2003. http://www.jerryjazzmusician.com/linernotes/miles.

"Miles Davis Biography in Full: Miles Dewey Davis III." *Biography.com* (1994–2010). http://www.biography.com/articles/Miles (4/25/2011).
"Miles Davis Biography." *8notes.com* (2000–2011). http://www.8notes.com/biographies/davis.asp.
"Miles Davis Biography." *The Rock and Roll Hall of Fame and Museum*. http://rockhall.com/inductee/miles (6/9/2011).
"Miles Davis Obituary." *Race Matters.org. The New York Times Company*, April 27, 2001. http://www.racematters.org/milesdavisobituary.htm.
"Miles Davis, Musical Dialogician." *Black Music Research Journal*, vol. III, issue 2 (Fall 1991): 255.
"Miles Davis, the Fifties." In *Jazz & Blues: The Definitive Illustrated Encyclopedia*, edited by Julia Rolf, 200. London: Flame Tree Publishing, 2007.
"Miles Davis: 1964–69 Recordings." *Coda* (May 1976): 8–14.
"Poetics of Sound, Miles Davis: 1954–1959." *Hear Music* (2005).
"Re: Cicely Tyson." *The New York Times Magazine*, January 31, 2021.
"Religion." In *Merriam-Webster's Collegiate Encyclopedia*, edited by Mark A. Stevens, 1360. Springfield, MA: Merriam-Webster, Inc., 2000.
"Rock and Roll Hall of Fame and Museum: Programs: Public Programs." *Press Room*, November 28, 2005. http://www.rockhall.com/museum/releases.
"The Jazz of Wayne Shorter: Serious Longevity." *The Economist*, November 16, 2013.
"Trumpeter Hubbard Dies at 70." *Las Vegas Review Journal*, January 1, 2009.
Adler, David. "The Man with the Golden Horn." *Jazz Times*, September 2004, 62.
Adorno, Theodor W. "On Jazz." *Discourse*, 12.1 (Fall/Winter 1989–90): 47–50.
Agoving, Michael J. "His [Miles Davis] Ensembles Epitomized Cool." *The New York Times*, March 13, 2016.
Albertson, Chris. "The Unmasking of Miles Davis." *Saturday Review*, November 27, 1971.
Albertson, Chris. Liner Notes to "Miles Smiles—Columbia Jazz, Contemporary Masters." Recording. New York: *Sony Music Entertainment, Inc.*, 1992.
Alkyer, Frank. "The Miles Files." *Down Beat*, December 1991.
Anderson, Lee J. "The Musings of Miles." *Saturday Review*, October 11, 1958.
Atkins, Ronald. "A Trumpet Fallen Silent." *The Guardian*, September 30, 1991.
Avakian, George M. "Where Is Jazz Going." *Down Beat*, September 1939.
Avakian, George. Liner Notes to "Miles Ahead, Miles Davis." Recording. *Columbia Records*, 1957.
Bailey, C. Michael. "Miles Davis: Miles Davis at Carnegie Hall." *All About Jazz*, June 1, 1998. https://www.allaboutjazz.com/miles.
Balliet, Whitney. "Jazz." *The New Yorker*, April 4, 1977.
Bambarger, Bradly. "Miles Davis' True Blue." *Billboard*, August 7, 1999.
Baraka, Amiri. Liner Notes to "Miles after Miles – Panthalassa: The Music of Miles Davis, 1969–1974." Recording. New York: *Sony Music Entertainment, Inc.*, 1998.
Battaglia, Andy. Review of "John Szwed: So What: The Life of Miles Davis." *ADCLUB*, February 28, 2003. https://aux.avclub.com/john-szwed.

Bauder, David. "Miles Davis Joins Rock 'n' Rollers." *Las Vegas Review-Journal*, March 14, 2006.

Belden, Bob, and John Ephland. "Miles . . . What Was That Note?" *Down Beat*, vol. 62, issue 12 (December 1995): 16. http://proquest.umi.com/pqdweb? index.

Berendt, Joachim-Ernst, and Günther Huesmann. *The Jazz Book: From Ragtime to the 21st Century*. Chicago, IL: Lawrence Hill Books, 2009.

Berger, Jonah. "Why 'Cool' Is Still Cool." *The New York Times*, November 22, 2015.

Bergstein, Barry. "Miles Davis and Karlheinz Stockhausen: A Reciprocal Relationship." *The Musical Quarterly*, vol. 76 (Winter 1992): 511.

Blumenthal, Bob. "Miles Glorious: The Man with the Brew." *The Boston Phoenix*, July 7, 1981.

Blumenthal, Bob. *Saxophone Colossus: A Portrait of Sonny Rollins*. New York: Abrams, 2009.

Bordowitz, Hank. "The Zen of Jazz Moves Keith Jarret." *Jazziz Magazine*, April/May 1993.

Bowden, Marshall. "Miles Davis Biography." *Jazzitude*, 2001/2002. http://www.jazzitude.com/milesbio.htm (9/13/2005).

Bowden, Marshall. "The Secret History of Miles Davis in the 1980s." *Jazzitude* (2001). http://www.jazzitude.com/milesdavis.

Boyd, Todd. "The Meaning of the Blues." *Wide Angle*, vol. 13, number 3 & 4 (July–October 1991): 57.

Brayton, Ed. "Miles Davis Redux." *Dispatches from the Culture Wares*, May 27, 2004. http://www.stcynic.com/blog/archives/2004/05/miles.

Breskin, David. "Searching for Miles: Theme and Variations on the Life of a Trumpeter." *Rolling Stone*, September 29, 1983.

Brodacki, Krystian. "Wayne Shorter Remembers Miles Davis." *Jazz Forum*, January 1992, 26.

Brodowski, Pawel, and Janusz Szprot. "Miles Speaks: I Don't Wanna be Like I Used to Be." *Jazz Forum*, 6 (1983): 38–39.

Brofsky, Howard. "Miles Davis and *My Funny Valentine*: The Evolution of a Solo." *Black Music Research Journal*, vol. 3 (1983): 32.

Byrnes, Sholto. "Blowing Up a Storm." *The Independent*, April 1, 2005. http://enjoyment.independent.co.uk/lowres.

Carter, Ron. Liner Notes, "Essay about My Funny Valentine." Recording. *Columbia Records*, September 25, 2004.

Carters, Gayle Jo. Quote by "Elijah Woods." *USA Weekend*, November 10–12, 2006.

Cheng, Jim. "'Blue' is a Different Kind of Look at Jazz Legend Davis." *USA Today*, October 9, 2000.

Chinen, Nate. "Jazz Apprentices Still Find Their Masters." *The New York Times*, July 22, 2012.

Chinen, Nate. "Recalling Miles Davis by Crossing Cultures." *The New York Times*, May 12, 2008. http://www.nytimes.com/2008/05/12/arts.

Clark, Cindy. "Kennedy Center Salutes America's Artists—With a Few Twists." *USA Today*, December 8, 2015.

Clark, Cindy. "The Night Belongs to Kennedy Center Honorees." *USA Today*, December 5, 2011.
Clark, Douglas. "Miles into Jazz-Rock Territory." *Jazz Journal*, vol. 30 (June 1977): 12–14.
Cole, Bill. *Miles Davis: A Musical Biography*. New York: William Morrow, 1974.
Cook, Mervyn. Photograph of W.C. Handy. *Jazz*. New York: Thames and Hudson, Inc., 1998.
Cook, Richard, and Frances S. Saunders. "Miles Too Popular." *New Statesman*, vol. 130, issue 4533 (April 16, 2001): 45. http://web17.epnet.com.
Cook, Richard. *It's About That Time: Miles Davis On and Off Record*. New York: Oxford University Press, 2005.
Cook, Richard. *Richard Cook's Jazz Encyclopedia*. London: Penguin Books, 2005.
Coryell, Julie, and Laura Friedman. "Miles Davis." In *Jazz-Rock Fusion: The People-Music*. New York: Delacorte Press, 1978.
Crips, George R. *Miles Davis: An Impact Biography*. New York: Franklin Watts, 1997.
Crouch, Stanley. "Play the Right Thing." *The New Republic*, February 12, 1990.
Crouch, Stanley. Liner notes to Shirley Horn's "You Won't Forget Me." Recording. New York: Clinton Recording Studio, 1990.
Crouch, Stanley. *The All-American Skin Game, or the Decoy of Race: The Long and the Short of It, 1990–1994*. New York: Pantheon books, 1995.
Culshaw, Peter. "A Talent for Making Music and Enemies: Hard Not to Like Him." *Brothers Judd Blog*, January 29, 2003. http://www.brothersjudd.com/blog/archives.
Dalzell, Rebecca. "Paris is for Jazz Lovers." *Las Vegas Review-Journal*, March 22, 2015.
Davis, Clive. "Gypsy of the Left Bank." *The Sunday Times*, July 25, 2010.
Davis, Francis. "Jazz-Religious and circus." *The Atlantic Month*, February 2000.
Davis, Gregory, and Les Sussman. *Dark Magus: The Jekyll and Hyde Life of Miles Davis*. San Francisco, CA: Backbeat Books, 2006.
Davis, Miles, and Quincy Troupe. *Miles: The Autobiography*. New York: Simon & Schuster Paperbacks, 1989.
Davis, Miles, and Scott Gutterman. *The Art of Miles Davis*. New York: Prentice Hall Press, 1991.
Davis, Miles. "The Moveable Feast." *Jazz Forum*, issue 3 (1983): 49.
De Luke, R. J. "Miles: Ever Changing, Ever Perplexing." *All About Jazz*, 1996–2005, 1. http://www.allaoutjazz.com/php/article.
Deffaa, Chip. Liner Notes to "Miles Davis: The Complete Concert, 1964 and My Funny Valentine, Plus Four & More—Columbia Jazz Masterpieces." Recording. New York: *Sony Music Entertainment, Inc.*, 1992.
Demichael, Don. "Miles Davis." *Rolling Stone*, December 13, 1969.
DeVeaux, Scott. "Constructing the Jazz Tradition: Jazz Historiography." *Black American Literature Forum*, vol. 25, issue 3 (Fall 1991): 528.
Dodero, Camille. "Lenny Kravitz Remembers the Greats Who Shaped His Life and Music." *Maxim*, September 2014.

Doershuck, Bob. "Miles Davis: The Picasso of Invisible Art." *Keyboard* (October 1987): 66–69.
Feather, Leonard. "Miles Davis' Miraculous Recovery from Stroke." *Ebony*, December 1982, 64.
Feinstein, Sascha, and Kathy Sloane. *Keystone Corner: Portrait of a Jazz Club*. Bloomington and Indianapolis, IN: Indiana University Press, 2012.
Fink, Jerry. "All That Jazz—And More." *Las Vegas Sun*, April 17, 2007.
Fink, Jerry. "No Desire to Settle Down." *Las Vegas Sun*, November 12, 2007.
Frankl, Ron. *Miles Davis*. New York: Chelsea House Publishers, 1996
Freeman, Philip. *Running the Voodoo Down: The Electric Music of Miles Davis*. San Francisco, CA: Backbeat Books, 2005.
Gabbard, Krin. "Signifyin(g) the Phallus: Mo' Better Blues and Representation of the Jazz Trumpet." *Cinema Journal*, vol. 33, issue 1 (Fall 1992): 47.
Gabbard, Krin. *Hotter Than That: The Trumpet, Jazz, and American Culture*. New York: Faber and Faber, Inc., 2008.
Gans, Charles J. "At 74, Jazz Pianist Hancock Remains Open to Possibilities." *Las Vegas Review-Journal*, October 30, 2014.
Gardner, Barbara J. "The Enigma of Miles Davis." *Down Beat*, January 7, 1960.
Gates, Henry L., Jr. *100 Amazing Facts about the Negro*. New York: Pantheon Books, 2017.
Gennari, John. "Jazz Criticism: Its Development and Ideologies." *Black American Literature Forum*, vol. 25, issue 3 (Fall 1991): 23. http://webliks2.epnet.com/Deli veryPrintsave.asp?tb (3/29/05).
Gere, Richard. "Dalai Lama: He Belongs to the World." *Time*, April 18, 2005.
Giddens, Gary. "Miles's Wiles." *The Village Voice*, August 5–12, 1981, 27.
Giddins, Gary. "Miles to Go, Promises to Keep." *Village Voice*, October 15, 1991.
Glasser, Brian. *In a Silent Way: A Portrait of Joe Zawinul*. London: Sanctuary Publishing Limited, 2001.
Goldberg, Joe. "Miles at 75." *Billboard*, vol. 113, issue 23 (June 9, 2000): 2 & 52. http://web17. epnet.com.
Goodman, George Jr. "Miles Davis: I Just Pick Up My Horn and Play." *The New York Times*, June 28, 1981.
Goodman, George W. "Sonny Rollins at Sixty-Eight." *The Atlantic Monthly*, July 1999.
Goodman, Jeremy. "Miles Davis." Silver Chips Online, February 16, 2005. http://silverchips.mbhs.edu.
Gourse, Leslie. *Wynton Marsalis: Skain's Domain, A Biography*. New York: Schirmer Books, 1999.
Granger, Greg. "Miles Davis and the Civil Rights Movement: The 1964 Lincoln Day Concert." *Something Else*, February 12, 2020. http://www.somethingelsereviews.com/milesdavislincoln.
Griffin, Farah, and Salim Washington. *Clawing at the Limits of Cool*. New York: St. Martin's Press, 2008.
Gundersen, Edna. "Miles Davis: The Complete Columbia Album Collection." *USA Today*, November 27, 2009.

Haley, Alex. "Miles Davis: A Candid Conversation with the Jazz World's Premier Iconoclast." Interview. *Playboy*, September 1962. http://www.honors.umd.edu/HORN269J.

Haley, Alex. Interviewer, "Miles Davis: A Candid Conversation with the Jazz World's Premier Iconoclast." *Playboy*, September 1962, 6. http://www.honors.umd.edu/HONR269J/archive/ Miles (5/10/2005).

Harlos, Christopher. "Jazz Autobiography: Theory, Practice, Politics." In *Representing Jazz*, edited by Krin Gabbard. Durham: Duke University Press, 1995.

Hayden, Thomas. "Of Hepcats and Cool Dudes." *U.S. News & World Report*, November 1, 2004.

Heckman, Don. "Miles Davis Times Three; The Evolution of a Jazz Artist." *Down Beat*, August 30, 1962.

Hentoff, Nat. "An Afternoon with Miles Davis." *The Jazz Review* (December 1958): 11.

Hentoff, Nat. "Miles: A Trumpeter in the Midst of a Big Comeback Makes a Very Frank Appraisal of Today's Jazz Scene." *Down Beat*, November 2, 1955.

Hentoff, Nat. "The Uniquely Creative Collaboration between Miles Davis and Gil Evans." Original Liner Notes to *Sketches of Spain*. Recording. New York: *Sony Music Entertainment, Inc.*, 1959.

Hentoff, Nat. Liner Notes to "Herbie Hancock's Speak Like a Child." Recording. *Manhattan Records*, A Division of Capitol Records, Inc., 1987.

Himes, Geoffrey. "Miles Davis: Forty Years of Freedom: The Legacy of Bitches Brew." *Jazz Times*, August 13, 2010. http://jazztimes.com/articles/26369-miles-davis.

Hine, Darlene Clark, William C Hine, and Stanley Harrold, eds. *African Americans: A Concise History*. New Jersey: Pearson Education, Inc., 2009.

Hirsch, Edward. *The Demon and the Angel: Searching for the Source of Artistic Inspiration*. New York: Harcourt, Inc., 2002.

Holman, Michael. "Miles Davis v. Wynton Marsalis: Jack Johnson in Jazz." *All about Jazz*, March 8, 2005. http//:www.allaboutjazz.com/php/article (6/11/2005).

Holman, Michael. "Miles Davis v. Wynton Marsalis: Jack Johnson in Jazz." *All About Jazz*, March 8, 2005. http://www.allaboutjazz.com/php/article.

Hopkins, Marc. "Miles Davis: Selling the Dark Price." *Jazz Times*, October 2006, 5. http://jazztimes.com/articles/17304-miles.

Hornbacher, Marya. "Return of a Virtuoso." *Smithsonian*, January 2006.

Hubner, Alma. "Must Jazz Be Progressive?" *The Jazz Record* (April 1944): 8.

Ianzito, Christina. "Interview: Cheadle Channels Miles Davis." *AARP: The Magazine*, April/May 2016.

Isacoff, Stuart. "The Genius of Miles." *The Wall Street Journal*, February 6, 2014.

Isler, Tom. "So What: The Life of Miles Davis Book by John Szwed." *Yale Review of Books*, March 11, 2020. http://yalereviewofbooks.com/so-what-the-life-of-miles.

Jackson, Anthony. "The New Dark Age." *Bass Player*, vol. 9 (Mar/April 1991): 78.

James, Michele. *Kings of Jazz: Miles Davis*. New York: A.S. Barnes and Company, Inc., 1961.

Jeske, Lee. "Miles Davis Felt Forum Review." *Down Beat*, April 1983.

Jones, Malcolm. "Still Chasin' the Trane." *Newsweek*, October 29, 2007.
Jones, Max. "The Return of Miles Davis." *Melody Maker*, June 21, 1980, 45.
Jones, Quincy. *Q: The Autobiography of Quincy Jones*. New York: Broadway Books, 2001.
Jones, Steve. "Instrumental to Her Voice: For Cassandra Wilson, Shades of Miles Davis." *USA Today*, March 26, 1999.
Kahn, Ashley. *Kind of Blue: The Making of the Miles Davis Masterpiece*. New York: Da Capo Press, 2000.
Kamiya, Gary. "A Master at Dangerous Play." *Salon Entertainment* (1998): 3. http://www.salon.com/ent/music/feature.
Kart, Larry. "Provocative Opinion: The Death of Jazz." *Black Music Research Journal*, vol. 10, issue 1 (1990): 78.
Kart, Larry. *Jazz in Search of Itself*. New Haven: Yale University Press, 2004.
Kelley, Robin D. G. "Miles Davis: The Chameleon of Cool, A Jazz Genius in the Genius of a Hustler." *The New York Times*, May 13, 2001. http://www.nytimes.com/2001/05/13/arts/miles
Kenan, Randall, ed. *James Baldwin: The Cross of Redemption: Uncollected Writings*. New York: Pantheon Books, 2010.
Kershaw, Tom. "Miles Davis's Religion and Political Views." *The Hollowverse*, March 15, 2013. https://hollowverse.com/miles-davis.
Kolodin, Irving. "Miles Ahead or Miles Head?" *Saturday Review*, September 12, 1959.
Laswell, Bill. "Miles into the Future: Re-Shaping the Music of Miles Davis." *Sound on Sound*, May 1998. http://www.soundonsound.com/sos/may98/articles.
Liebman, David. Liner Notes to "Dark Magus: The Legacy of Columbia Jazz." Recording. New York: *Sony Music Entertainment*, 1977.
Lingan, John. "Jazz on European TV." *The New York Times Magazine*, December 2, 2018.
Litweiler, John. "Transition: Miles Davis and Modal Jazz." In *The Freedom Principle: Jazz After 1958*. New York: William Morrow and Company, Inc., 1984.
Litweiler, John. *The Freedom Principle: Jazz After 1958*. New York: William Morrow and Company, Inc., 1984.
Long, Daryl N. *Miles Davis for Beginners*. New York: Writers and Readers Publishing, Inc., 1992.
Lotus, Flying. "Psychedelic Funk and Fusion Barreling Into the Future." *The New York Times*, October 12, 2014.
Luther, Claudia. "Bandleader Artie Shaw Dies." *Las Vegas Review-Journal*, December 31, 2004.
Majors, Richard, and Janet Mancini Billson. *Cool Pose: The Dilemmas of Black Manhood in America*. New York: Lexington Books, 1992.
Mandel, Howard. "Miles Davis' New Direction is a Family Affair." *Down Beat*, September 1980.
Mandel, Howard. "Sketches of Miles." *Down Beat*, December 1991.
Marchese, David. "Cicely Tyson on Racial Dynamics and Hollywood." *The New York Times Magazine*, January 17, 2021.

Marchese, David. "Interview with Sonny Rollins on Whether Great Musicians Make Good People." *The New York Times Magazine*, March 1, 2020.

McCall, Cheryl. "Miles Davis." *Musician, Player, and Listener*, vol. 41 (March 1982): 38–41.

McCleary, Kathleen. "Jazz: The Multi-Cultural Beat Goes On." *Parade*, August 2, 2015.

McDonough, John. "Jazz in Black and White." *The Wall Street Journal*, August 13, 1999.

McFarland, Scott. "Miles Davis: The 'Electric' Years." *Perfect Sound Forever* (August 1997). http://www.furious.com/pervect/miles.html (2/16/2006).

McGee, Tiffany. "Chris Botti: My Favorite Jazz Albums." *People Magazine*, October 8, 2007.

Mercer, Mitchell. *Footprints: The Life and Work of Wayne Shorter*. New York: The Penguin Group, 2004.

Milkowski, Bill. "Miles Plays Gil." *Down Beat*, October 1991.

Miller, Paul E. "Roots of Hot White Jazz Are Negroid." *Down Beat*, April 1937.

Minkel, J. R. "The Roots of Creativity." *Scientific American Mind*, June/July 2008.

Mnookin, Seth. "The Keys to the Future." *Newsweek*, March 10, 2003.

Monson, Ingrid. "Monk Meets SNCC." *New Perspectives on Thelonious Monk, Black Music Research Journal*, vol. 19, issue 2 (Autumn 1999): 188.

Moody, Nekesa M. "Lil Jon Works to Expand his Kingdom of Crunk." *Las Vegas Review-Journal*, November 23, 2004.

Morgenstern, Dan. "Miles in Motion." *Down Beat*, September 3, 1970.

Morton, Brian. *Miles Davis*. London, England: Haus Publishing Limited, 2005.

Murphy, Chris. *Miles to Go: Remembering Miles Davis*. New York: Thunder's Mouth Press, 2002.

Murray, Charles S. "Interview: Miles Davis; Cat Who Walks by Himself." *The Observer*, vol. 40, sec. 5, issue 40 (June 18, 1989): 4–6.

Neergaard, Lauran. "You Do Say: Brain Scans Show Jazz's Back-and-Forth Works Like Conversation." *Las Vegas Review-Journal*, February 20, 2014.

Nemeyer, Eric. "The Magical Journey—An Interview with Wayne Shorter." *Jazz Improv*, vol. 2, issue 3 (2000): 72–82.

Nisenson, Eric. "Now's the Time!!! 25 Years of Bitches Brew." *Jazziz*, 12/6 (June 1995): 70.

Nisenson, Eric. *Round about Midnight: A Portrait of Miles Davis*. New York: Da Capo Press, 1996.

Nisenson, Eric. *The Making of Kind of Blue: Miles Davis and His Masterpiece*. New York: St. Martin's Press, 2000.

Ouellette, Dan. "Bitches Brew." *Down Beat*, vol. 66, issue 12 (December 1999): 3. http://proquest.umi.com/pqdweb?index.

Pareles, Jon. "Miles Davis, Trumpeter, Dies: Jazz Genius, 65, Defined Cool." *The New York Times*, September 29, 1991. http://www.nytimes.com/1991/09/29/nyregion/miles.

Pareles, Jon. "Miles Davis: The Alchemist and the Terrorist." *The New York Times*, October 4, 1991.

Patterson, Spencer. "Davis' 'On The Corner' Is No Pedestrian Effort." *Las Vegas Sun*, April 8, 2005.
Pond, Steve. "Soundtracks & Scores: All That Jazz." *Movie line*, December 1996, 36.
Quarles, Benjamin. *The Negro in the Making of America*. New York: Collier books, 1969.
Queliett, Dan. "Dark Price in Twilight." *Down Beat*, vol. 68, issue 5 (May 2001). http://proquest.umi.com/pqdweb.
Radano, Ronald M. "The Jazz Avant-Garde and the Jazz Community: Action and Reaction." *Annual Review of Jazz Studies*, vol. 3 (1985): 74.
Ramsey, Doug. "Miles Davis." In *Jazz Matter: Reflections on the Music & Some of its Makers*. Fayetteville: The University of Arkansas Press, 1989.
Ratliff, Ben. "A Jazz Innovator During His Late, Funky Phase." *The New York Times*, August 3, 1997. http://www.nytimes.com/1997/08/03/arts.
Reich, Howard. "Completely Hot: Live at the Plugged Nickel' Shares Miles Davis' Incendiary Gig with the World." *Chicago Tribune*, June 18, 1995.
Riggs, Ransom. "The Genius of Miles Davis: Explained!" *Mental Floss*, August 15, 2008. https://www.mentalfloss.com/blogs/archives/16692.
Roach, Max. Comments in "Sonny: Memories of Miles." *Musician, Player, and Listen*, vol. 41 (March 1982): 44.
Rockwell, John. "Miles Davis: Theme with Restless Variations Built In." *The New York Times*, December 27, 2002.
Rosenbaum, Joshua. "Kurt Elling: Keeping the Jazz Faith." *The Wall Street Journal*, November 13, 1998.
Russonello, Giovanni. "A Symbol of Jazz's Past, Aiming to Shape its Future." *The New York Times*, July 28, 2019.
Saal, Hubert. "Miles of Music." *Newsweek*, March 23, 1970.
Sandow, Greg. "From Miles Davis to Bjork, THEY'VE Loved Stockhausen." *The Wall Street Journal*, December 19, 2007.
Schudel, Matt. "Jazz Drummer Roach Dies." *Las Vegas Review-Journal*, August 17, 2007.
Schwendener, Peter. Giddens's Quote in "Miles Davis: The Loss of Lyricism." *Tri-Quarterly* (Winter 1987): 161–164.
Shatz, Adam. "Cool in Every Way." *The New York Times*, December 29, 2002. https://www.nytimes.com/2002/12/29/books.
Shepard, Lucius. "Miles Davis: He Was a Hero Descending, Never Flinching from the Experience." *Nation*, vol. 277, issue 3 (July 21/28, 2003). http://web17.epnet.com/deliveryprintsave.
Shipton, Alyn. *Jazz Makers: Vanguards of Sound*. New York: Oxford University Press, 2002.
Shriver, Jerry. "1959 Saw Jazz Take Giant Steps in Pop Culture." *USA Today*, June 30, 2009.
Shriver, Jerry. "For Rollins, The Spirit of Jazz Is Freedom." *USA Today*, May 6, 2011.
Silver, Marc. "Wynton Marsalis: The Herald of Our Swinging Heritage." *U.S. News & World Report*, October 30, 2006. http://www.usnews.com.

Smith, Christopher. "A Sense of the Possible: Miles Davis and the Semiotics of Improvised Performance." *The Drama Review*, vol. 39, issue 3 (Fall 1995): 41.

Span, Paula. "Musicians, Friends Honor Jazz Legend Miles Davis." *The Washington Post*, October 6, 1991.

Spencer, Charles. "Let Yourself be Seduced by Jazz." *The Daily Telegraph*, July 26, 2010.

Stein, Stephanie. "Kenny G: Songbird in Full Flight." *Down Beat*, January 1988.

Tallmer, Jerry. "Twenty-Five Years in the Making: Village Resident with New Documentary on Miles Davis." *The Villager*, vol. 74, issue 27 (November 10–16, 2004). http://www.thevillager. com/villager_08 (6/11/2005).

Tate, Greg. "Silence, Exile, and Cunning: Miles Davis in Memoriam." In *Flyboy in the Buttermilk: Essay on Contemporary America*. New York: Fireside, 1992.

Tate, Greg. "The Electric Miles." *Down Beat*, part two, August 1983.

Tayler, William. "Jazz: America's Classical Music." *The Black Perspective in Music*, vol. 14, issue 3 (1986): 21.

Taylor, Billy, and Teresa L. Reed. *The Jazz Life of Dr. Billy Taylor*. Bloomington, IN: Indiana University Press, 2013.

Teachout, Terry. *POPS: A Life of Louis Armstrong*. New York: Houghton Mifflin Harcourt, 2009.

Tesser, Neil. "Blowing on Empty: Miles Davis at the Altar of Show Biz." *Reader*, February 18, 1983.

Tillet, Salamishah. "Hitting the Beat on the Offbeat." *The New York Times*, April 24, 2016.

Tingen, Paul. "Miles Beyond." *The Last Word Original Liner Notes*, April 2001. http://www.miles-beyond-com/last.

Tingen, Paul. "Miles on Target: The Making of Tutu." *Jazz Times*, March 2002.

Tirro, Frank. "Constructive Elements in Jazz Improvisation." *American Musicological Society*, vol. 25, issue 2 (Summer 1974): 285.

Tomlinson, Gary. "Miles Davis: Music Dialogician." *Black Music Research Journal*, vol. 11, issue 2 (Fall 1991): 249.

Tooks, Lance. *Between the Devil and Miles Davis*. New York: NBM Publishing, Inc., 2004.

Trescott, Jacqueline. "The Poet in Pursuit of Two Legends." *The Washington Post*, November 22, 1989.

Troupe, Quincy. "Miles Davis: Our 1985 Interview—Cool is As Cool Does, and in This First of a Bitchin' Brew on the Man with the Horn, We Discover the Birth of the Cool. Dig?" *Spin*, September 28, 2019. https://www.spin.com/ featured/ miles-davis.

Troupe, Quincy. *Miles and Me*. Los Angeles, CA: University of California Press, 2000.

Turner, Douglas. "Miles and Me: An Interview with Quincy Troupe." *African American Review*, vol. 36, issue 3 (Fall 2002): 429. http://web17.epnet.com.

Tynan, Kenneth. "Miles Apart." *Holiday*, February 1963.

Ullman, Michael. "Miles Davis in Retrospect." *New Boston Review* (May/June 1981): 18.

Varga, George. "The Miles Davis Interview." *Overseas*, July 1985.
Veal, Michael E. "Miles Davis's Unfinished Electric Revolution." *Raritan*. EBSCO Publishing, 2002.
Vogel, Eric. "Jazz in Nazi Concentration Camp." *Down Beat*, December 7, 1961.
Walser, Robert Walser. "Out of Notes: Signification, Interpretation and the Problem of Miles Davis." In *Jazz among the Discourse*, edited by Krin Gabbard, 165. Durham and London: Duke University Press, 1995.
Ward, Geoffrey C., and Ken Burns. "Miles Davis." *Jazz: A History of America's Music*. New York: Alfred A. Knopf, 2013.
Watrous, Peter. "Jazz View: A Jazz Generation and the Miles Davis Curse." *The New York Times*, October 15, 1995. http://query.nytimes.com/gst/fullpage.
West, Michael J. "Ornette Coleman Transformed, Transcended Jazz." *Las Vegas Review-Journal*, June 15, 2015.
Williams, Martin. "Miles Davis: A Man Walking." In *The Jazz Tradition*. New York: Oxford University Press, 1970.
Williams, Richard. "On Top of All the Beat." *The Times*, April 28, 1983.
Williams, Richard. *The Man in the Green Shirt: Miles Davis*. New York: Henry Holt and Company, Inc., 1993.
Williams, Tony. Liner Notes to "A Tribute to Miles." Recording. Burbank, CA: *Qwest Records*, 1992.
Wilmer, Valerie. "Controlled Freedom is the Thing This Year." *Down Beat*, March 23, 1967.
Wood, Elijah. "Quote on Miles Davis." *USA Weekend*, November 10–12, 2006.
Woods, Phil. Foreword. Larry Fisher. *Miles Davis and David Liebman Jazz Connections*. Lewiston, NY: The Edwin Mellen Press, 1996.
Yanow, Scott. "Miles Davis." *Jazz Heritage Society* (1990): 15.
Yanow, Scott. "Miles Essentials." *Jazz Heritage Society* (1990): 15.
Yanow, Scott. *Trumpet Kings: The Players Who Shaped the Sound of Jazz Trumpet*. San Francisco, CA: Backbeat books, 2001.
Yudkin, Jeremy. *Miles Davis, Miles Smiles, and the Invention of Post Bop*. Indianapolis: Indiana University Press, 2008.
Zanger, Mark. "Miles Davis Blowing Hot and Cool at 56." *The Real Paper*, August 11, 1976.
Zwerin, Mike. "From Jazz to Pop to Reggae to Jazz." *Internal Herald Tribune*, July 11, 1989.
Zwerin, Mike. "Rio Women and Colorful Squares by Miles Davis, the Painter." *International Herald Tribune*, July 11, 1988.

Index

acoustic jazz, 94, 128, 132, 149
Adderly, Cannonball, 16, 22
Adorno, Theodor, 129
African: life, 59; Research Foundation, 52; rhythms, xix
African American(s), xv, 146, 155; culture, 164; man, 42–43; music, 45
Afro-Americans, 143
Albertson, Chris, 95, 127
album, jazz, 35, 62
altered state, 145
Alton, IL, 1, 6, 10, 160
America, blacks, 77
American music history, 154
apprenticeship, 17
Armstrong, Louis, xi, xviii, 4–5, 37, 42, 60, 148, 159, 164
Ascenseur pour l'échafaud, 80
Astaire, Fred, 41
audiences, 21, 25; jazz, 89
Avakian, George, 3, 78
avant-garde, 85–90, 93, 121
Avery Fisher Hall, New York, 52

Bailey, Michael, 15
Baker, Kathy, 159
Baldwin, James, 53, 77
ballads, 31, 60–62, 66, 68, 122, 163
Balliett, Whitney, 58

Bambarger, Bradly, 62
band member(s), 22, 24, 69
Baraka, Amiri (LeRoi Jones), xv, 94, 127
Basquiate, Jean-Michel, 156
Batman, 155
Bebop, xix, 11, 17, 41–42, 78, 94, 149, 168
Beethoven, 38
Berendt, Joachim-Ernst, 10
Bergstein, Barry, 109
Billboard Award, 159
Billson, Janet Mancini, 43
Billy Eckstine Orchestra, 9
Birdland jazz club, 51
Bitches Brew, 4, 17, 87, 94–95, 114–15, 123, 129
black: Americans, 31, 53; artists, 43, 53; church, 60; cultural nationalists, 53; identity, 53; jazz man, 25, 38, 42–43, 65; jazz messiah, 144; jazz musician, 94; music, 80; musician, 53–54, 65, 98, 100; rockers, 90; trumpeter, 2
Blakey, Art, 17
blues, 37, 45, 57–60, 146; superstars, 125
bluesy pain, 117
Blumenthal, Bob, 16, 105
Bohemian, 81; chic, 47

bop, pyro technicians, 3
Bossa Nova, 123
Botti, Chris, 132
Bowie, Lester, 61
Breskin, David, 77
Brown, Clifford, 2, 11
Buchanan, Elwood, 1
Byrd, Donald, xviii
Byrnes, Sholto, 128

Carnegie Hall, 38, 52
Carter, Ron, 16–17, 116
Cayton, William, 158
Chambers, Jack, 22
Chambers, Paul, 16, 21, 101
charlatan, jazz, 153
Cheadle, Don, 51, 100
Cheng, Jim, 59
Chinen, Nate, 17, 35
chords and notes, 87, 94
Chrisp, George, 44, 54, 97
Church: of jazz, 79, 106, 165; of Miles Davis, 116
civil rights, 52–54, 100
Clark, Douglass, 130
Clark, Terry, 2, 9
classical jazz, 68
Cole, Bill, 45, 67, 99
Cole, Nat King, 58
Coleman, Ornette, 30, 86, 164
Collier, James, 116
Coltrane, John, 16, 21, 29, 66, 70, 164, 166
Columbia Records, 78
community, jazz, 153
concerts, 22, 38, 122
contemplative state, 36
contemporary: jazz trumpeters, 144; music, 90, 122, 144, 148
Cook, Richard, 15, 45, 148
cool jazz, 68, 78, 80
Corea, Chick, 29
Coryell, Julie, 163
criticism, 27–28, 35
critics, jazz, 94, 131–32

Crouch, Stanley, 85, 114, 128–29, 131–32, 149
cultural: icons, 20th century, 154; nationalists, 53

Dalai Lama, 165
Davis, Cheryl, 2
Davis, Clive, 82
Davis, Erin, 2
Davis, Gregory, xvii, 2, 38
Davis, Irene, 82
Davis, Sammy, 58
death, Davis's, 67
Debussy, 137
Deffa, Chip, 35–36
Denver, Colorado, 160
Doerschuck, Bob, 30
Doobop, 141, 157
Doo-Bop, rap album, 116
doo-wop, 149
Down Beat, 115, 159
drug-fueled period, 98, 100
Duke University, 144

East St. Louis, Ill, 1, 9, 42, 97
Easy Mo Bee, 149
Eddie Randall's Blue Devils, 2, 9
Ed Dwight('s), 160; Studio, 103
Education Project, 52
Eldridge, Roy, 10
electric: funk, 146; fusion, xix; instruments, 88, 94; music, 94, 146
Elling, Kurt, 79
Ellington, Duke, 42, 100, 137, 148, 156, 159–60, 164
Ellison, Ralph, 23
embouchure, 29, 114, 116
entertainers, black, 71
epicenter of jazz, 154
esoteric musical path, 124
establishment, jazz, 86
European: countries, 65–69, 72; jazz fans, 65, 72
Evans, Bill, 16, 166
Evans, Gil, 12, 45, 123, 137

existentialist, 23, 77, 82, 97
expatriates, 77
exquisite music, 68

faith, jazz, 156, 164
fans, jazz, 35–36, 60, 65, 68, 70, 102, 123, 130–31, 154–55
Feather, Leonard, 59
fetishistic outfits, 44
Frankl, Ron, 140–41, 168
freedom, jazz, 85–86
free jazz, 85
Freeman, Moran, 159
Freeman, Philip, 89
French: people, 77–78; singer, 80; woman, 81–82
funk, 149
funkatude, jazz, 146
fusion: jazz, 93–94, 149; jazz rock, 87, 93, 131–32, 148; music, 153

Gabbard, Krin, 31
Gabriel, Archangel, 36, 168
The Gallery in Cork Street, 157
Gardner, Barbara, 70
Garland, Red, 21, 101
Garrett, Kenney, 116
Gates, Henry Louis, 43
Gelbard, Jo, 157
Gennari, John, 130
genre boundaries, 27
Germany, Karlsruhe, 66
Giddins, Gary, 90
Gillespie, Dizzy, 2, 9–11, 37, 108, 113, 143
god, jazz, 141, 154
god-like musician, 150
godly: message, 163; music, 159; trumpet, 36
Goodman, George, Jr., 36
Gordon, Dexter, 42
gospel traditions, 31
Gourse, Leslie, 132
Grammy Award, 160
Granger, Greg, 52
Grateful Dead, 115

Grēco, Juliette, 80–82, 97–98, 118
Griffin, Jasmine, 93
Griot Museum, St. Louis, Missouri, 160

Hackett, Bobby, 9
Haley, Alex, 52, 79, 128
Hampton, Lionel, 160
Hancock, Herbie, xvii, 16, 45, 59, 67–68, 166
Handy, William Christopher, 46
harebrained musical ideas, 149
harmonic jazz, 94
Harmon mute, 58–59, 69
Hendrix, Jimi, 114
Hentoff, Nat, 45
hip-hop: music, 149; and Rap, 4–5
Hirsch, Edward, 165
hole-in-the wall clubs, 125
Holiday, Billie, 12
Holland, Dave, 165
Hollywood Bowl, 122
holy: or evil force, 72; grail of music, jazz, 97; Jazz Sepulcher, Church, 159; music, 36; spirit, 163
Holzman, Adam, 124
Horn, Shirley, 37
Horne, Lena, 131
Hot Fives, 60
Hubbard, Freddie, 115
Huesmann, Günther, 10
hybrid, rock and jazz, 121

iconoclast, musical, 143
idiosyncratic blues, 59
improvisation, 10–11, 17, 29, 36, 59, 144–45
improvisational, 29, 35, 53, 62, 69, 78, 127
improvisers, 130
intellectuals, Parisian, 77
interracial relationships, 80
Isle of Wight, 125
Isler, Tom, 106

Jackson, Anthony, 132
Jackson, Jesse, 168

Index

Jackson, Michael, 46, 90, 122, 153
Jackson State University, ix
James, Michael, 28, 70
Jarrett, Keith, 167
jazz, xv, 1–3, 5, 35, 57, 68, 85, 88, 94, 97, 144, 164–65; bluesy, 60; church, 115, 133, 149, 156; club, xviii, 11, 159; community, 98; critics, 5, 24, 94, 113–14, 116, 123, 129–30, 149; disciples, 16; enthusiasts, xii; fans, 103; folklore, 82; fusion, 94–96; genre, xv, 17; god, 16, 53, 65; man, 44, 51, 62; master, 67; messiah, 51, 144; music, x, 29, 78, 88, 102–3, 123; musician, 57, 61, 67, 78, 93–95, 99, 105, 109, 124, 143, 159, 168; music world, 97; orthodoxy, 129; police, 128; purists, xi, 18, 89, 93, 128–29; rhythms, 88; rock music, 88, 93, 114, 127, 129–30, 153, 167; standards, 18; trumpeter, x, 5, 9, 61, 69, 116, 123; world, x, xi, 62, 98, 143
jazzy blues, 57
Jeske, Lee, 122
jheri curl hairstyle, 44
Jim Crow, 52, 168
Johnson, Jack, 101, 157, 159
Jones, Philly Joe, 21, 101
Jones, Quincy, 60, 82, 137–38, 140
Julliard School of Music, 9, 132, 156
JVC Jazz Festival, 154

Kahn, Ashley, 46, 58, 60
Kart, Larry, 146
Kelley, Robin, 59, 69
Kenny G, 115
Kielce, Poland, 160
Kind of Blue, 35, 59–62
Knighthood, Legion of Honor, 160
Knights of Malta, 160
Kolodin, Irving, 57
Kravitz, Lenny, 90

landscape of jazz, 150
Lauper, Cyndi, 123, 153

Lee, J., 101
Left Bank, 77
life and politics, 27
Lincoln: Abraham, 52; Center, 132; Day Concert, 52
Lingan, John, 72
Lorman, Ron, 72
Los Angeles (LA), 90, 141

Mabry, Betty, 2, 44
Macero, Teo, 122
Male, Louis, 79
Malibu, California, 139, 141
Mandel, Howard, 113
Marsalis, Branford, 164
Marsalis, Wynton, 42, 93–94, 128, 130–32, 166
Martin Committee trumpets, 139
Mayors, Richard, 43
McCleary, Kathleen, 57
McGhee, Howard, 11
McLaughlin, John, 166
McLean, Jackie, 100
melodic order, 30
melodies and choruses, 89
Mifune, Toshiro, 107
Miles: Ahead, 51; magic, 70
Milkowski, Bill, 140
Miller, Marcus, 43, 116, 149, 159
Millstadt, East St. Louis, 100
mind-boggling jazz, 72
Minkel, J. R., 145
missed notes, 27–28
modal, 29, 35, 46, 94, 144; clichés, 30
Monk, Thelonious, 12, 143
Monson, Ingrid, 53
Montreux, 133, 138–40, 160; jazz fans, 140; Jazz Festival, 137, 139
Moody, Nekesa, 4
Morgenstern, Dan, 114
motifs of blues, 31
Murphy, Chris, 76, 102, 118
Murray, Albert, 59
Murray, Charles, 137
Murray, James, 85

music: god, 21; jazz, 81
musical: form, black American, xvii; territory, 121; work, past-collegiate, 17
musicians, jazz, 17, 21, 24, 41

Napoleon-looking jackets, 44
nationalists, black cultural, 53
Navarro, Fats, 2, 11
Neergaard, Lauran, 61
Negro chic, 41
Nerlino Gallery, 157
new (jazz) paradigm, 29
Newport Jazz Festival, 21, 101
New York, 2, 82, 98, 122, 154, 157
Nice, France, 76, 160
Nisenson, Eric, 23, 25, 46, 87, 163–64
Nobs, Claude, 137

organizations, civil rights, 53
orthodoxy, jazz, 132, 144

Pareles, Jon, 31, 59, 75, 167
Paris, 97–98; France, 75, 77–80, 82
Parisians, 75, 80–81
Parker, Charlie, 3–4, 9–12, 17, 29, 31, 44, 60, 98, 143–44, 156
path-breaking trumpeter, 37
Patterson, Spencer, 146
performances, 27, 37; European, 72
permutations, blues, 61
Peterson, Oscar, 168
Philharmonic Hall, 52
Picasso, 42, 157–58
plateau, jazz, 60
Playboy (magazine), 128
Poland, Kielce, 71, 117
political activism, 168
Pond, Steve, 79, 80
Prince (the late singer), 90, 149, 153
Prince of Darkness, xvii, 15, 94–95, 113
processed hair, 43
psychedelic rock, 89
pure jazz folks, 130
purists, jazz, 131, 133, 140, 149

R&B, 130
racial equality, 77
racism, 65, 86; systemic, 53
racist America, 75–76
Radano, Ronald, 86
Raney, Phil, 130
rapturous music, 144
Ratliff, Ben, 70, 160
Reeve, Christopher, 159
Reich, Howard, 35, 66
religion, jazz, 156
religious chants, 35
rhythms, call-and-response, 35
Riggs, Ransom, 9, 12, 65
Roach, Max, 148, 168
Robinson, Sugar Ray, 101
rock, 157; rock jazz, 89, 149; and roll, 125, 149; and Roll Hall of Fame, 148–49, 166
rockers and hipsters, 90
Rockwell, John, 3, 31
Rollins, Sonny, 3, 16, 18, 100, 164, 166
Roney, Wallace, 138–40
Round About Midnight, 101
Royal Festival Hall, England, 118
royalty, 169
Russonello, Giovani, 17

Salle Pleyel Concert, 80
Santa Monica, California, 149
Santana, Carlos, 115, 124–25
Sartre, Jean-Paul, 77
Satoh, Kohshin, 45
scalar, 46, 77
scales and chords, 69
Schwendener, Peter, 123
Scott De Veaux, 164
Shatz, Adam, 58
Shepard, Lucius, 165
Shipton, Alyn, 11
Shorter, Wayne, 16–17, 29–30, 35, 38, 87, 125, 155
Silver, Horace, 42
singers, jazz, 58
slaves, black American, 35

Smith, Christopher, 127
social: activists, 52; music, x, xvii, 1, 17, 30, 36, 68, 70, 78, 87–89, 94–95, 97, 105–6, 109, 116, 123, 125, 132, 143, 148–49, 153–57, 159–60, 164, 166, 169
solo(s), 30, 36; jazz, 145
southern struggle, 53
Spanish-flavored music, 159
spectrum, jazz, 54
spiritual experience, 145
standards, traditional jazz, 93
St. John's Hospital and Health Center, 149
St. Louis, 2, 28
Stockhausen, Karlheinz, 108–9
St. Peter's Church, New York, 168
struggle, African American, 53
Sullivan Law, 52
superhuman, 144
supernatural sound, 25, 60
Supreme Being, 125
Sweden, women, 70
Switzerland, 160
systemic racism, 53
Szwed, John, 41–42, 147

Tate, Greg, 149
Taylor, Frances, 2
Taylor, William, 5, 17
Teachout, Terry, 37
Terry, Clark, 2, 9, 17, 108
Tillet, Salamishah, 100
Tingen, Paul, 153, 158
Tirro, Frank, 144
tradition, jazz, 79, 86, 90, 94, 116, 131, 145
transformation, 149
Troupe, Quincy, 28, 42, 52, 139
trumpet: improvisations, 90; music, 66; player, 30, 36, 38, 60, 65, 67, 69, 78, 114–15, 128, 144, 154; sound, 28; voice, 27, 139
trumpeter, jazz, 35, 61–62, 75, 116, 123
tunes, jazz, 60

Tynan, Kenneth, 115, 131, 143
Tyson, Cicely, 2, 69, 106, 117–18, 125
Tyson, Mike, 158

Ullman, Michael, 105
Uncle Tom, 24, 93
unconventional technique, 29
United States, 54, 65, 75, 77, 79–80, 93, 100, 116, 156
University of Virginia, 164
unreconstructed black man, 43

Vancouver Jazz Festival, 131
vibrato-free, 11, 58

wah-wah trumpet, 88
Walser, Robert, 27
Warner Brothers, 124
Washington: Salim, 93; University, St. Louis, 53
white: European, 81; producer, 75; racists, 147; rule, 168; society, dominant, 86; supremacists, 53; woman, 80
Williams, Martin, 25
Williams, Richard, 82, 93, 115
Williams, Tony, xv, 16, 166
Wilson, Cassandra, 3, 145
Wood, Elijah, 5
Woodlawn Cemetery, Bronx, NY, 141, 160
World Heavyweight Boxing Championship, 158

Yale University, 147
Yanow, Scott, 102
young musicians, 21
YouTube, 72
Yudkin, Jeremy, xviii, 46

Zanger, Mark, 4
Zawinul, Joe, 88
zealots, jazz, 70
Zoo-suit, 44
Zwerin, Mike, 154, 157

About the Author

Earnest N. Bracey is a retired Army Lieutenant Colonel and professor of Political Science and Black American History at the College of Southern Nevada. He earned a doctorate from George Mason University and his PhD from Capella University. Dr. Bracey is the author of *The Moulin Rouge and Black Rights in Las Vegas, Fannie Lou Hamer: The Life of a Civil Rights Icon,* and *Daniel "Chappie" James: The First African American Four-Star General.*

www.ingramcontent.com/pod-product-compliance
Lightning Source LLC
Chambersburg PA
CBHW061714300426
44115CB00014B/2682